Woman of Color, Daughter of Privilege

Woman of Color, Daughter of Privilege

Amanda America Dickson,
1849–1893

Kent Anderson Leslie

BROWN THRASHER BOOKS
The University of Georgia Press
ATHENS AND LONDON

© 1995 by The University of Georgia Press
Athens, Georgia 30602
All rights reserved
Designed by Erin Kirk New
Set in ten on fourteen Linotype Walbaum

The paper in this book meets the guidelines for
permanence and durability of the Committee on
Production Guidelines for Book Longevity of the
Council on Library Resources.

Printed in Canada

05 04 03 02 01   P   7 6 5 4 3

Library of Congress Cataloging in Publication Data

Leslie, Kent Anderson.
Woman of color, daughter of privilege : Amanda America Dickson,
1849–1893 / Kent Anderson Leslie.
p. cm.
ISBN 0-8203-1688-1 (alk. paper)
ISBN 0-8203-1871-X (pbk.: alk. paper)
1. Dickson, Amanda America, 1849–1893. 2. Mulattoes—Georgia—
Hancock County—Biography. 3. Hancock County (Ga.)—Biography.
4. Plantation life—Georgia—Hancock County—History—19th century.
I. Title.
F292.H3L47 1995
975.8′623041′092—dc20
[B] 94-17033

British Library Cataloging in Publication Data available

Contents

Acknowledgments

THE TELLING OF THIS STORY has been a long and arduous journey that could not have been accomplished without the expertise and encouragement of a great many people. The journey began in a graduate class at Emory University on the southern lady led by Beverly Guy-Sheftall. Beverly recognized that Amanda America Dickson's life was important and retrievable, and she encouraged me to begin searching in out-of-the-way places, beginning with ancient agricultural histories of Georgia, which recorded information about Amanda's famous father, David Dickson, the "Prince of Georgia Farmers." The Dickson family wealth made it possible to find information in archives. The archivists I encountered were generous guides to their special domains. Sister Mary Alice Chineworth of the Oblate Sisters of Providence Convent in Baltimore introduced me to the treasures in their records, which date from 1828. Dale Couch and Virginia Shadron of the Georgia Department of Archives and History directed me to obscure sources which only they knew existed. Linda Mathews and the staff of Special Collections at Emory University answered an endless number of requests for original documents with grace and speed. The reference librarians at Emory University directed me to obscure clues with efficiency and good humor. Dovie Patrick of the Special Collections Department at Atlanta University offered crucial information about Amanda Dickson's years at the university. Kevin Swanson, director of state and local records at the Maryland State Archives, patiently directed me through the nineteenth-century court records until we found the divorce proceedings for the case of Nina Pinchback versus Nathan Toomer. Larry Gulley of the University of Georgia Special Collections made me laugh as he directed me to the hidden corners of Georgia history. Alice O. Walker of the Augusta–Richmond County Public Library made it possible for me to find the local history of black families in Augusta. Most knowledgeable of all about the history of Hancock County was archivist Merita Rozier, a lifelong scholar and teller of tales. Professional help also came from Fred Zimmerman, photographer, who traveled with me to Sparta.

Scholars of southern history read early drafts of the story and contributed insight and helpful criticism. They included Virginia Bernhard, Willard Gatewood, Michelle Gillespie, Suzanne Lebsock, Catherine Clinton, Rudolph Byrd, Adele Alexander, John Rozier, Florrie and Jim Corley, Connie Currie, Ginger Gould, and Jim Roark. Other helpful readers included Dickson family members Jean Jackson, Tanya Sims, Harrell Lawson, and Julia Orr and coercible friends, Gene George, whose life is an inspiration to me; Elizabeth Stevenson, a gentle scholar and teacher; Patricia Hilden, who served on my dissertation committee; Pattie Mallory, a lifelong mentor and friend; and Alice Hickcox, who has been an ever-present resource.

Members of the Dickson family patiently told me their stories and shared with me photographs, jewelry, and sterling silver that had belonged to Amanda Dickson. Family members included Jean Jackson, the keeper of the family treasures; Shirley Franklin, who directed me to my most valuable source, her grandmother-in-law Kate Holsey Dickson and her great-grandmother Julia Frances Dickson; Harrell Lawson, who organizes the Dickson family reunion every year and who inducted me into the family as an honorary member; and Alberta Goode, Julia Orr, and Dr. Julia Hall, who told me all they could about the different branches of the family. Other African-Americans invited me into their homes and blessed me with their hospitality: Juanita Washington, Rosa Bailey, Kate Hunt, Nathaniel and Mrs. Dickson, Peaches Armstrong, Mr. and Mrs. Walter Rollins, Alberta Goode, and Mrs. Tommy Youngblood.

A handful of Hancock County scholars graciously offered me a share of their vast knowledge. They included Clifford White, Lee Dickens, John Rozier, John Bryant, Forrest Shivers, Mark Shultz, Dorothy Morgan, and Gordon Smith.

The management of this entire enterprise was done by competent, professional book people—editors, including Virginia Ross, Barbara Merchant, Madelaine Cooke, Kim Cretors, Trudie Calvert, and Karen Orchard. I am grateful for their careful attention to this project.

Many faithful friends have stood by me through all these years, enlivening my life with letters, lunch breaks, fishing trips, long conversations, gardening, and simple kindness. I am grateful to them all, most especially Elizabeth Rucker Weathersby, who has been my soul mate since our youth, which was a long time ago.

I would like to thank Grace and Ernest Lindley for carefully protecting extra copies of the manuscript as it evolved, an archival task that began in 1981. The Lindleys made it possible for me to sleep at night knowing that both our houses would not burn down at the same time. Doris Ragsdale and Christine Ezzard helped me keep my house in order.

I would especially like to acknowledge my debt to my typist, Catherine Wilburn, whose kindness, patience, and expertise guided me through the tangled early drafts. The grace and good spirit of this wonderful lady will remain with me always.

John and Dorothy Rozier served as editors, friends, and guides to the untold mysteries of Sparta and Hancock County. I enjoyed their conversation immensely, not to mention the tea and cookies.

Adele Alexander became my friend and companion on this geographical and spiritual journey. While traveling the byways of Hancock County I enjoyed her crystal-clear intellect and the questions she asked as she searched for the ghosts of her own people. Her acceptance and encouragement will always be a blessing.

Alice Hickcox read and reread the text with the patience of an Old

Testament scholar. Her careful suggestions, her presence at lunch, her spirit lifting, and her theological comments encouraged me to continue on this complex journey. From her I learned to operate a computer and the blunt fact that the Old South needs a theological perspective.

A significant transformation occurred when Woody Hickcox began the process of scanning the typed manuscript into digital form. I might never have finished if he had not done that.

My dissertation adviser, Jim Roark, guided me through the process of finding my own voice. He read and reread the manuscript, offering helpful criticism and encouragement with wisdom and good humor. During the most powerful intellectual process of my life, he remained steadfast in his role as mentor, giving freely of his time, his vast knowledge of southern history, and his ability to nurture confidence in others.

I would like to thank my family for traveling with me—Bob for the life he has shared and Kate and Jennie for their growing up, which was a blessed relief from the academic world.

Lastly, I am grateful to Amanda America Dickson for her story, which illuminates the complexities of real life in the Old South.

The mistakes are my own.

Woman of Color, Daughter of Privilege

Introduction

White faces, pain-pollen, settle downward through a cane-sweet
mist and touch the ovaries of yellow flowers.
—Jean Toomer, *Cane*, 1923

❦

ONE DAY IN THE MIDDLE of February 1849, David Dickson rode
across his fallow fields. A wealthy man in his early forties, large and
heavyset, he wore his long black hair straight, Indian style. As he rode,
he spotted a young female slave playing in a field. Dickson knew the
slave. She belonged to his mother. She was, in fact, a great favorite of
his mother's. Deliberately he rode up beside the slave child and reached
down and swung her up behind him on his saddle and, as a member of
her family would remember 140 years later, "that was the end of that."
The slave's childhood ended as Amanda America Dickson's life began,
on that day when her father raped her mother.

Amanda America Dickson was born on November 20, 1849, on the
Dickson home place in southeastern Hancock County, Georgia. She
spent her infancy, childhood, and early adulthood in her white father's
household, inside the boundary of his family, as his daughter. She married a white Civil War veteran and had children of her own. She inherited her father's enormous estate and eventually moved to Augusta,

Georgia, where she died amid luxury and comfort, at home in the wealthiest section of the city. An exploration of Amanda America Dickson's story from several perspectives will show that her personal identity was ultimately bounded by her sense of class solidarity with her father, that is, by her socialization as David Dickson's daughter,[1] her gender role as a lady, and her racial definition as a person to whom racial categories did not apply. How did these definitions affect the life choices of an elite lady of color in nineteenth-century Georgia?

Information on Amanda America Dickson's life has been difficult to locate. Unfortunately, no personal written material remains. Consequently, her story had been remembered from the outside, from the views and perspectives of others. The single most valuable view of Amanda Dickson's life came from her granddaughter Kate Louise Dickson McCoy-Lee, a well-educated, well-traveled mulatto woman. Kate McCoy-Lee was born in 1894, one year after Amanda Dickson's death. Her sources of information included Julia Frances Dickson, Amanda's mother; Kate Holsey Dickson, Amanda's daughter-in-law and Kate McCoy-Lee's mother; and Aunt Mary Long, Amanda's life-long personal servant. The oral history that Kate Dickson McCoy-Lee remembered not only provided valuable information about Amanda America Dickson, but it also revealed a perception of the family that defines itself as elite and black. It is the story of a lady who lived outside the categories of race, in a world defined by class.[2]

The legal records that were generated by David Dickson's wealth also record Amanda America Dickson's story. Wills, deeds, and court cases appeared and reappeared during the course of David Dickson's rise to wealth and prestige and, after his death in 1885, when his white relatives and his mixed family argued over who should inherit his vast estate. The richest of these documents is the transcript of the trial contesting David Dickson's will. In this unique document able lawyers for both sides asked Dickson's employees, former slaves, friends and acquaintances, and both his families to describe the most private and personal relationships in the Dickson household.

Because of the controversial nature of David Dickson's will and the unusual size of his estate, newspapers in the South and as far distant as New York and Cleveland covered the trial closely. These sources relate Amanda Dickson's story from another perspective, the sensational. Precious few African-American newspapers have survived from this era, but those that have took notice of Amanda Dickson's origins and her enormous inheritance.

Older texts on agricultural reform in the South have not been useful in providing information on David Dickson's "outside" family.[3] These authors say very little about Dickson's personal life, and much of what they do say is incorrect. For example, in a footnote Ralph B. Flanders presents the following often quoted misinformation:

> David Dickson was as unusual in his marital relations as he was in the planting industry. According to one of his close friends, while a young man he became attached to a mulatto girl, about his age, who was a wait- ing maid in his father's house. Falling heir to this slave upon the death of his father, Dickson lived with her as man and wife, becoming the father of several mulatto children. So open was Dickson in this respect that he was banned from polite society. Upon his death in 1885 he left his entire estate, some half million dollars[,] to his concubine, who bore his name, Amanda A. Dickson.[4]

This information is incorrect in several revealing ways. Amanda America Dickson was David Dickson's daughter, not his concubine. Julia Frances Dickson, Amanda America's mother, was twenty-seven years younger than David Dickson and belonged to his mother, Eliza- beth Dickson. David Dickson's close friend must have known the facts in this story, either from direct experience or from the information that filled the local newspapers. Was Amanda America's relationship with David Dickson less threatening as a lover-concubine than as a daughter?

These kaleidoscopic points of view provide a glimpse into a world of conflicting ideologies and expectations where what was forbidden in the abstract existed in reality. This glimpse is afforded by the fas- cinating story of a woman, born of a slave mother and a white father, whose life engaged the interlocking issues of race, class, and gender in the nineteenth-century South, both before and after the Civil War, both under slavery and emancipation. Her story reflects light into both the black and white communities in that time and place. It is a story in which the strong wills of an elite white father and a slave mother, coupled with lifelong personal relationships and extensive economic obligations, interacted to annul the boundaries of race for the sake of a daughter, not necessarily a family.

Antebellum southerners recognized the conflict between the ideology of racial slavery and their use of the metaphor of the family to organize social relationships. In 1864 Judge C. J. Lumpkin of the Georgia Supreme Court commented: "Which of us has not narrowly escaped petting one of the pretty little mulattoes belonging to our neighbor as one of the family?" Herein lay a terrible dilemma. These "pretty little mulattoes belonging to our neighbor" were sometimes members of the family. On an ideological level, these walking contradictions might be explained away as the products of the "lustful entrapments" of black women, as the "frolics of the lower classes," or as frail creatures who would die out as a result of natural selection. In reality, however, individuals had to deal with each other on a personal level. It was on this level that the conflict between the ideology of race and the ideology of the family caused human anguish. As E. Franklin Frazier has observed: "Neither color caste nor the law of slavery could resist altogether the corrosive influence of human feeling and sentiment generated in these lawless families."[5]

This conflict was present when children were denied as well as when affection was acknowledged, creating a barrier in relationships between individuals, between mixed families and their extended black and white families, and between mixed families and their larger communities. These conflicts brought home to nineteenth-century southerners the contradictions that riddled their dominant ideology. The boundaries of race were unsustainable. Southerners never resolved this dilemma. They simply declared "race" an absolute in the abstract and maintained a semblance of order at the expense of both logic and feelings. Because human affection knows no racial boundaries, how did southerners manage not to care for each other as friends, as parents, as lovers, as grandparents, as aunts and uncles? How did white southerners persuade themselves that they ought to abandon their children to chattel slavery? In essence, those white individuals who did so were

abandoning English common law, which dictated that the child should
follow the condition of the father, and returning to a principle of Roman
law, which dictated that the child should follow the condition of the
mother. The latter judgment set up a kinship system that functioned at
the mercy of an economic order. Eventually that economic order elimi-
nated the possibility of legal slave marriages and disavowed any legal
relationship between slave parents and their children.[6]

Scholars have effectively argued that in the early colonial period of
American history, between the arrival of the first African slaves in 1619
and the decade of the 1650s, a series of factors combined to retard the
formation of a social and economic order that would define the differences between slaves and indentured servants in racist terms. In the
first half of the seventeenth century, death and disease ran rampant in
the colonies. For newcomers, life expectancy averaged seven years after
coming to the colonies. In addition, servitude was almost universal. In
Virginia during this era the category of "service" contained at least
eight types: white indentured servants, white servants without inden-
tures (those brought to the New World voluntarily and those brought
involuntarily), Christian Negro servants, Indian servants, mulatto servants (whose servitude was a penalty for having a white mother and an
Indian, African-American, or mulatto father), Indian slaves, and Negro
slaves. As the seventeenth century progressed, southern colonists tried
to influence one another's behavior through the law. Eventually the
law declared black slaves "slaves for life" regardless of whether they
were Christians. In 1662 the Virginia legislature passed a law that declared that the child of a white man and a Negro slave should follow
the status of the mother, and other colonies followed suit. With this law
the colonists relinquished the possibility of defining slavery as limited
to a specific time, even one lifetime. Free colonists also gave up the
possibility of defining a separate class or caste for children of a free
father and an enslaved mother.[7]

This social and economic order was not inevitable. In Brazil, for
example, where Spanish and Portuguese conquistadors came without
their families to conquer the natives, a separate caste was established
for mulatto children so that white citizens did not define their mulatto

children as slaves. Conversely, the North American colonists defined a system of slavery based on a theoretically absolute dichotomy of black and slave, white and free. There would be no space for mulatto children in the social pattern, no "mulatto escape hatch," no middle ground where "new people" might be something besides black. In colonial North America, the law simply placed these children on the other side of a boundary that erased their relationship to a white parent. In reality, some found that price too dear to pay.[8]

By the nineteenth century, the law prohibited mixed families everywhere in the South except in South Carolina. Georgia law prohibited "interracial" marriage, or legal miscegenation, from 1750, when slaves were first lawfully admitted into the colony, until 1979. The colonial statute also outlawed "interracial" sex, declaring that if the court convicted any white man of "lying with" a female Negro or black or any white woman of "lying with" a Negro or black, these individuals would be fined ten pounds sterling, British money. Conversely, the law prescribed corporal punishment for black or Negro individuals charged with the same offense. As time passed, the statute dropped miscegenation from the original prohibition but continued to outlaw interracial marriages. As a result, individuals involved in interracial sexual relationships were always liable to prosecution under the fornication laws.[9]

The Civil War did not change this situation. In *Scott* v. *Georgia* (1869), the Georgia Supreme Court indicted Charlotte Scott, "an unmarried woman of color," for "cohabitating and having sexual intercourse" with Leopold David, an unmarried white man, born in Lyons, France. The Scotts claimed to have been legally married by a black preacher, but they could not produce a marriage certificate. In the ensuing trial Charlotte Scott's daughter testified that "it was so considered by the family, that they were married, and all the family have looked upon them as man and wife." The court ruled this testimony out of order and concluded that Charlotte Scott was guilty of fornication. In justifying the decision, the court stated, "The offspring of these unnamed connections are generally sickly and often effeminate and are inferior in physical development and strength to the full blood of either race." By 1890 the court had abandoned the sickly mulatto argument as a premise for forbidding interracial marriages and had adopted a straightforward racial purity stance. In *Tutty* v. *Georgia* (1890), Charles Tutty was indicted for "the statutory crime of fornication" with Rose Ward, a "woman of African Descent and formerly a slave," on the first day of April 1889 and "at other times." On April 15, the Tuttys traveled to the District of Columbia and were legally married there. They then returned to Chatham County, Georgia, for fear that their lives would be in danger if they returned to their home in Liberty County. Nevertheless, the state of Georgia issued an indictment on the grounds that if a marriage relationship was forbidden in the state, all such marriages of citizens of the state were void no matter where they were performed. The Circuit Court for the Southern District of Georgia ruled in favor of the state with the comment that "by a settled policy of the State, a policy adopted with the purpose to preserve, as far as the laws may accomplish that result, the purity and distinctiveness of the races inhabiting the state, it is declared that the marriage relation between white persons and persons of African descent is forever prohibited, and such marriages are null and void." The law reiterated that all interracial sexual relationships were punishable as acts of fornication.[10]

As these legal cases demonstrate, individuals who tried to establish lasting monogamous sexual relationships, or other family relationships, across racial lines might expect to suffer reprisals. Before and after the Civil War, these individuals were faced with formidable challenges that varied from outright violence, to threats of violence, to ostracism by both the black and white communities, to benign neglect, or to the problem of maintaining an agreed-upon "will not to notice."[11] Nevertheless, some nineteenth-century southerners transcended the imaginary boundary of race and the fear of this array of reprisals and formed intimate relationships. They could accomplish this feat because a fundamental tension existed within antebellum southern society. The power of the master within slavery as a social system functioned without clearly defined limits. A person who had the legal power to beat another human to death, to sell other human beings, to separate husbands from wives, and to separate mothers from children might be motivated by lust, affection, or his or her own ego to transcend the South's ethical code of honor. These autocrats were sometimes able to use personal relationships in an organic society and a web of economic obligations to confound the very system that had empowered them.

These transgressions included the entire gamut of human sexual behavior from the heterosexual and homosexual rape of slave children and adults, to incest, to the formation of lasting relationships between individuals who could or would have willingly consented had they been outside the slave-master-mistress social and economic system. We will probably never know how often these categories of relationships occurred in the antebellum South though accounts of biracial heterosexual rapes by white males abound in the slave narratives. The case described in the text *Celia, A Slave* demonstrates with chilling clarity that neither Bertram Wyatt-Brown's concept of honor, nor Steven Stowe's concept of manners, nor the law effectively protected a slave from the lust of a determined master or mistress. For honor and manners were not the glue that held the Old South together but the anesthesia that kept it from flying apart.[12]

Documented cases of incestuous relationships between masters and their slave kin are rare, but the example of James Henry Hammond serves to illustrate the casualness with which at least one master took the possibility of incest with his property. Writing to his son, Hammond remarked:

> In the last will I made I left to you . . . Sally Johnson the mother of Louisa & all the children of both. Sally says Henderson is my child. It is possible, but I do not believe it. Yet act on her's rather than my opinion. Louisa's first child *may* be mine. I think not. Her second I believe is mine. Take care of her & her children who are both of *your* blood if not mine & Henderson. The services of the rest will I think compensate for indulgence of these. I cannot free these people & send them North. It would be cruelty to them. Nor would I like that any but my own blood should own as slaves my own blood or Louisa. I leave them to your charge, believing that you will best appreciate & most independently carry out my wishes in regard to them. Do not let Louisa or any of my children or possible children be the Slaves of Strangers. Slavery *in the family* will be their happiest earthly condition.[13]

Addressing the frequency of lasting relationships between "consent-ing" adults, Herbert Gutman has commented that southern court rec-ords containing divorce suits in which slaves are mentioned as corre-spondents suggest that meaningful affairs, if not common, "were not rare." Scholars have documented cases of lasting relationships between white men who held state and national office and black women, for in-stance, Marcus Winchester, mayor of Memphis, and the beautiful free quadroon mistress whom he married, and Richard M. Johnson, the vice-president of the United States under Martin Van Buren, and Julia Chinn, who was the mistress of his household. Sylvia Hoffert relates the story of Ralph Quarles, a Virginia planter, who maintained a lasting relationship with a slave concubine and their four mulatto children. At his death Quarles freed the children and their spouses. The most promi-nent cases of this sort in Georgia were the Healy family of Macon and John Hope's family from Augusta. Elite white women in the Old South also took note of these relationships. Ella Gertrude Clanton Thomas of Augusta, Georgia, commented in her diary on June 26, 1869, "A colored woman a very bright mulatto is living in the neighborhood with Mr. Towns who rents a portion of Mr Ware's land. . . . This relationship is so common as to create no surprise whatever." Probably the most noted example of a master's power to sustain an intimate sexual re-lationship with a slave woman is Thomas Jefferson's relationship with Sally Hemmings.[14]

White parents' reactions to their "outside" children varied from cruelty to affection. It cannot be denied that the great majority of whites ignored their mulatto offspring, as did their white families and the white community. The reactions of those white parents who did not deny their children also fell along a spectrum, from simple everyday favors that made life more bearable (or unbearable), to a position in the big house, to manumission, to manumission with expatriation and financial security, to packing up everything and everybody and mov-ing to a place where parents and children could form a family. For those who stayed in the South, a white parent, usually a male, might establish a biracial family and maintain his outside family until he married. Or he might maintain two families, one white and one mixed, as was the case with the Durham family of Greene County, Georgia, in which the male children of both families were educated as doctors. Or a white parent might maintain a public role as a bachelor and have a "mixed" family as his only one, as did Stephen Griffith of Pickens County, Georgia, who left his estate to his daughter Amanda Griffith and her mother, Lina, "formerly my faithful domestic servants." Surely the rarest of all these cases was the one in which a white parent stayed in the South with his or her mixed family and acknowledged this family as his or her only family, leaving these individuals the family wealth.[15]

The most useful sources containing examples of these intimate interracial relationships are Helen Tunnicliff Catterall's *Judicial Cases Concerning American Slavery and the American Negro* and Caroline Bond Day's *Study of Some Negro-White Families in the United States*, both published in 1932.[16]

Catterall records cases involving slavery that reached the supreme courts of the states. Of the 435 cases that reached the high court in Georgia, Catterall describes 21 in which one could reasonably suspect that intimate interracial relationships existed.[17] In two cases masters accorded special status to female slaves and their children. In *Ingram* v. *Fraley*, Ingram, a "bachelor," left his estate to his brother-in-law Fraley, stating that he had the "utmost confidence" that Fraley would carry out his wishes to treat all of his Negroes with humanity, particularly a mulatto family, "to which testator, for reasons not necessary to be repeated, had a strong affection."

In eight of the cases, masters manumitted mulatto women and their children or willed them property. All of these cases occurred after 1801, which meant that manumission had to take place outside the state of Georgia. If a will stated that a slave was to be manumitted and then taken to a free state, the court could declare the will null and void. In *Cleland* v. *Waters* (1854), Thomas J. Waters enumerated forty-four slaves whom he wanted taken out of the state "to such place as they may select" and there be manumitted. The court records reported that "a number of those mentioned were lineal descendants of testator."

In four cases, mulatto children claimed that they had a white mother in order to substantiate their claims to free status. In 1856, Joseph Nunez, reported to be mulatto, died and his executor sued to recover

slaves he had inherited from his father, James Nunez, also reported to
be mulatto. The court ruled against Joseph, reminding the legal profession that "the status of the African in Georgia, whether bond or free, is
such that he has no civil, social or political rights or capacity, whatever,
except such as are bestowed on him by statute; that the act of manumission confers no other right but . . . freedom from the dominion of
the master, and the limited liberty of locomotion."[18] Consequently, free
persons of color had no right to bequeath slaves to others.

In June 1856, Joseph Nunez's administrators tried again to retrieve
the slaves, admitting that some of them, the children of Patience, were
Joseph Nunez's children. They claimed that Nunez's mother was a
white woman, "and a pretty one too," and that his father was an American of Portuguese ancestry who "passed as a white man." They also
argued that Joseph Nunez had always been treated as a white man; that
he worked as a clerk in a counting room; that he kept "as good company
as anybody in the neighborhood; that he could dance "very gracefully";
that he often went to white balls and parties; and that he dined with
whites. Nevertheless, the court ruled that because Joseph Nunez had
applied for a guardian as a free person of color, he was therefore a free
person of color and unable to "convey" slaves to a guardian; hence he
could not protect his children who were born of a slave mother.[19]

Caroline Bond Day's *Study of Some Negro-White Families in the
United States* summarizes the author's investigation of 246 mixed families, of which 243 were established before the Civil War and 3 were
established after the war. Eighty-nine percent of the histories were of
families from the southeastern United States and 45 percent were from
Georgia. As one might suspect, 230 of the prewar relationships Day recorded were between white men and black women, although thirteen
of the cases involved white women and black men. In these latter cases,
all except one of the relationships constituted legal marriages.[20]

Of Day's 246 mixed families, descendants in 102 bore the same sur-
names as their fathers, grandfathers, or great-grandfathers. In only
eighteen of the recorded families was the black family the only family
of a white antecedent.[21]

Unfortunately, Day was primarily interested in the anthropological characteristics of these families: individuals' height, weight, shoulder breadth, arm length, measurements of facial features, and health. Nevertheless, her study provides some of the most useful clues to the histories of mixed families in the nineteenth-century South.

Historical texts on mixed families in the nineteenth-century South fall into three categories. The first deals with isolated communities of Creole families that define themselves as either white or not black. Among the first group, Gary Mills and Sister Frances Jerome Woods have traced the history of the Creole descendants of Marie Therese Coin Coin of Isle Bravelle, Louisiana, through ten generations. According to Mills, this mixed family survived as a special group because of its position in an essentially French-Anglo culture, its geographic isolation, its complex family networks, and, "most significantly, the wealth of the people brought them education and culture, the two factors which proved to be the bridge between the colony and the more genteel elements of whites which dominated parish society."[22]

The second deals with mixed families and individuals within the general context of southern culture. Among the second group, Michael P. Johnson and James L. Roark have examined the free mulatto population of antebellum Charleston. Johnson and Roark argue that these families maintained their separation from the poor free black and slave populations through a complex set of strategies, that is, their kinship with elite whites and consequently their personal acquaintance with powerful individuals in Charleston (personalism), their usefulness to the white community (expertise), and their establishment of a separate social structure all worked to enable separation. For these families, protection in this urban society came from the goodwill of aristocratic whites.[23]

Johnson and Roark also shed light on the issues of survival for mixed families through their study of the family of William Ellison, a wealthy mulatto planter in Sumter County, South Carolina. While Ellison was a slave, his master trained him as a ginwright and allowed him to buy his freedom and the freedom of his wife and daughter. The free status of his wife meant that Ellison's three sons were born free. According to Johnson and Roark, Ellison protected his mixed family by making himself indispensable to the white elite. His scrupulous attention to the manners of survival, coupled with the Ellison family expertise in making and repairing gins, created a safe place for a time, which enabled Ellison to exploit the plantation regime and become a wealthy planter.

The third category of historical texts that deal with mixed families contains the stories of these families from the inside out. These texts include Thomas O. Madden and Anne Miller's *We Were Always Free*, Kathryn L. Morgan's *Children of Strangers*, Pauli Murray's *Proud Shoes*, and Adele Logan Alexander's *Ambiguous Lives: Free Women of Color in Rural Georgia, 1789–1879*. All these texts chronicle the self-definition of mixed families from the perspectives of the families themselves.[24]

Madden's *We Were Always Free* traces the Madden family history from the birth of a mulatto infant, Sarah, to a white indentured servant named Mary Madden in Spotsylvania County, Virginia. Sarah's father remains nameless, identified only as probably a slave of James Madison. From Mary to T. O. Madden, the family struggled to establish itself as free and respectable. They accumulated wealth, land, and eventually status as educated people, successfully separating themselves from slaves before the Civil War and poor African Americans after the conflict.

Conversely, Morgan remembers the stories of her great-grandmother Caddy, who had been born a slave. Caddy's stories appear in different versions, but the message to the family remains the same: "You have to fight every inch of the way to be free." Caddy's family rejected its white ancestry and defined itself as black against white. Pauli Murray's *Proud Shoes* records the story of her aristocratic mulatto grandmother Cornelia Smith Fitzgerald, her African-American grandfather Robert Fitzgerald, and their descendants. As the mulatto daughter of one of *the* white Smiths, Cornelia Fitzgerald was raised in her father's household. There she learned that because of her aristocratic white background, "she was inferior to nobody," a notion that, according to Murray, made it impossible for her grandmother to adjust later to her "Negro status." When Murray describes herself as standing "very tall in proud shoes," she pictures herself standing in the shoes of her African-American grandfather, choosing to define herself as black and proud.[25]

Adele Logan Alexander's *Ambiguous Lives* records the stories of women in mixed families of material privilege, families in which fathers acknowledged their paternity and protected their children from racial definitions as a necessity. The Hunt-Logan family valued education and decorum as a way to transcend racial definitions. Alexander chronicles the struggles of her grandmother Adella Hunt Logan in her effort to live with racial ambiguity as an independent adult, making the choice between retreating into a world of "private privilege" or accepting the challenges of becoming a part of the black community.[26]

The purpose of this book is to remember Amanda America Dickson's story and use it to ask questions about the intersection of race, class, and gender in the life of an elite mulatto lady and her family in nineteenth-century Georgia. This story does not reflect the defiance of Caddy's stories in *Children of Strangers* or the pride in blackness by choice of Pauli Murray in *Proud Shoes*. It does reflect Madden's concern for status and the racial ambiguity of Adella Hunt Logan's life. Amanda America Dickson's story takes these ambiguities one step further in forging a definition of self as raceless and consequently alone, without a nuclear family or an extended family, as a "no nation."[27]

Exceptions to the Rules

I never should have been a slave for my father was a gentleman.
—An unnamed candidate for a postwar constitutional convention

IF IT IS TRUE that public sentiment, not abstract ideology, controlled the amount of miscegenation that took place in the nineteenth-century South, then what factors combined to create a place where an elite white male could rape a slave child and raise the offspring of that act of violence in his own household? If we include the sentiments of the slave community in this observation, we are left with a complex question. A partial answer lies in the geography, history, and socioeconomic arrangements that evolved in Amanda Dickson's place, a place where she was both protected and trapped. What factors influenced the amount of miscegenation and the kinship relationships that were tolerated? What factors allowed for exceptions to the rules? [1]

Amanda America Dickson's birthplace, Hancock County, Georgia, is in the fertile so-called black belt of the state, 125 miles south and east of Atlanta, between the pre–Civil War capital of Milledgeville and the river-port city of Augusta (Map 1). The geography of nineteenth-century Hancock County was suitable for the development of a plantation culture based on the production of cotton using slave labor. The

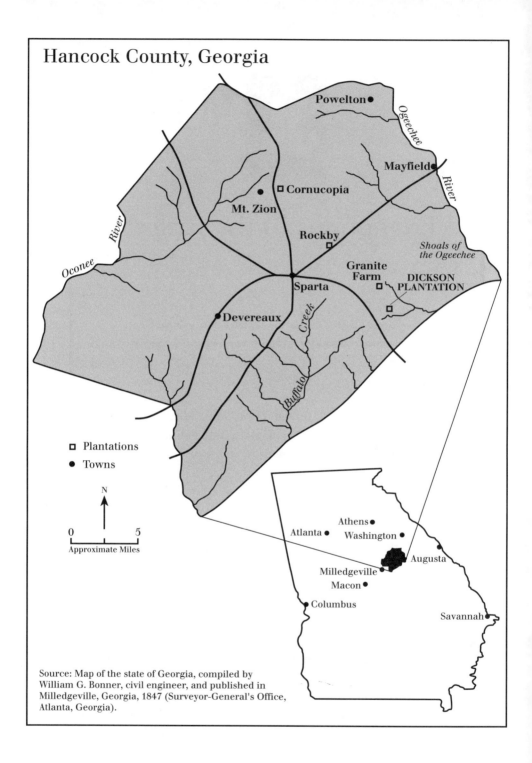

Hancock County, Georgia

Powelton

Ogeechee

Mayfield

River

Cornucopia

Mt. Zion

Rockby

River

Oconee

Shoals of
the Ogeechee

Granite
Farm

DICKSON
PLANTATION

Sparta

Devereaux

Creek

Buffalo

□ Plantations

● Towns

N

0 ———— 5
Approximate Miles

Athens
Atlanta   Washington

Augusta

Milledgeville
Macon

Columbus

Savannah

Source: Map of the state of Georgia, compiled by
William G. Bonner, civil engineer, and published in
Milledgeville, Georgia, 1847 (Surveyor-General's Office,
Atlanta, Georgia).

land was relatively flat, with gently sloping hills and plentiful water in creeks and rivers. The climate provided farmers and planters with a growing season that exceeded the two hundred days required for cotton. Heavy rainfall in the spring coupled with light showers in the summer and fall months provided adequate moisture. Small accumulations of snow appeared rarely in the winter and quickly melted. The summers in that section of Georgia were sometimes oppressive with long spells of hot, humid weather aggravated by the presence of gnats, which flourished in the southern part of the county, below the fall line.[2] The fall line passes through the county on an east-west axis so that the land is distinctly different on either side of that boundary. In the north, hardwood forests abound, producing fertile land as a result of an accumulation of organic material. In the southern part of the county, the pine barrens, the soil varies from sandy, with occasional granite outcroppings, to bright red clay. Farmers and planters in the nineteenth century had to replenish the soil in this section of the county to produce any crops at all, especially a staple crop as greedy as cotton.

Before the coming of the Europeans, Hancock County had been inhabited for centuries by Native Americans, whose culture was imminently susceptible to European diseases, technology, and cunning. Native American tribes had established boundaries for their nations and traded, negotiated, and killed one another over who had the right to use, not own, the land.

In the sixteenth century, wandering Spaniards visited the area in search of gold and the illusive fountain of youth. Led by the powerful chief Ocute, Hernando DeSoto and his band of adventurers tramped across the land, following trading paths created by Native Americans. During this era game was plentiful, if not fountains of youth, and even large animals such as buffalo abounded.[3]

By the seventeenth century Euro-Americans had established themselves as traders in the area. They remained the only white presence until 1732, when the British established the colony of Georgia. Eventually visitors began to arrive, including the naturalist William Bartram, and then settlers or families who intended to support themselves through agriculture. The first such family was that of Captain Benjamin

Fulsam, his wife, one son, and three daughters. In 1773 Creek Indians killed the Fulsams and destroyed their farm. Other land-hungry settlers followed and transformed the wilderness into a frontier. Settlers moved up the creeks and rivers from coastal Georgia and cleared land for agriculture, pushing the boundary between users of land and owners of land farther and farther west. As a consequence, acts of violence between Native Americans and whites were common. The United States government and the state of Georgia began a curious process of justification by negotiating a series of treaties with various cooperative Creek Indian chiefs such as the "tame chief" of the Tallahassee and the "fat chief" of the Cusseta. Although Indians and colonists signed the treaties of Augusta (1782), Shoulderbone Creek (1786), and Colerain (1796), hostilities did not cease until 1828, when the state and national governments declared all claims of the Indians null and void.[4]

Between the establishment of Hancock County by the state of Georgia in 1793 and the official end of Indian hostilities in 1828, the county emerged from its frontier status and became an "incubator," a place where poor to middling settlers congregated while waiting to move on to land in the middle and western parts of the state. Farmers who had accumulated a surplus of capital bought up the fertile bottomlands of the county and stayed put. The white population of the area reached 9,605 in 1800 and steadily declined thereafter with only slight variations in the trend for the next 150 years, reaching 1,831 in 1990. Conversely, the slave population increased from 4,835 souls in 1800 to 8,137 in 1860, 4,242 males and 3,895 females (see Table 1.1).[5]

As Hancock County's citizens transformed the area from a wilderness to a frontier and then to a settled community, a parallel process was taking place which profoundly affected the community's economic and social patterns. In the late eighteenth century, Europeans and North Americans wore hot, itchy wool garments. Cotton was not available as a substitute because laborers could not separate cotton seeds from cotton fibers economically. In the last decade of the eighteenth century, Eli Whitney and others invented effective cotton gins, and the cotton market exploded. That explosion was accompanied by the evolution of a plantation regime based on the extensive use of slave labor and

Table 1.1. Population Growth in Hancock County, 1800–1990

Year	White	Slaves	Free black	Total	Percent black
1800	9,605	4,835	16	14,456	33.6
1810	6,849	6,546	25	13,330	48.6
1820	5,847	6,863	24	12,734	54.1
1830	4,603	7,180	37	11,820	61.1
1840	3,697	5,915	47	9,659	61.7
1850	4,210	7,306	62	11,578	63.6
1860	3,871	8,137	36	12,044	67.6
1870	3,645		7,672	11,317	67.8
1880	5,044		11,943	16,989	70.3
1890	4,739		12,410	17,149	72.4
1900	4,649		13,628	18,277	74.6
1910	4,917		14,268	19,189	74.3
1920	5,136		13,221	18,357	72.0
1930	3,725		9,345	13,070	71.5
1940	3,581		9,183	12,764	71.9
1950	2,984		8,068	11,052	73.0
1960	2,518		7,461	9,979	74.8
1970	2,360		6,659	9,019	73.8
1980	2,060		7,406	9,466	78.2
1990	1,831		7,077	8,908	79.4

Sources: John Rozier, *Black Boss: Political Revolution in a Georgia County* (Athens: University of Georgia Press, 1982), 197; United States census.

the parallel evolution of a racist ideology which justified that regime. The processes of civilizing its inhabitants and the evolving of a plantation regime took place at the same time in Hancock County. Some individuals and families became very wealthy at the expense of others. Between 1802 and 1860 the total number of slaveholders in the county declined from 819 to 410. The average number of slaves held by each slaveholder increased from about 6 in 1802 to about 20 per unit in 1860. In 1802, 656 slaveholders, or 80 percent of the total, owned fewer than 10 slaves while 28, or 3 percent of the total, owned 20 or more. By 1860, 182 slaveholders, or 44 percent of the total, owned fewer than 10

Table 1.2. Growth of the Plantation System and Slavery
in Hancock County, 1802–1860

	Number of Slaves							
Year	3	4–9	10–19	20–49	50–99	Over 100	Number of slaveholders	Number of slaves
1802	68	288	135	26	2	—	819	4,823
1807	378	323	185	45	3	—	934	6,424
1813	227	222	136	64	4	—	653	5,612
1821	229	208	145	88	8	—	678	6,331
1825	197	147	107	86	13	2	552	6,315
1835	145	132	107	77	17	2	480	5,680
1840	86	272	163	106	28	3	658	5,915
1850	105	133	131	90	20	3	490	7,306
1860	84	98	87	106	28	7	410	8,137

Source: Forrest Shivers, *The Land Between: A History of Hancock County, Georgia, to 1940* (Spartanburg, S.C.: Reprint Company, 1990), 73.

slaves, while 141, or 34 percent, owned 20 or more bondspersons (see Table 1.2).[6]

By 1830 the county had established itself as a cotton-growing region. By 1840 it produced twice as much cotton as any of its nearest competitors in Georgia. As a consequence of this prosperity for some, in 1860 Hancock County was the home of more slaveholders owning forty or more slaves than any neighboring counties except Columbia, which was located near the urban center of Augusta (Richmond County). By 1860 the leading fifty-six planter families, or 5 percent of the families in Hancock, owned more than half the land and 40 percent of the slaves. The average value of their real and personal property was approximately $70,000. At the end of the antebellum period, based on income per capita, excluding slaves, Georgia was the richest state in the Union and Hancock County was one of its richest counties. In sharp contrast with the relative wealth of the county as a whole, approximately one-third of the white families in the county owned land but no slaves, and approximately one-third owned neither land nor slaves.[7]

Table 1.3. A Comparison of the Economic Status of Planter, Farmer, and Nonagriculturalist White Families in Hancock County in 1860

Occupational group	Number	Total in families	Percent owning realty	Percent owning slaves	Percent owning other personal property
Planters and farmers					
$10,000	56	267	100.0	100.0	100.0
$1,001–$9,999	220	1,049	100.0	92.2	100.0
$0–$1,000	85	379	100.0	41.6	91.7
Professional	48	195	62.4	54.1	77.1
Merchants	29	101	50.0	45.0	75.9
Tradespeople	116	414	13.7	7.7	26.9
Overseers	139	367	1.4	6.4	20.8
Farm laborers	198	610	1.2	0.016	8.4
Factory workers	96	157	0.9	0.0	0.0
All others	110	276	0	0	0

Source: James C. Bonner, "Profile of a Late Ante-Bellum Community," *American Historical Review* 49 (July 1944): 671.

Table 1.3 compares the economic status of planter, farmer, and non-agriculturalist white families in Hancock County in 1860. All of the planters and farmers who were worth more than $10,000 owned both real estate and slaves. In the middle group of agriculturalists, those worth between $1,001 and $9,999, slightly fewer than 8 percent owned real estate but no slaves. These relatively prosperous individuals may represent a segment of the population that refused to buy slaves. Of the poorer farmers, those worth $1,000 or less, all owned real estate, but only 41.6 percent owned slaves. Outside the planter-farmer category, 54.1 percent of the professional people in the county, 45 percent of the merchant families, 7.7 percent of the tradespeople families, and 6.4 percent of the overseer families owned slaves. Of the 1,097 families represented in the table, only 350, 32 percent or approximately one-third, owned slaves in 1860.[8]

The two-thirds of Hancock County families who owned no slaves were composed of approximately 18 intermediate farm families, 49 lesser farm families, 22 professional, 16 merchant, 107 tradespeople, 131 overseer, 198 farm laborer, 96 factory worker, and 110 "other" families. These 747 families were approximately 68 percent of the white families in the county. Who were the 110 families of "others," those who owned no real estate, owned no slaves, and had no occupation? Certainly some of them were respectable hunter-gatherers who lived on marginal land that no one owned. Others may have fallen into the categories of Bobtails, Sandhillers, and Rag Tags, individuals who were described by Daniel R. Hundley in 1860 as "ignorant, lazy, prone to snuff dipping and of the Hard Shell persuasion" but who might more accurately be described as families who simply lived outside the cash economy.[9]

Both the cash and the subsistence economies in Hancock were based primarily on agriculture. Some people made a living, and some made a profit. The most important crops produced in Hancock County in 1849 were cotton and corn, with smaller amounts of wheat, oats, peas, rye, barley, and nuts. Cotton averaged 550 pounds per acre, which made Hancock the most productive county in the area except for neighboring Putnam, whose farmers and planters averaged 600 pounds per acre. Land values in Hancock County ran as high as $20.00 per acre, although most sales fell within a range of from $2.50 to $3.00 an acre. These average land prices made Hancock County land the cheapest in the area, at least the land that anyone was willing to sell (Appendix C.1).[10]

It is clear from this examination of the evolution of an economic order in Hancock County that, given an appropriate climate, available land, and a captive labor force, the inhabitants of this place worked out economic arrangements that were grossly inequitable. By 1860 fifty-six planter families, or 5 percent of the total number of families in the county, owned half the land and 40 percent of the slaves. Two-thirds of the families in the county owned no slaves, and 433, or 39 percent of the total, owned less than $100 worth of personal property. The community vested the planter class with both the control of a disproportionate share of the wealth and with almost absolute legal power over a large segment of the labor force. These slaveholders could buy and sell human beings with impunity. They could separate wives and husbands, parents and children on the basis of economic expediency. They could administer corporal punishment up to the point of death. In fact, the law required that slaves submit without "remonstration," as children submit to punishment by their parents. And they could maintain their labor force at a subsistence level. Herein lay a great deal of power for those who could force labor as opposed to those who were wage earners. It would seem logical to presume that such a disproportionate distribution of wealth and the capacity of planters to command the labor of such a huge work force would combine to place the planter class in imminent danger of rebellion by the rest of the white population. This does not appear to have happened in Hancock County. A partial explanation can be found by briefly exploring the social institutions and social conventions that evolved with plantation slavery.

In 1849, when Amanda America Dickson was born, Hancock County remained relatively isolated. Three towns were located in the area: Sparta, with a population of 700, Powelton, with a population of 150, and Mount Zion, with a population of 200. No railroad operated in the county at that time. The stagecoach did pass through and stop at the Drummer's Hotel, on its way from Augusta to Milledgeville and Macon, and the mail arrived sporadically at six post offices: Devereaux's Store, Long's Bridge, Mount Zion, Powelton, Rock Mills, and Shoals, in the southeastern part of the county.[11]

In 1850 Hancock County had a white population of 4,210, a slave population of 7,306, and 62 free persons of color. One-fourth of the white population lived in towns and three-fourths lived in the country; population density was about seven people, or one family, per square mile. The black population of Hancock County was almost entirely composed of slaves, 75 percent of whom lived on farms with 19 or fewer bondspersons. Of the 490 slaveholders in 1850, 56, or 11.4 percent, were women. The average plantation was worked by 15 slaves. Only 113 of the 490 slaveholders were planters with 20 or more bondsmen and women. Of these planters, 11 were women; Mrs. E. E. Bell was the mistress with the largest number of slaves—43. By 1860, the number of slaves had increased to 8,137, while the number of slaveholders had decreased to 410, of whom 51 were women, or 12.4 percent, and 12 were planters. Nancy Watts owned 112 slaves in 1860, Mary Sasnett owned 76, and Mrs. W. E. Terrell owned 74.[12]

By the last decade before the Civil War, Hancock County had become a settled community with enough surplus wealth to support churches and schools. A visitor described it as a place where "fine breeds of livestock, improved tools, neat horizontal tillage, well-fed slaves, and the genteel quality of its people were the county's well-known assets." In this era social life for the white citizens of Hancock County re-volved around the family, visiting friends and relatives, the church, and the educational institutions. Sparta was the home of one Presbyte-rian, one Methodist, and one Baptist church, plus a male and a female academy. Powelton could boast of two churches and one academy for females, and Mount Zion was the home of the Reverend Nathan Beman's famous school. In addition, in the county at large, there were twenty common schools. Nine Methodist, nine Baptist, two Presbyte-rian, and one Protestant Methodist church served the religious needs of the people in the hinterland, in some cases both black and white, as was also true in Sparta. Nine of the Methodist churches in the area had mixed congregations ranging from 25 to 46 percent "colored" in 1851 and from 25 to 56 percent "colored" in 1860. In 1860 two of the Baptist churches, Horeb and Darien, had more black members than white (Appendix C.2).[13]

In addition to churches and basic education, the citizens of Han-cock could boast of higher education for their white citizens. In 1831 the Sparta Female Academy was founded. It offered five disciplines of study: language, mathematics, history, geotics, and philosophy. The academy advertised itself as a no-nonsense institution. Young ladies who were not serious about their studies were advised not to apply. The catalog warned that the single object of the school for the pupil was "not personal display in dress and jewelry, idle amusement and useless visiting, attentions of the wealthy, learned, influential or any others . . . but physical, intellectual and moral culture." The young lady

who could not find in the "toil" of her studies "high and rational enjoyment for the usually short period of school life, cannot enroll herself
among the pupils of the Seminary with any fair prospect either of an
honorable or useful distinction." The Sparta Female Academy did not
intend to educate young women to be "ladies" in the ornamental, useless sense. It intended to guide young women into finding "high and
rational enjoyment" in difficult intellectual "toil." [14]

The Sparta Female Academy not only provided the citizens of the
region with a first-class school for their daughters; it also attracted well-
trained teachers. Sereno Taylor, director of the school, was popular in
the community, even though he played the violin, an instrument the
rural Baptists and Methodists believed "to have been 'devised by the
evil Spirit' to encourage dancing." [15]

The Sparta Female Academy may have included among its students
the elite mulatto children of Judge Nathan Sayre, one of the founders
of the institution and a member of its board of directors. Judge Sayre
was a prominent politician and lawyer in Sparta who had emigrated to
the area from the North sometime in the 1820s. By the 1830s the Georgia legislature had appointed Sayre solicitor general for the Northern
District of Georgia and the electorate had placed the judge in the state
house and senate. By the 1830s Nathan Sayre also had established a
lasting relationship with Susan Hunt, a free woman of color. Nathan
Sayre and Susan Hunt Sayre had two daughters, Susan II and Mariah. [16]

In July 1839, Mary E. Moragne, a traveler and diarist, visited the
Sparta Female Academy. As an honored guest, Moragne attended an
examination on astronomy in which "the young ladies went with per-
fect ease through all the mysteries of Aries, Aquarius, Sagittarius, Arc-
tus, Antarctus, Pleiades, Orion, etc. etc., all of which seemed to me
like blowing bubbles into the air through a hollow rod, and likely to
be about as useful to them." Moragne then observed a cacophonous
collective musical recital using twelve pianos after which the head-
master sent for two "young ladies." Moragne described one of the per-
formers as having "large, dark eyes, soft and beautiful as a Turkish
dream of Houri" and the other as "a little dark complexioned girl."
This "interesting couple" then proceeded to play in concert "the most

beautiful and difficult airs and overtures." After the concert these two talented musicians were "surreptitiously whisked away" without the honored guest ever learning their names.[17] Adele Alexander has convincingly argued that these extraordinary, dark-complected musicians were Susan II and Mariah Sayre.

Judge Nathan Sayre's daughters were not the only blacks in Hancock County who were not treated as slaves. Some individuals listed themselves as free in the census, some registered as free with the county ordinary, as required by law, and some were so thoroughly protected by white paternalists that they did neither, as was the case with the Sayre children. In 1850 the census taker in Hancock County listed sixty-one people as free; however, in 1855, only twenty-four, or approximately 40 percent of these same individuals, registered with the ordinary. Among those listed in the 1850 census, the ratio of free females to males was twenty-seven to thirty-four. Nine individuals, or 15 percent of the total number of free persons of color, were mulatto. The census taker listed fifty-two free persons as black. In the county at large, 2.6 percent of the free population was listed as mulatto, compared with 8 percent in Georgia and 13.2 percent in the nation as a whole. According to the census of 1850, thirteen free persons of color lived in white households. Three of the males owned property ranging in value from $150 to $800.[18]

The census taker of 1860 registered thirty-seven people of color as free, seventeen females and twenty males; six were listed as mulatto and thirty-one as black. Only 41 percent of these individuals registered with the ordinary. Two of them lived in white households. In this census two females owned property, Cresa Ruff "a planter," worth $1,000, and Nancy Wadkins, worth $2,000, including two slaves, one eighteen-year-old black female and one two-year-old black male.[19]

A close examination of the Register of Free Persons of Color reveals either that free people were coming and going frequently or that registration was haphazard. Twenty-five individuals registered in 1855, the first year that a register was kept by the ordinary of Hancock County. By 1862 only three of those listed in 1855 remained, while ten individuals from 1856 did not register and none of the people who registered in 1860 were present. Lucretia, or Cresa, Ruff registered every year from

1855 to 1862, except 1859, but Nancy Wadkins never appears. The law required these individuals to register so as to protect their free status. If some people did not register at all and others did not register on a regular basis, it is reasonable to conclude that some free persons of color in Hancock County did not feel obliged to follow the dictates of the law or did not feel that their freedom needed this protection. The existence of elite free persons of color such as Susan II and Mariah Sayre, who did not register with the county ordinary or with the census taker, and the haphazard registration of other free persons of color indicate that, at least in Hancock County, Johnson and Roark may have overstated their case when they commented that "in the American South the small number of free mulattoes found that the racism of the white majority exerted steady downward pressure on all free people of color, mulattoes and blacks alike, barely allowing them a footing in freedom and always threatening to push them backward into bondage."[20]

There were other exceptions to the abstract rules that were intended to control the behavior of slaves and free people of color in Hancock County. Formal, institutionalized education for these individuals was nonexistent in Hancock County in the antebellum period. As early as 1820, Georgia law forbade the teaching of reading and writing to slaves. By 1829 the law prescribed a fine of up to five hundred dollars, or a whipping, for any slave or free person of color who could read or write or any white person who taught a slave or free person of color to read or write either printed or written characters. Nevertheless, slaves did learn to read and write from other slaves, from slaveholders, and from white children who had access to an education. Such was the case with Bishop Lucius Henry Holsey of Hancock County, who was born the slave of his father, James Holsey, and Louisa, of "pure African descent."[21]

In his autobiography, Holsey, a future Christian Methodist Episcopal bishop, recalled that as a young man of fifteen he felt "an insatiable craving for some knowledge of books, and especially I was anxious to learn to read the Bible." But he added sadly, "I was a slave and could not attend school, and it was considered unwise, if not dangerous, for slaves to read and write." Nevertheless, Holsey was determined to learn to read and write "at all hazards." Because of his slave status, Holsey's first problem was to accumulate enough cash to purchase books without giving the appearance of stealing from his master. He solved this problem by collecting rags and selling them for enough money to purchase two Webster *Blue Back Spellers,* a common school dictionary, Milton's *Paradise Lost,* and a Bible. These he described as "more precious to me than gold." The next problem was to find someone who would teach a slave the alphabet. "The white children and an old colored man" rescued Holsey from this dilemma. Each day Holsey would carry a leaf from one of the spelling books with him and when he was sitting in a carriage, walking in the yard, or using a hoe or a spade, he would take out his spelling leaf, catch a word, and commit it to memory. At night the future bishop would gather pine knots and pine roots, kindle a fire in his small room, turn over on his back to catch the light, and review his lessons.[22]

Somewhere, somehow, some of the black citizens of Hancock County, both slave and free, learned to read and write. In 1850 the census taker recorded that twenty-three, or 88 percent of the twenty-six adult free persons of color who resided in the county, were literate. In the 1860 census, fifteen of the twenty adult free persons of color, or 75 percent, registered as literate. Among the families who became prominent as freedmen, the Huberts, the Hunts, the Barneses, the Harrisons, and the Dicksons all contained literate family members. In the last decade before the Civil War the powers that be perceived education for persons of color to be dangerous. Nevertheless, some individuals found a way around the law, and the community tolerated these exceptions.[23]

By 1850, other organized social institutions for whites flourished in Hancock County in addition to churches and schools. One of the county's most famous agricultural organizations was the Hancock County Planters' Club. The club was founded in 1837 by eighteen "gentlemen," including ten prominent planters, two justices of the peace, the county sheriff, the clerk of the Inferior Court, two prominent schoolteachers, and the judge of the Superior Court, Nathan Sayre (Appendix C.3). At its organizational meeting the club elected William Terrell, one of the largest slaveholders in Hancock County, its first president. Joel Crawford, another leading planter, drafted a constitution that stated that the purpose of the club was to "advance the cause of agriculture, and to improve the practice of agricultural husbandry." Membership was open to those who subscribed to the constitution and paid one dollar annually. The original members of the club were "planters or professional men with considerable property in planting and other interest." Between 1837 and 1847, however, the club increased its membership to eighty and its rolls included "men of modest means."[24]

The men who founded and supported the Hancock County Planters' Club did so in response to the twin curses of cotton production and the accompanying soil depletion and emigration. In 1843 Eli Baxter, a member of the club, stated that all the choice lands in the county were occupied and what remained was depleted to the point of exhaustion: "At every point the eye meets the evacuated and dilapidated mansion and worn-out and exhausted plantations. Fields that once teemed with luxuriant crops are disfigured with gaping hillsides, chequered with gullies, coated with broom-straw and pine, the sure indices of barrenness and exhaustion—all exhibiting a dreary desolation." The lament continued: "Heretofore we have contemplated the gradual and certain deterioration of our lands with a careless indifference. Cheap and apparently inexhaustible supplies of rich land lay upon our borders. . . . But the choice lands in desirable locations are all occupied . . . and there is no alternative, but in expatriation, or [to] remain and be content with a lean and scanty subsistence."[25] The Hancock County Planters' Club offered an alternative to these bleak choices—replenishing the land.

In spite of a sense of urgency about the need for agricultural reform, the Hancock County Planters' Club was exclusive in one respect. It did not include women. In 1859 the club made an exception by making Martha Lewis, a widow, an honorary member so that she could receive a silver cup for growing the best acre of corn that year. Lewis responded to the club's invitation, using the third person: "She tenders due acknowledgment for this attention shown her by the club but whilst she confesses that she is much gratified, she would still desire to decline, if it means no disrespect, the conspicuousness which the ceremonies of a public presentation would give her." Nevertheless, she concluded that she would "comply with the wishes of the club."[26]

In the last decade before the Civil War the Hancock County Planters' Club was endeavoring to preserve a way of life. Through fairs and treatises on agriculture its members hoped to demonstrate an Old World idea, that planters and farmers could replenish the land and stay put. Nevertheless, white citizens continued to leave the county at an alarming rate.

In addition to the important social institutions, including churches, schools, and an agricultural club, society in Hancock County was held together by social conventions that evolved along with "civilization" and the plantation regime. Foremost among these was what David Potter has described as personalism. The people who stayed in the county knew one another and what to expect from their neighbors. Some knew each other and their families all their lives, across racial and class lines. In 1885, during the trial to decide the validity of David Dickson's will, the Superior Court of Hancock County summoned thirty-seven witnesses to testify. These individuals were Dickson's slaves, employees, business associates, relatives, and friends. Ten of them testified that they had known David Dickson all their lives. The six former slaves who testified declared that they had known Dickson an average of forty-three years. Twenty-nine white employees, business associates, relatives, and friends testified that they had known Dickson for an average of twenty-six years. Comments like "ever since I have known myself," "as long as I recollect," and "ever since I was a boy" appeared frequently in the court record.[27]

Manners and a shared sense of what Bertram Wyatt-Brown has termed honor, "essentially the cluster of ethical rules, most readily found in small communities, by which judgments of behavior are ratified by community consensus," minimized differences in status among whites in the county. According to Wyatt-Brown, individuals of high social status addressed those of lower status with directness and respect as whites and vice versa. In addition, status inequities among whites were minimized by notions of hospitality and generosity, which worked in both directions. Wyatt-Brown found that deviance from the accepted norms could be tolerated only if the offender "somehow conveys a sense of powerlessness, otherwise the nonconformist, whose misdeeds may be real or socially conjured up, faced ostracism or worse." In this system of honor, miscegenation and the formation of a white-mulatto kinship relationship within the elite class would constitute a violation of community norms, a "danger in the margins."[28] The relationship between Amanda America Dickson and her father disproves Wyatt-Brown's assumption that everyone who transgressed racial taboos in the antebellum South was "ostracized or worse." As we shall see, David Dickson sometimes behaved in an imperious manner, and though he may have been ostracized by a segment of the population in Hancock County, he certainly was accepted by other segments of this complex community.

This, then, was Amanda America Dickson's place, a place where black slaves outnumbered white citizens by almost two to one; a place where education, culture, and even luxury were available to a small minority of a ruling race; a place where enough was available for everybody to subsist; a place where people often knew each other all their lives. How did these factors combine across racial and class lines both to impose order on human behavior and to make it possible for the community to tolerate exceptions to that order in the elite class?[29]

A Story

Now I am an orphan.
—Amanda America Dickson, immediately after the death of David Dickson

DAVID, JULIA FRANCES, AND AMANDA AMERICA DICKSON'S
stories represent threads that intertwine to form a pattern, a pattern
distorted by the tensions between racial ideology and family, between
paternalism and exploitation, and between power and the control of
power in an interdependent community. As a consequence, Amanda
America Dickson's life unfolded within the boundaries of her father's
social and economic power, her mother's conflicting loyalties, and her
own evolving sense of self. The story of this family's struggles spans
almost all of the nineteenth century, bracketing the beginning and the
end of the plantation regime in Hancock County, the Civil War and
Reconstruction (the New South for some, the nadir for others), and the
complete disfranchisement of black Georgians by 1908.

Close analysis of the pattern of these lives reveals the processes by
which David Dickson created a web of interlocking social and economic relationships, accumulating enough power to transgress a fundamental social taboo. Julia Frances Dickson's story shows the conflicting loyalties that are reflected in her relationship to David, to Amanda,

and to her own black family. Amanda America Dickson's story is complicated because there are several contradictory versions of it. The African-American Dickson family oral history presents a picture of an elite "lady," in the ornamental sense (Appendix A.1). David Dickson's will, however, speaks of Amanda America in a respectful tone that acknowledges that she possessed "sound judgment." The contemporary newspapers that discuss Amanda America's story after David Dickson's death describe her as an oddity, a contemporary oxymoron, a wealthy black "lady." Finally, the Dickson will case transcript describes Amanda America Dickson as a person whose blackness was mitigated by her father's relationships in the community at large. This chapter describes the dilemmas the actions of these individuals posed for the community in which they lived, beginning at the end of David Dickson's long and productive life.

David Dickson died suddenly on February 18, 1885. He had taken his morning ride over his farm and returned home complaining that he felt cold. After lying down, he became unconscious and died in a few minutes. In an obituary the *Augusta Chronicle* described Dickson as a person who had been widely known throughout the South "as the foremost of all her agriculturists and the man above all others who had contributed most to the development of the farming interests of this section." He was "a man of mark," who had "amassed a large fortune." The author concluded by saying that Dickson's "death will be deeply regretted by a wide circle of friends."[1]

David Dickson's hometown newspaper, the *Sparta Ishmaelite*, dealt with his death on a more personal level. It described Dickson as a man of "vast information" and "unfailing will," who "gave no reasons for the positions he took or for the duties required of those he controlled. His will was law and his judgment infallible as far as they were concerned. He would not tolerate opposition." The editor of the *Ishmaelite* then mused, "What he did and what he failed to do, the debts and credits of a long and active life have gone to record. That record, as it stands in its entirety, as the only true will and testament, has gone to probate in the courts above without possibility of caveat." Hidden within these obituaries are subtle clues to the complex story of David

Dickson, his white family, his outside family, and the community of which they were all a part. The debits and credits of his long and active life might serve as Dickson's true will and testament in the heavenly courts, where nothing could be changed; however, Dickson's earthly last will and testament would create such a storm that a host of his white relatives would try to change it and the community of his family, friends, and acquaintances would have to face a reality that some of them had censured, some had ignored, and some had accepted.[2]

David Dickson was born on January 6, 1809, on a small farm in the southeastern part of Hancock County, in the same simple country house in which he would die seventy-six years later. He was the tenth child of Thomas Dickson and the fourth child of Thomas's second wife, Elizabeth Sholars Dickson (Appendix B.2). The Dickson house was small and the Dickson household lively. By the time David was five years old, his siblings included five brothers and half-brothers and seven sisters and half-sisters, some of whom were married and had children of their own. Because the family farm was nine miles from town in a sparsely populated county,[3] the Dickson children were necessarily homebodies, a pattern of living that extended into the adult lives of three of the several children of Elizabeth Dickson. Rutha, born in 1805, David born in 1809, and Green, born in 1814, never permanently moved away from the Dickson home place.

There were no frills in the Dickson household. The land that the family worked was poor. Nevertheless, the family was not economically marginal. Some of the children learned to read, and the family extracted enough profit from the land for Thomas to leave approximately 170 acres of land, at least nineteen slaves, and $500 in cash to his wife and children when he died in 1827.[4]

Very little information is available concerning David Dickson's childhood. His formal education probably did not exceed what he could learn in an old field school. We do know that David Dickson was more than simply literate. As an adult he composed long and informative letters to the agricultural press, which were published and drew a wide audience. In some of these letters Dickson described his crop yields and profits per acre in minute detail using calculations that required complex record-keeping skills and a high level of mathematical reasoning.[5]

An incident in David Dickson's later life demonstrated his devotion to his mother. Dr. E. W. Alfriend, who became the Dickson family physician in 1854, described the relationship between David Dickson and his mother: "Well sir, they were perfectly affectionate as far as I know. Mr. Dickson was not a demonstrative man, and the only occasion on which I ever saw him shed a tear was on the occasion when he thought his mother was going to die, and I thought so too." Dr. Alfriend described David Dickson's reaction to this grave situation: "He was in her room and seemed to be very much interested in her; and he wept; and that was the only time I ever saw him give way to his feelings."[6]

David Dickson's earliest recorded recollections of his childhood indicate that he went to work as a young person and that he was observant. He noticed while plowing and hoeing corn or "cutting the roots of plants" that he could see "the effect of hot days behind him in less than thirty minutes, wilted plants." According to the young Dickson, the damage would continue for days, "more or less according to the seasons." Dickson commented that "even with the hoe, digging around corn, and hilling up, I could see the corn wilt at once, in hot dry weather; and the corn would fire more or less, and sometimes be prevented from silking well. How was this to be prevented?" And most revealing of all, "I formed my opinion then, and put it in practice as soon as I commenced planting." Even though the Dickson family owned slaves, the male children went to work plowing as youngsters. As a worker on his father's farm, David Dickson did not feel free to make suggestions about improving the family farming methods. He determined to wait until he was independent.[7]

When David was eighteen years old, his father died, leaving property to his wife, Elizabeth, and to each of his "beloved" children. Elizabeth received approximately 170 acres of land between the Ogeechee and the Little Ogeechee; one-third of the horses, one-fourth of the cattle, one-fifth of the hogs; two beds; all the furniture; one-third of the working and farm tools; one year's support; three blacks; Bock and her child; Ephraim and a girl Mary; and during her lifetime, the slaves Jonathan, Tom, and Isaac. Each of Thomas's oldest five children received ten dollars, and each of the youngest eight received cash and one or two slaves. David received "two likely young Negroes, that is to say, one likely young fellow and one likely young wench, or their value in likely Negroes; also one good feather bed, bedstead and furniture, and seventy-five dollars in cash to be delivered to him at the time of his marriage or at the age of twenty-one years." By dividing his estate among his wife and all of his children, Thomas Dickson dispersed the family wealth. The oldest children received ready cash while the younger children received cash and a meager beginning as slaveholders. Neither Elizabeth nor any of the children received enough inheritance to maintain their standard of living without working themselves or controlling the profits from the work of others.[8]

David Dickson did not marry as a young man, and therefore he received his share of the estate in 1830, at the age of twenty-one. With that inheritance, which he later valued at $1,200, Dickson began his career as a merchant, trading and lending money out at interest, with an eye toward eventually becoming a planter. The census of 1840 lists him as a thirty-one-year-old male living at the Dickson home place with his mother, who was described as the head of the household. David Dickson also maintained a room in the house of his sister Lucinda Dickson Rogers in the county seat of Sparta so that he could also carry on his business enterprises. In 1840 David Dickson owned six slaves and no land in Hancock County. We can presume that he was either hiring out his slaves or maintaining them on the Dickson farm. In 1840 Elizabeth Dickson owned twelve slaves, approximately 160 acres in Hancock County, and 150 acres in the Cherokee strip.[9]

By 1845 David Dickson had accumulated an estate worth $25,000 and was in the initial stages of transforming himself from a plowboy to a merchant to a planter (Appendix C.4). In 1841 he had owned ten slaves and no land. By 1845 he owned forty-five slaves and 1,000 acres of land. By the end of 1849, Dickson owned 2,010 acres of land, some of which he had purchased for as little as fifty cents an acre, and fifty-three slaves. Only seven individuals in Hancock County owned more than fifty-three slaves in 1849.[10]

The section of the county where the Dickson family homesteaded and where David Dickson established his largest plantation was composed of poor land. In one of the few instances in which David Dickson

made an effort to be humorous, he described his land as commencing
on "granite hills" in Hancock County and running to "rotten lime-
stone" in Washington County, "containing some of every kind of land
in Middle Georgia—from red rocky hills to a blowing sand—from mulatto soil to pipe-clay. I tell you, if a man can make corn and cotton
on blowing sand, he can make it anywhere above water, off of a solid
rock." [11] The secret to David Dickson's success on this land lay in his
good judgment, the extensive use of commercial fertilizers, and a system of labor that taught each laborer to be an expert.

In 1850 David Dickson still lived on the Dickson home place with his
mother, his unmarried sister Rutha, and his unmarried brother Green.
Each of them also owned slaves: Elizabeth, twelve; Rutha, thirteen; and
Green, thirteen. One of Elizabeth's slaves was David's infant daughter,
Amanda America Dickson. [12]

Amanda America was also the daughter of Julia Frances Lewis Dickson. Julia Dickson is described in the African-American Dickson oral
history as a small, copper-colored person with soft hair and beautiful
teeth, a woman who was "very temperamental and high-strung" (Appendix A.1). [13] At the time of Amanda America Dickson's birth, November 20, 1849, Julia Dickson was thirteen and David Dickson was forty.

We do not know what reactions the violence of Amanda America
Dickson's conception evoked. Years later, David Dickson commented
that Julia had been a waiting maid in his mother's house and that
he had "let his foot slip." According to the African-American Dickson
family oral history, Julia never forgave David for the rape, for forcing
her to have sex with him at such an early age. Julia was a "great pet"
of Elizabeth Dickson's so what was Elizabeth's reaction to this violent
event? Deborah Gray White has observed that sometimes genuine affection flowed between white mistresses and slave children, as was the
case with Frankie Goole and her mistress, who warned her to "always
be a good girl, en don't let a man er boy trip me." In fact, Elizabeth
could not protect the child Julia, whom she owned, from rape by her
own son. Julia Dickson's mother, Rose, and her two brothers, Seab and
John C. Lewis, were also living on the Dickson plantation at this time
and were probably aware of the rape. Their reaction is unknown. Years

after abolition, Bishop Lucius Henry Holsey commented that "the way amalgamation has been brought about in the Southern States is enough to make the bushman in the wild jungles blush with shame." [14]

We do not know whether Amanda America Dickson was born in the Dickson home place or in Julia Dickson's house in the yard. Nor did anyone record her naming. America is certainly a patriotic, and consequently ironic, name for a slave. It does not seem likely that Julia Frances Dickson named her daughter Amanda America. Perhaps her father or grandmother gave her the name. Perhaps they were expressing their own patriotic view of the sectional conflict that raged over slavery in the territories at the time. Were they expressing their belief that in America this child could be brought into their family in spite of her color, that she could be rescued from slavery and racial categories by their individual wills, even in the South?

After Amanda America was weaned, she was taken from her mother, another act of violence against Julia Dickson as tragic as the rape itself. Thereafter the child lived in her white grandmother's room, sleeping in a trundle bed that Elizabeth Dickson had made especially for her. She lived in that same room, in the white Dickson household, until her grandmother's death in 1864.[15] One wonders what arrangements would have been made if Amanda had been a grandson instead of a granddaughter.

Later in his life David Dickson reflected on the decision to bring Amanda America into the Dickson household. He declared that he believed it was his duty to care for his daughter and that he wanted her to be with him. Perhaps these feelings prompted Dickson to take the infant into his household. Perhaps Elizabeth Dickson made the decision to separate Amanda America from her mother in an effort to make amends for her son's loss of control, or perhaps she simply wanted the company of her grandchild and could obtain David's cooperation. One of Elizabeth Dickson's grandsons commented that he had "never seen a man in all his life who was as kind to his mother as [David] was; I have never seen any person any kinder; there was nothing he could do for her but what he was ready to do it." Perhaps David and Elizabeth made the decision together to create a "family" that excluded the mother.[16]

During the antebellum period in the South, it was not unusual for a master or mistress to bring a slave into a white household. According to Mary Chesnut, her mother-in-law slept with two servants in the same room, in case she needed attention during the night, and two servants in the next room as guards. In the case of slave children, as Elizabeth Fox-Genovese has observed, "It was widely believed that the best way to develop good house servants, who were notoriously difficult to come by, was to raise them." Likewise, Ella Gertrude Clanton Thomas observed in her diary that a slave child whom she knew was "a bright, quick child and raised in our family could have become a good servant. As it is she will be under her mother's influence and run wild in the street." In the case of Amanda America, the servant was an infant. For a time at least, she would have to be cared for in a family of older white people.[17]

Between Amanda America's birth in 1849 and Elizabeth Dickson's death in 1864, several other members of the white Dickson household formed intimate connections with slaves and tenants alike. Observers remembered Green Dickson as very different from his older brother. Green was short, about five feet seven inches tall, and thin, while David was six feet tall and weighed approximately two hundred pounds. David was generally remembered as a very sober man, while Green was remembered as "wild and reckless" and given to drink. The relationship between David and Green was stormy on several counts. During the Dickson will case trial, James M. Dickson, a witness for the white relatives who were contesting the will, was asked about the "state of feelings" between David and Green at the time Amanda America was born. Did Green threaten to kill David "because he had put this nigger Julia over his mother?"[18] Unfortunately, the question was stricken from the record.

In 1850 Green made out a will, and shortly thereafter he died. His will declared that because his "collateral kin" did not need any aid, he felt it was his duty to assist and maintain "certain persons." Green then directed his executor, his older half-brother James Dickson, to permit Nancy Lewis (white) and her present children to stay on his farm and have the use of as much land as they might need, with the privilege of firewood, "as long as she shall conduct herself with propriety in the opinion of the said executor, and she shall take proper care of said children." Green warned, "Whenever her conduct, in the opinion of said executor, shall require it, He shall take the exclusive possession of said place (land), stock, etc. and make other provisions for said children and their support." Green gave his executor a black girl named Jane Wilder, who was reputed to be his daughter. Subsequently he left slaves to each of Nancy Lewis's children, Ellen, Elizabeth, Susan, and John W. Lewis; to Charlotte Lewis's child, Pleasant; and to the two youngest children of Martha Lewis, Sis and Joseph, "to be selected by each of said children on his or her marriage or attaining age and then to become his or her property." Green left the remainder of his estate to the same children in equal portions. Green instructed his executors to hire out his slaves and apply the proceeds of such hiring "to the support and education in an economical mode of all the aforesaid children." As a last effort to provide autonomy to the female children, Green directed his executor that "if any of the above named female children marry, her legacy and portion shall be conveyed to a trustee for her separate use free from the claims of her husband." Green saw it as his duty to provide for the control of Nancy Lewis's behavior by a male and for the financial independence of Nancy Lewis's female children from their husbands via a legal instrument. Obviously, Green did not trust Nancy Lewis in particular or husbands in general.[19]

David Dickson's sister Rutha's relationship with her slaves appears to have been less intimate and more paternalistic, maternalistic in this case. Rutha Dickson died in 1855. In her will she left all of her slaves to her mother, "in consideration of the great kindness shown to me and the unwearied attention bestowed on me by my dear mother during the many years of affliction, I give and bequeath unto her all my property consisting of Negroes (twenty), debts due to me, money, and the interest I have in my deceased father's estate." Rutha "enjoined" her mother to "continue to my Negroes the same kind treatment they have always received at my hand and to give each of them who may be grown twenty dollars per annum as a token of my kind remembrance of them." The will then appointed James Thomas and Rutha's brothers, Thomas and David, as executors and instructed, "The word five erases twenty underlined and the word gratuity [the] underlined per annum." Rutha then signed her will with an X, indicating that she could not write her own name or know about the substitutions to her will unless someone read them to her. Someone may have changed Rutha's instructions without informing her of the alterations. This seems most likely because Rutha was on her deathbed when she dictated her will. Someone was setting limits on the generosity that Rutha wanted to extend to her slaves after her death.[20]

The white Dicksons also set limits on the generosity they were willing to extend to each other. In 1860 Elizabeth Dickson, at the "special instance" of David Dickson, divided her property, including thirty-six slaves, among her children. In return David promised to support his mother in a "handsome and comparable manner during her natural life and to pay her annually $200 to enable her to appropriate the same to charitable purposes such as she shall select." In the event that David died first, Elizabeth was to select slaves from his estate for her use. David instructed his executors to provide Elizabeth with a carriage and enough money to make her "entirely comfortable, not to exceed $2000 per annum."[21]

From her birth in 1849 until her grandmother's death in 1864, Amanda America Dickson remained legally a slave. During this time period, it would have been virtually impossible for Elizabeth or David to free Amanda and still keep her with them in Georgia. As early as 1801 the state of Georgia had outlawed manumission within the state, except by petitioning the legislature, a process that became more and more restrictive after 1818. Before 1859 masters and mistresses could free their slaves outside the state while they were alive or outside the state via their wills. Amanda Dickson could have been freed in another state, but she could not have legally returned to Georgia as a free person of color. For Elizabeth and David to keep Amanda America with them on the Dickson home place, the child remained a slave and continually at risk, vulnerable to her grandmother's and her father's mortality.[22]

In the event of the deaths of her grandmother and her father, mechanisms existed to protect Amanda America from being sold on the auction block. Either one of them could direct their executors to take the

child to a free state and manumit her there. A much more dangerous arrangement would have been to bequeath Amanda America to
someone they trusted. Two of David Dickson's brothers made special
provisions for female slaves by directing that they be given or sold to
specific individuals and instructing these individuals, either in a deed
or by a will, to give the children special care. David's older brother John
made out a deed bequeathing the mulatto girl Caroline, aged seventeen, worth $1,600, to David. David did not register the deed until
John's death. Likewise, Green Dickson willed Jane Wilder, who was
reputed to be his daughter, to his older half-brother James Dickson. If
David and Elizabeth had died before 1865, the only protection from
chattel slavery that Amanda America would have had in the state of
Georgia would have been the loyalty of David's or Elizabeth's executors and that of her new owner. Elizabeth and David Dickson took that
risk and kept Amanda America in the slave South.[23]

When Amanda America Dickson was born, the white Dickson household was composed of older, widowed, or never-married white people.
Elizabeth Dickson was seventy-two when her granddaughter was born,
David was forty, Rutha was forty-three, and Green was thirty-five. All
of them lived in the same house, though Green seems to have come
and gone. This nuclear family of older white people treated Amanda
America like a slave child, a servant, a pet, and a member of the family.

According to both the African-American Dickson family oral history and white observers, Amanda America spent most of her childhood and youth in her grandmother's room. Julia Frances Dickson
observed that Amanda stayed there night and day, studying her books
and doing "whatever she was told to do." Dr. E. W. Alfriend, the Dickson family doctor, observed that Amanda America was "very devoted"
to her grandmother and "very comfortably situated" in her grandmother's room.[24]

Some evidence supports the thesis that Amanda was treated like a
servant by her white relatives, although she was weaned and then taken
from her mother and placed in Elizabeth Dickson's room. As an infant
she could not have played the servant role. When asked what Amanda
did, one of David Dickson's nephews commented that "she was about

the house like any other child would be; helped at sweeping the floor and such as that." When asked about the feelings of Elizabeth Dickson toward Amanda, the same relative responded that "[Elizabeth] had the kindest feelings towards Amanda."[25]

Although she may have performed some duties that would typically be performed by servants, the evidence suggests that some members of the white Dickson household treated Amanda America as they would a pet, as someone to love and spoil, behavior very much like the care and "loving fascination" with children that Jane Turner Censer argues was common within elite planter families but not possible in relationships between these families and slave children. According to the African-American Dickson family oral history, Amanda America was the "darling of David Dickson's heart." He "adored her" and "gave her everything in the world. He had her bathed in sweet milk to lighten her skin. He allowed her to claim newborn slaves as her own and name them whatever she liked." Everyone on the plantation called her "Miss Mandy," including her father, and, one would presume, her mother. "She was his pampered darling." Because Amanda America Dickson was a mulatto and a slave, this description of child rearing seems tragic. It is a picture of a raceless "little princess of the hinter isles" raised in a make-believe world. Curiously, the African-American Dickson family oral history does not record this situation with regret.[26]

Some evidence suggests that the white Dickson household provided for Amanda America Dickson as though she were a member of the family. She learned to read and write, which was certainly a luxury for any girl child of the time. Elizabeth, Rutha, and Julia were illiterate. Green and David were not. Scholars have observed that antebellum southern fathers often took charge of their daughters' formal education.[27] Perhaps Amanda America learned to read and write from her father. Their signatures are very similar.[28]

During the Dickson will case trial, it became evident that Amanda shared many of her father's characteristics. This evidence supports the thesis that David "took Charge" of his daughter's education. Judge J. C. Simmons commented, "[Amanda America] favored Mr. Dickson in her personal appearance, her manner of speech, and general management of business." According to the African-American Dickson family oral history, tutors came to the Dickson plantation to teach Amanda America. They specifically remembered that she read *Camille*, a play written in 1852 by Alexander Dumas the Younger, himself a mulatto. Ironically, the play deals with a young courtesan in Paris who was doomed to be "ostracized from polite society." [29]

While residing within the boundaries of the white Dickson household, Amanda America learned the skills and manners appropriate to her family's class. As a child she learned to play the piano; to dress with subdued elegance, including the display of jewelry; and to behave like a "lady," in the educated though ornamental sense. Amanda America Dickson also learned to manage business transactions in the manner of her very successful father and to retain control of her own financial affairs after marriage. We do not know who her friends were as a child or as an adult. We do not know if or how the family of Elizabeth, David, and Amanda protected themselves, especially Amanda, from chance encounters with individuals who were not aware of their unorthodox arrangements. And we do not know how Julia Frances Dickson reacted to having her daughter raised as a mulatto slave who was addressed by everyone, including her mother and white father, as "Miss Amanda" or "Miss Mandy."

While Amanda America was growing up and spending most of her time reading in the big house, her mother lived a very different life. Julia Frances Lewis Dickson began her life as a slave living in a "nigger" house in the yard with the other servants. It was a large frame building, two stories high, with three to five rooms. By 1857 Julia Dickson was living in another house on the edge of the yard that was "a little better furnished." Julia lived upstairs in this second house, in a room partitioned off from the other servants. Her mother, Rose, had an adjoining room separated from Julia's space by a door.[30] From these residences, Julia Frances Dickson moved in and out of the white Dickson household as a slave with a privileged position.

Between 1849 and 1863, David Dickson prospered. His slave force grew from 53 to 160. All of these individuals had to be housed and fed and clothed, and Julia Dickson was part of the great organic structure that made this possible. One of David Dickson's nephews remembered that Julia "waited in the house and minded the table, and so on." He added that "after the child [Amanda] was born, [Julia], was confined a good deal nursing the child and while she was nursing the child she did a good deal of sewing; after that period ceased she was active about the house under the direction of my grandmother like any other slave would be." Julia Dickson described her own work as follows: "I assisted in making up the beds, swept the yards and did anything else about the house and garden." [31]

During the last decade before the Civil War, Julia Dickson gave birth to two more children by two different fathers, one of whom was black and one of whom was white. In 1853, when Julia Dickson was seventeen, she delivered Julianna, nicknamed Juan, whose father was another Dickson slave, Joe Brooken the wagoner. Thirteen months later, when she was eighteen, she gave birth to another child, Lola, whose father was "Doc Eubanks," a white man. Lola died as a small child. These early pregnancies compromised Julia Dickson's health. E. W. Alfriend, the Dickson family doctor from 1854 to 1861, remembered that he "never missed a year that I didn't attend [Julia] in some sickness." [32]

In addition to these sexual relationships, Julia maintained an intimate relationship with David Dickson that was more than simply sexual. Other slaves and at least one white employee on the Dickson plantation observed a relatively open show of affection between Julia and David. They were present when David lifted Julia down from her horse and kissed her. They also observed David kissing Julia on other occasions. [33] In addition, other members of the plantation community and several of David Dickson's relatives observed David and Julia behaving as intimates, sitting in the parlor or by the fire in David Dickson's bedroom, talking over business and other matters of concern to them both.[34] During the Dickson will case trial, when Julia Dickson was asked by the attorneys for the caveators about these multiple sexual relationships, the following exchange took place:

Q. Did anybody else have anything to do with you [sexually] except the men who were the father[s] of these children?
A. No, sir.
Q. You say it mighty weak? Julia?
A. I can say it strong.
Q. You just confined your favors to those three?
A. To those three.
Q. And to Joe Brooken?
A. I don't know anything about confining myself; I was not a bad woman.[35]

As Julia reached adulthood and Elizabeth Dickson became more and more infirm, the younger woman assumed control of the household. Along with another mulatto slave, Lucy, Julia stood guard over the keys to the plantation and presided over the kitchen. In essence, Julia became David Dickson's housekeeper. In this role she was described by Dr. E. W. Alfriend as "a very attentive business woman about the house." In fact, said Dr. Alfriend, "I became very much attached to the woman."[36]

Anne Goodwyn Jones has observed that there existed a role for a black woman in white antebellum southern homes as "mammy," a person who "became the nurturant, all-giving mother figure, beloved because she threatened the hierarchy of neither race nor sex." In the white Dickson household, Julia Frances Dickson was, in certain respects, the antithesis to Jones's ideal "mammy." She "attentively" controlled the domestic sphere of David Dickson's domain while maintaining an overtly intimate relationship with the master. She was in Deborah Gray White's terms both the mammy, serving as surrogate mother to her own child, and the Jezebel, the mistress of the master. Did this arrangement threaten labor management on the Dickson plantation, where Julia controlled the access of her own kin both to the necessities of life and the few luxuries that were available? How did it affect white people who transacted business through her? Viewed as political acts,

these arrangements threatened the essential myths of the racial hierarchy of chattel slavery, the moral superiority of all whites, the myth of
beastliness of all blacks, and finally, the myth of racial purity, a myth
that Mary Douglas has claimed was an essential "enemy of change, of
ambiguity and compromise."[37]

During Amanda America Dickson's childhood years, David Dickson became wealthy and famous. By 1860 he was the richest planter
in Hancock County, with 150 slaves in his own name (Appendix C.4);
350 cattle, 100 of which were milk cows and 37 of which were oxen;
600 hogs; 200 sheep; and 57 horses and mules. Of his 150 slaves, 55
were "hands" and 60 were "little Negroes under the age of ten." By
1860 David Dickson's plantation was self-sufficient. All the corn and
meat that were needed were produced at home along with wagons,
carts, plows, shoes, wool, and slaves' clothing plus 666 bales of cotton
weighing approximately 425 pounds each.[38]

In addition, by 1860 David Dickson had become famous as one of
Georgia's most innovative and successful farmers. In the early 1850s,
C. W. Howard, the editor of the widely read *Southern Countrymen,*
which later became the *Southern Cultivator,* "discovered" Dickson.
Howard praised Dickson in his publications and invited him to publish
letters describing the Dickson method of farming in both journals. As
a result, by 1861, Dickson was labeled in the agricultural publications
of the day as the "Prince of Georgia Farmers" and described as "the
person most responsible for agricultural reform in the region."[39]

At the end of the decade of the 1850s, one skeptical visitor to the
Dickson plantation wrote a long, insightful article for the *Southern Cultivator* describing his conversion to Dickson's method of farming. The
author, signed only as "An Empty Corncrib," described David Dickson's plantation as composed of "poor pine land," presided over by
a "humble, unpretending planter," who, "surrounded by his success,
seems to have no greater pleasure than to impart to others all that he
has learned by years of experience, close application to business, and
continuous and patient investigation." The visitor went on to describe
meeting David Dickson, "a man dressed in a neat summer suit, sitting
on an unpretentious porch, with a naturally fair complexion, though

somewhat burnished by the sun's rays, and a face indicating reflection and will, when not lit up with a genial smile of hospitality and welcome with which he greets his guest, a man of leisure." After meeting David Dickson, the author and his company were treated to a five-year-old apple cider cordial, watermelon, a comfortable dinner, and a guided tour of the plantation. They "sallied forth" through large, flat fields of corn and cotton, fields at rest, and fields in which Dickson was growing experimental crops.[40]

The experiments that these and other visitors came to the Dickson plantation to observe were based on a "scientific method" of farming that David Dickson had helped to create. Between 1840 and 1860, agricultural reformers began to approach planting from the point of view of permanent residents. They realized that if the citizens of the region were going to maintain stable communities, farming practices would have to become more respectful of the land. As Dickson put the case, "In addition to the present profit that is derived from the use of guano and other fertilizers, I consider it our moral duty to increase the productiveness of the land equal to the increase in population. Succeeding generations should find it as easy to live as the present, and we should look upon ourselves as being only tenants at will."[41] As a result of this change in philosophy, by 1860 a successful method of planting had evolved that included deep contour plowing in preparation for planting, shallow cultivation, crop rotation, heavy applications of both animal and commercial fertilizers, the careful management of labor, and economic independence, or self-sufficiency.

David Dickson made several valuable contributions to the evolution of this new system. First, he advocated an experimental approach to farming: "I believe in natural laws, study nature; trace all things from cause to effect, and effect to cause." Second, Dickson claimed to be the first farmer in the region to use imported Peruvian guano experimentally and then on a large scale. He described the use of this commercial fertilizer and the results of experiments on relatively poor land in his letters in the *Cultivator*. According to the agricultural press, Dickson also demonstrated that slave laborers could be taught to become expert operatives who took pride in their work and worked efficiently without supervision. Finally, Dickson, through his letters to the agricultural publications and the hospitality he extended to anyone who wanted to "come see for themselves," demonstrated that the new plan worked.[42]

Dickson's contributions to the agricultural revolution in the region were useful to the ruling class in more than just an economic sense. Clearly, he became a very wealthy man by using a scientific approach to planting on poor land. His wealth became a source of pride for other citizens of Hancock County. Articles by and about David Dickson appeared not only in the agricultural press but also in the regional newspapers. Citizens of the county invited their friends to come see the "Modern Mecca of farming," and David Dickson entertained them royally. By 1859, "L. of Babewake," in a letter to the *Southern Cultivator*, invited anyone who doubted the prosperity of Hancock County farmers to visit, and "in half a day from here I can put you down at Dixon's [Dickson's] and the general opinion is that you will not—need not—desire to go any further. You'll see the elephant." In addition, the local newspaper, the *Sparta Ishmaelite*, used David Dickson's success to brag about Hancock County at the expense of Oglethorpe and other plantation counties.[43]

The story of David Dickson's fame and fortune was also useful to the planter class in Hancock County in another, more subtle way. By introducing commercial fertilizers and demonstrating that they could be used economically, David Dickson provided a method for farmers on marginal land to make a better living without wearing out the soil. Consequently, the agricultural press exhorted poorer individuals to be hopeful and content, which would contribute significantly to maintaining a stable white population and the plantation regime.

The planter class was indebted to David Dickson for demonstrating that slave labor could be profitable without the extensive use of overt violence. Contemporary newspapers, Dickson himself, and, ironically, twentieth-century white agricultural historians who defended slavery as a system all claimed that Dickson's slaves took pride in their work and consequently worked without supervision, much less coercion. According to the *Southern Cultivator*, "The truth is, his hands see that they beat their neighbors, and people are constantly coming to see their fine crops, and they feel a pride in their success, and indeed that our plantation shall not be beat." David Dickson himself declared that "no system can prosper without learning all the operations and laborers to be experts. The first thing to do in regards to any of the operations of labor, is to teach the laborers how to do it; the next thing, to do it with more ease and efficiency, and to learn to do better and better work every day." Dickson boasted that "I have in five minutes, learned a hand to pick one hundred pounds more of cotton per day than he has picked on the previous day, and from that point he will continue to improve." In this argument David Dickson solves the problem of managing slave labor through the simple expedient of overcoming ignorance and instilling pride.[44]

Mid-twentieth-century agricultural historians have argued that Dickson's most significant contribution was his demonstration that slaves could be taught to become expert operatives who worked without supervision. Perhaps this assumption was true for some slaves, but it is unrealistic to presume that it was true for all of Dickson's slaves. In 1886, when one of Dickson's former slaves, Matthew Dickson, was asked if Dickson whipped his slaves, he replied, "Yes sir, most of them down there." Joe Brooken, another Dickson slave, declared that "[the slaves] all had to obey [David Dickson]." Peaches Armstrong, an elderly black citizen of Hancock County, the granddaughter of two Dickson slaves, Raibun and Julianna Youngblood, described the situation for slaves on the Dickson plantation as "terrible." The "mens would go off to get more children and leave those women in charge; they treated people like pigs; fed people out of a trough and would not let anybody have sugar." According to Eula Youngblood, the wife of Tommy Youngblood, child of Amanda Dickson's half-sister Julianna and Raibun Youngblood, David Dickson "created a class system among his slaves with drivers whose status put them above the other slaves. There was a whipping post on that plantation. When I think of those times I smile to keep from crying."[45]

In addition to misrepresenting labor relations on the Dickson plantation, later agricultural historians also distorted David Dickson's relationship with the Hancock County Planters' Club. These historians assumed that David Dickson was excluded from the club because of his open liaison with "his concubine Amanda A. Dickson." Amanda A. Dickson was not David's concubine but his daughter, and the Hancock County Planters' Club was founded in 1837, twelve years before Amanda America was born, at a time when David Dickson was a relatively poor merchant. Its only requirement for membership was that a prospective member pay one dollar and support the constitution. By 1860 the club advertised for members in the public press and held its meetings out of doors. In all probability, David Dickson was not excluded from the club but chose not to join. As Dickson wryly commented, "I do not plant for premiums, or for silver cups [which the Planters' Club awarded at its annual fairs] but for good dividends and plenty of corn to feed my friends' horses when they honor me with a visit."[46]

By the 1850s David Dickson was one of the main attractions at the Hancock County Planters' Club annual fairs. In 1859 the editors of the *Southern Cultivator* reported that "a run of persons were drawn to the fair in hopes of eliciting information from Mr. Dickson." They continued, "To many of them, he was compelled to reply that they would find his system fully stated in the *Southern Cultivator*." Ironically, the *Southern Cultivator* then apologized for relating that David Dickson had denied some requests for visits to his plantation. "Under ordinary circumstances, this particularity of detail as to the private affairs of an individual would be in bad taste and must be unpleasant to the subject. But emigration is depopulating old Georgia—her lands have gradually depreciated in saleable value." According to editors of the *Cultivator*, "Mr. Dickson had shown us that a fortune could be made on Georgia lands and in the process the land be restored to its original fertility. The thanks of the South are due to this gentleman."[47]

As David Dickson became wealthier by exploring the new system of agriculture and a chattel slave system of labor, a parallel process intensified, which eventually threatened both his wealth and his private social arrangements—the argument over slavery in the new states and territories. By the late 1850s and the dawning of the 1860s, David Dickson realized what lay ahead. In a letter to his friend James Thomas on April 8, 1865, Dickson reiterated the predictions he said that he had made before the Civil War had begun: "That we never would get any peace by fighting; that Lincoln would issue the proclamation freeing the slaves and arming them after he found that our resistance was permanent; that he [Lincoln] would do more by fire and theft than the sword; and that Davis would never yield to any compromise. He [Davis] would have all or none."[48] If David Dickson saw what the war would bring as clearly as he says he did, he must have felt anxiety for both his wealth and the special place he had maintained for Amanda America Dickson. Ahead loomed the prospects of both poverty and a new social order.

In 1861, when the war erupted, Amanda America Dickson was twelve years old. At that time her household consisted of her grandmother, who was eighty-four years old, and her father, who was fifty-two. Having spent her childhood in the white Dickson household, mostly in her grandmother's room, she may have been unaware of the impending crisis. After all, she lived in the household of a powerful patriarch-paternalist, a man who had protected her from other ambiguities and anxieties. By the end of the war in 1865, however, Amanda America, at the age of sixteen, must have been aware of her uncertain future.

What Julia Frances Dickson thought about the impending crisis is unclear. She was twenty-five years old when the Civil War broke out. She was also a slave. One of her living daughters had been taken from her and benefited materially from the slave system while the other, Julianna Youngblood, had not. In fact, Julianna, Julia's mother, Rose, and her brothers John C. and Seab Lewis were Dickson slaves. Julia's privileged position as the Dicksons' housekeeper rested on David Dickson's wealth, which rested on the backs of his slave labor force, Julia Dickson's kin.

At the beginning of the Civil War, Hancock County escaped the ravages of battle; nevertheless, planters' lives changed drastically. The "agricultural revolution" came to a halt as planters grew crops to provision the Confederate army. The newspapers no longer contained letters from and about David Dickson and his farm as a "modern Mecca" but were full of news of the war. Planters no longer came from "all over the county" to visit David Dickson.

Though David Dickson claimed to have been a reluctant secessionist, he supported the Confederate cause. By his own reckoning, he sold eight hundred bales of cotton to the Confederacy and a "large amount" of bacon and grain. In 1863, he paid $27,000 in taxes to support the rebellion, leading one observer to describe his contribution as "almost sacrificial." "[Dickson] delivered to the Confederate Government 400 bales of cotton for which he got bonds which were never paid; and after the first year of the war he planted no cotton, but raised provisions for the Army, and for most of which he received no pay, not even Confederate money." [49]

While the war raged in other parts of the South, slave unrest became apparent in Hancock County. Linton Stephens, a resident of Hancock County and the brother of Alexander H. Stephens, vice-president of the Confederacy, observed in September 1863: "Our Negro population is going to give us trouble. . . . I believe that the institution of slavery is already so undermined and demoralized as never to be of much use to us, even if we had peace and independence today." [50]

As a manifestation of this deterioration, slaves in Hancock County began to run away and then to revolt. The slave woman "Savannah" was the first "to go over to the Yankees." Shortly thereafter, sometime in March 1863, "at corn planting time," a group of slaves who had previously met to trade wine and tobacco formed a military unit. They met once a week at night, in an old field. They began by swearing everyone to secrecy. According to a member of the band, they all held up their hands and swore to die before telling what they had heard or seen. The group elected officers—Dick Shaw as captain, John Cain as lieutenant, Spencer Beasley as next "head man," and Mack Simmons last. All four were skilled workmen. Cain and Shaw were painters, Simmons a blacksmith, and Beasley a shoemaker. The company continued to meet through the summer at night, in the old field. They drank blackberry wine "occasionally," drilled, and, no doubt, talked about freedom. According to members of the company, John Cain said that they ought to be free and they would have to fight for their freedom. His plan was to "fight their way through" to Sparta, enter "private houses" and take arms and ammunition, then "fire" Sparta and head for the Yankee troops. Dick Shaw wanted to band together and head for the Yankees and to attack only if the group was attacked.[51]

On September 13, 1863, "a very dark night," the company met and divided into two groups. It is not clear what happened next except that John Cain fired a shot at Allen Stevens, a white farmer, hitting his hat. After the shooting, "everybody ran." Eventually the authorities arrested the ringleaders, Cain, Shaw, Beasley, and Simmons, and incarcerated them in the county jail. Thirty other individuals were whipped and released. In November 1863, all four of the ringleaders were tried in the Superior Court of Hancock County, convicted of attempting to incite an insurrection, and sentenced to hang. Mack Simmons and John Cain were executed. The governor commuted the sentence of Spencer Beasley to four hundred lashes because 120 of the "best citizens of Hancock County" petitioned for mercy. The court recommended clemency for Dick Shaw, who was beaten and released. When Cain and Simmons were hanged, northern troops under the command of General William T. Sherman were only months away from their invasion of Hancock County.

Mary Roxie Lane Edwards, the daughter of Colonel Andrew Jackson Lane, one of the largest slaveholders in Hancock County before the Civil War, was seven years old at the time and described the situation at the Dickson plantation in a story she wrote as an adult. The story begins with the appearance of a young grandson who implored his grandmother, Mrs. Edwards, to tell him about the old days in Hancock County. Obligingly the grandmother began by explaining that she had grown up at Granite Hill, her father's plantation, located ten or twelve miles from "Mr. David Dixon's [Dickson's] place." Edwards described the Dickson place as "housing hundreds of Negroes who worked 30,000 acres of land, a place with so many houses that it looked like a town." She then described the relationship between her family and David Dickson on a personal level: "Mr. Dixon was a great friend of my father and admired my mother and sisters very much. His servant, going for the mail every day, passed Granite Hill and always stopped with something that Mr. Dixon sent—a big rattlesnake watermelon, a basket of grapes, a lamb, or strawberries, something he thought that we might not have." [52]

Edwards also described David Dickson's special attention to her as a child. "He often had our family down to spend a day and, although I was a very little girl, he would send me a special invitation. This was a great deal of pleasure to me, and he certainly did know how to entertain a child." David Dickson arranged for special entertainment for her while she visited the Dickson plantation. "He always had a certain young negro woman to take charge of me and look after me. That was all she had to do that day. She would fix the prettiest popcorn I have ever seen, make candy for me, peel sugar cane and crack nuts and play with me." Edwards also recalled that after dinner, "[the young black woman] would take a large basket of food for the fish, and the dinner bell, and we would go and stand on the bridge over the pond and ring the bell for fish to come to their dinner." According to Edwards, "[the fish] would come as fast as they could. The water would look as though a whirlwind had struck it. I thought it was fine fun to ring that bell." [53]

Mary Roxie Lane Edwards then told about the ravages of war. Her father had been wounded in Virginia and had recuperated in the home of a Mrs. Grainer. When "Col." Lane finally returned home to Granite Hill, he brought Mrs. Grainer's daughter with him, and "Mr. Dixon got up a big dinner party in her honor and invited us all down for the day." Unfortunately, General Sherman's troops arrived in the southern part of Hancock County the same day, and the dinner was lost to the Yankee soldiers: barbecued hog, lamb, shoat, veal, beef, chicken, hominy, sparrowgrass salad, sweet potato pie, roast turkey, lemon pie, scuppernong wine, blackberry jam, and rice and gravy. Mary Roxie Lane Edwards explained that the troops did not burn the Dickson home place or capture David Dickson because "Mr. Dixon's old mother was there" and David Dickson had "some mighty fast horses and knew all the plantation roads." [54]

This rather lighthearted story about a grave situation makes it clear that David Dickson was not excluded from a monolithic "polite society" in Hancock County. In 1864, when Sherman and his marauding troops passed through Hancock County, Amanda America was fifteen years old and living in the Dickson household and yet Edwards reports that Colonel Andrew Jackson Lane and David Dickson were "great friends." The Lane family, including wife and daughters, were often invited to visit the Dickson plantation for the day. Even the fish were trained to entertain guests. According to Mary Roxie Lane Edwards, David Dickson was a wealthy, hospitable man and a fine neighbor.

Amanda America Dickson may have played the role of servant on these occasions. She may have been the "young Negro woman" who spent the day entertaining Mary Edwards by making popcorn and candy and peeling sugarcane and cracking nuts. Surely, if Amanda America had played the role of daughter and had sat at the dinner table with everyone else, the storyteller would have noticed, but she might not tell the tale.

In addition to the festive dinner, the invading Yankee troops carried away or burned three hundred bales of cotton, oats, wheat, machinery, fifty-five mules, and "a large quantity of provisions." David Dickson commented that he "had felt General Sherman, if not seen him."[55]

We do not know where Amanda America Dickson was when the Yankee troops liberated the Dickson plantation. The African-American Dickson family oral history relates that Julia was on the plantation and helped to bury the silver.[56] If Mary Roxie Lane Edwards's story is true, it appears that the Dickson household, including the infirm eighty-seven-year-old Elizabeth, did not flee to any distant place but continued to live on the home place and to entertain neighbors graciously.

On August 20, 1865, nine months after Sherman and his troops marched through Hancock County, President Andrew Johnson declared that "peace, order, tranquility and civil authority now exist in and throughout the whole United States of America." The Civil War had ended. David Dickson lost his investment in a captive labor force, all his crops and provisions, his machinery, and all his stock. He still owned his plantation, though Sherman and his troops had subjected the land to a scorched-earth policy.

In 1865, Julia Frances Dickson was twenty-nine years old and a free woman. She was free to leave the Dickson home place, free to leave her position as "housekeeper," and free to terminate her sexual relationship with David Dickson. No mention is made in the African-American Dickson family oral history, of which Julia Frances Dickson is the primary source, of Julia's feelings toward David except that she never forgave him for forcing her to have sex with him at a tender age and that she "ruled David Dickson with an iron hand." According to what the family chose to remember, control in the domestic sphere constituted Julia Dickson's revenge. Other evidence also suggests that Julia Frances Dickson was a formidable person who could exercise power and make choices. Former slaves, white employees on the plantation, and Dickson relatives all remembered that Julia controlled the keys to the Dickson plantation, which meant that she controlled the distribution of sugar, whiskey, meat, clothes, medicine, and other valuable items. They also observed that Julia Dickson sometimes managed the "ultimately sensitive and symbolic responsibility" of handling money in transactions with renters and merchants.[57]

Julia Frances Dickson chose to stay on the Dickson plantation. Perhaps she was reluctant to leave the place. She had grown up there, a "special pet" of Elizabeth Dickson's. Perhaps she stayed because of her position of responsibility in the operation of the Dickson plantation. Perhaps she stayed because David would not allow Amanda America to leave or because Amanda America would not leave. Perhaps she stayed because she did not want to leave David Dickson.

In 1865 Amanda America Dickson was sixteen years old. Her white grandmother had been dead a year. Her father's empire lay in ruins, and she faced the possibility of being poor for the first time in her life. She had always been treated as essentially free from slavery, but she was also trapped in the domain of her white family. The material privileges that she enjoyed were the result of the enslavement of others. She may have been afraid of those others. She may have been afraid of poverty. Or she may have put her trust in the belief that her father was still in control.

With the end of the war another segment of Hancock County's population was free—Confederate soldiers were free to come home.

Among the returning soldiers was Charles H. Eubanks, David Dickson's nephew. Eubanks enlisted in the Hancock Confederate Guards, Fifteenth Regiment, Georgia Volunteer Infantry, in 1861 and fought until he was paroled on April 21, 1865, at Farmville, Virginia. Eubanks was born in Georgia in 1836. Before he went off to war, he had lived all his life in Hancock County, and there is evidence that he spent a good deal of time on the Dickson plantation. In 1865, Charles Eubanks was twenty-nine years old, the same age as Julia Frances Dickson. Some time in 1865, Amanda America Dickson began an intimate sexual relationship with Charles Eubanks, which is not remembered in the Dickson family oral history as "forced." By choosing to marry her first cousin, Amanda America abandoned the slave-sanctioned preference for endogamous marriage and adopted the white convention of consanguine marriage. By May of 1865 Amanda America Dickson Eubanks was pregnant with her first child, Julian Henry, born in 1866.[58]

Because of existing antimiscegenation laws, Charles Eubanks and Amanda America Dickson could not legally marry in the state of Georgia. One of the first laws passed by the Georgia legislature after the Civil War reinstated a prohibition against interracial marriage. The African-American Dickson family history records that David Dickson arranged the marriage and took the couple to Baltimore to be married, but there are no records of the marriage in the Maryland State Archives. A newspaper account, published after David Dickson's death, states that the marriage took place in Boston, but there are no existing records there either.[59]

According to the African-American Dickson family history, David Dickson gave the couple a plantation on the banks of the Oostanaula River, near Rome, in Floyd County, Georgia. In fact, on February 2, 1866, Charles H. Eubanks purchased seventeen and seven-tenths acres of land on the Oostanaula for $600. In 1870 the couple had a second son, Charles Green. Aunt Mary Long, Amanda America Dickson Eubanks's personal servant, remembered seeing Amanda and Charles Eubanks with their small sons and their nurses crossing the river on a ferry as they left to go live on their own "plantation."[60]

As Amanda America Dickson Eubanks attempted to establish an

existence independent of her father, David Dickson began the process of financial recovery. Initially, Dickson lamented that he was planting "cautiously, not caring to save money until we had a government that would protect us in person and property." On September 4, 1865, David Dickson begged the pardon of the United States; "I am now satisfied [that] the rebellion is at an end and that slavery is forever gone. I propose to come back to the old government, if permitted."[61] This action was necessary for Dickson to regain control of his property, excluding his slaves, and to be able to vote or run for public office, which he never did.

The "old government" proved to be an evolving institution in the South immediately after the Civil War. The citizens of Hancock County worked out a new system of economic order amid violence and intimidation at levels that varied with the presence or absence of federal troops. Initially, acts of violence against black citizens were sporadic and unorganized. In 1866 individual white men killed three black men in the county but were acquitted in each case on the basis of justifiable homicide. By 1868 the Ku Klux Klan appeared, and acts of violence against black citizens became more organized and frequent. Testifying before a joint congressional committee, Eli Barnes, who was a black representative in the Georgia legislature, stated that it got to be a "common thing" for black men to report that night riders had visited their homes and "played mischief there," molesting wives and daughters, "playing wild generally" with families.[62]

A beating that occurred in Hancock County in 1870 illustrates the brutality that some black families faced in this era. On April 25, 1870, Frank Watkins (black) wrote a letter to the same Eli Barnes and to W. H. Harrison, Hancock County's other state representative, to report that his daughter Ida had been "outrageously and brutily [brutally] beaten" by John Hall (white). Watkins had been working in the fields at the time, and when he returned he found his daughter near death, her head "beaten to a pulp." In all too human disbelief, Watkins asked Hall why he had not come to him first; Hall replied that he "consulted no damn Negro about beating thare [their] children." Finally, Watkins expressed his hopelessness: "I can and will make an affadavit [affidavit] to this murderous affare [affair] and produce witnesses: but I know thare [there] will be nothing done so I will not ishare [issue] no warrant until I hear from you." [63]

By the end of 1870, the white citizens of Hancock County had regained control of the electoral process through fraud and the U.S. government's reluctance to intervene. Nevertheless, acts of violence against the persons of blacks and the property of whites, including David Dickson, continued. The issue was one of control.

After the war, Dickson and other planters had to face the reality that their legal power to control the labor of black families had been greatly reduced. This lack of dominance manifested itself in the abandonment of the gang labor system and the flight of black women and children from the fields. By 1869, prominent black politicians began to articulate a traditional work ethic for black families. They advocated that wives work in a private domestic sphere: "Believing in the teachings of the Bible, as well as those of nature, and following the customs of all civilized people, this convention of black Delegates [in Macon in 1869] urges upon the men of the State, in behalf of their wives and daughters . . . that they take their wives from the drudgery and exposure of plantation toil as soon as it is in their power to do so." Because there was no great proliferation of cooperative communities like the one at Mound Bayou, Mississippi, most families of freed people faced the prospect of becoming independent economic units. [64]

While black families were exerting their power to rearrange labor relationships by removing women and children from the fields, David Dickson lamented the unavailability of those very laborers: "The present system of labor does not exceed 60 percent of slave labor, involving fully a loss of one-third of the labor of men going to villages, railroads, mining, and other enterprises." Indeed, "One-half of the women and children are absent, housekeeping, idling, and other things. Under the slave system, the women and children were the mainspring of cotton raising . . . [now] each family must have its housekeeper and washer, and must send to mill, if they only send a half bushel of corn." [65] For David Dickson, freedom was inefficient.

At first, Dickson organized his labor force in "companies" of six to eight workers. By 1870 he had been forced to abandon this effort and turn to a tenant system, working from twelve to sixty-five hands on ten thousand acres of land. Dickson had firm convictions about the management of labor after the war just as he had before. "The best method of hiring, I consider to be wages—[with] a contract setting forth the duties of each party. The policy of managing freedmen is, to act firmly, and truly, and honestly with them, and to require them to do the same." In addition, "never pay them more than half wages till the end of the time for which they contracted to work." Dickson believed that on plantations of any size, "the actual necessaries should be kept, and sold to the freeman at a profit sufficient to pay all risk and interest on the money." In practice, "Those who work shares should divide the profits and responsibilities with the land owner. The rent of the land should pay for the horsepower, machinery and tools. The laborer should have one third, he finding his own hoe and axe, it being impossible to keep such things as plantation tools." And finally, "The whole direction of the laborers, the management, gathering and the sale of the crop should be held by the landowner." Despite this clear conviction about where the final authority ought to lie in the management of all labor, Dickson observed, "The Negroes have notions of their own."[66]

Employing the black labor force was more satisfactory, Dickson argued, than importing foreign labor. "The Negro we have with us, and we cannot get rid of him if we would. They will not die out, as most of our Northern friends and many of our people think. The next census [1870] will show a large increase." Dickson then argued that "the only way to make it tolerable for them to live amongst us, is to give them employment. With full employment, they will steal less, be more law-abiding, and a less nuisance in every way. Do we want more labor, and for what?"[67]

There is evidence that David Dickson was not ostracized because of his outside family during this period of reorganization as historians have presumed. In December 1868, the State Agricultural Society invited Dickson, along with nineteen other prominent planters, to attend a meeting of cotton planters in Macon, Georgia. In January 1869, the *Southern Recorder* reported that the newly reorganized State Agricultural Society had invited Dickson to become its first president but that he had declined. The *Recorder* declared that "Mr. Dickson is a gentleman of retired habits and prefers to preside over his plantation to anything else."[68]

Dickson's enterprises prospered after the Civil War, as they had before. Experienced blacksmiths manufactured plows on the Dickson plantation, which were advertised and sold through the *Southern Cultivator,* providing a profit of $10,000 in 1869. Dickson also sold a commercial fertilizer called the "Dickson Compound" and offered discounts of 10 percent to planters who would recommend it to others. After the war this compound was mixed and shipped by the Dickson Fertilizer Company of Augusta, the directors of which were described by a Dun & Bradstreet agent as "some of our best men." In his letters to the agricultural journals, Dickson also recommended "Dickson's Select" seed, which he marketed from Covington, Georgia.[69]

By 1870 David Dickson was back on his feet financially. From that year until his death in 1885, Dickson's net worth increased each year, from $72,920 in 1870 to $276,030 in 1885.[70] His fame increased with the publication in 1870 of *A Practical Treatise on Agriculture.* This three-hundred-page tome consisted of twenty-nine chapters on the "science of farming" plus twenty-seven of David Dickson's letters, which the *Southern Cultivator* had published between February 1859 and October 1869. *A Practical Treatise* offers insight into David Dickson's motives as a farmer and as an individual. In these articles Dickson exhorted young men to follow the noble cause of farming, advertised his products, mentioned his accomplishments in a self-deprecatory way, and defended himself, though he claimed that he would not, by citing the testimony of his many visitors.

Though David Dickson claimed that his motives were pure, he seems to have been eager to brag about his accomplishments in the public press and overly anxious about criticism of his extraordinary claims. In 1869 he stated: "I will not reply to any criticism on my views hereafter, as I have no interest to serve that is not common to every planter, to-wit: the prosperity of the South. I have never held office, and do not wish to do so. I speak and write simply what I believe is in the true

interest of the cotton planter, without regard to pleasing or displeas-
ing." Nevertheless, Dickson claimed that he was the first to introduce
guano in the "cotton states"; that he could train a laborer to pick seven
hundred pounds of cotton, or three good bags, a week; that he could
grow two bales of cotton per acre on "old land," which was "nothing to
laugh at"; and that before the war his hands had earned for him $1,000
each per year. David Dickson claimed that his system of farming never
failed. If there was a failure, it was "in the man; if carried out to the
letter, it will not fail." To prove his claims of extraordinary productiveness, David Dickson cited the authority of his visitors. He described
them as "my many visitors from all parts of the country," "gentlemen
from all parts of Georgia," or as "the 100 gentlemen in Hancock," all
of whom would endorse his method.[71]

His public writings show a distinctive pattern. He said he did not care
what other people thought. Then he made extraordinary claims about
his accomplishments and, to verify his claims, cited the authority of the
many gentlemen who had seen his crops. When this pattern is considered in the light of David Dickson's personal life, a paradox emerges.
David Dickson invited anyone and everyone to observe his agricultural
successes. At the same time, he maintained an outside family, which we
can reasonably assume would be offensive to someone. It would seem
much more logical for him simply to have lived well and quietly.

In 1870, the same year that David Dickson began to increase the size
of his estate, he experienced an act of violence, not by the white community at large but by the black community at home. On a Saturday
night in late September 1870, armed black citizens burned David Dickson's largest gin house. Dickson described the situation to his cotton
factor, S. D. Heard: "The Negroes here say that the Yankees and home
radicals tell them to organize, kill and burn, to suppress the Ku Klux. . . .
Nearly all the Negroes on my place are opposed to this deviltry, because they have something to lose; a few, I suspect, because they have
nothing, are guilty. And of their guilt I have some evidence." Dickson
then described the barn burning. "Last Saturday night an armed force
of Negroes came upon my plantation and burned the largest gin-house
I own. It was forty-eight-feet square and contained three gins, two

screws and a scaffold; the latter was built the same day it was burned. Four Negroes had cotton in it, from two to nine bales each, of which they owned two-thirds." Dickson lamented: "I had in it about thirty bales in all; about 3,000 bushels of cotton seed. I lost between four and five thousand dollars." The Superior Court records of Hancock County show that Arthur Chapple, Lawson Sasnett, and Scott Amop were tried for arson on October 14, 1870. Arthur Chapple was convicted of burning two gin houses, one of which belonged to David Dickson, and was sentenced to two sequential terms of six years at hard labor in the state penitentiary. Lawson Sasnett was convicted but recommended to the mercy of the court, and Scott Amop was declared not guilty.[72]

The 1870s were momentous years for Amanda, Julia, and David Dickson for reasons other than the gin-house burning. In October 1870 Amanda America gave birth to her second son, Charles Green. According to the African-American Dickson family oral history, shortly thereafter Amanda America and her two children returned to the Dickson plantation. Amanda explained the situation to her father with the comment, "I want to live with you, 'Papie.'" Charles Eubanks attempted to retrieve his wife and was met with a "stormy" reply. "He never came back." The census of 1870 lists Eubanks as living with his mother, Elizabeth.

Nevertheless, according to Julia Frances Dickson, after the separation, the boys remained close to their white grandmother and visited at the Eubanks's home in Hancock County. No mention is made of a divorce. David Dickson arranged for Amanda and her sons to take the Dickson surname. David Dickson then took them to New Orleans and "had them declared white." One wonders why David Dickson did this and then returned to Hancock County. Their recollection of these events illustrates the conviction by the African-American branch of the Dickson family that David Dickson could transform his mulatto daughter and his mulatto grandchildren into a white daughter and white grandchildren and then return to a community that knew of their racially mixed heritage. The only way this family could have escaped the public stigma of race would have been to abandon their place.

According to the African-American Dickson oral history, David

Dickson loved the little boys, called them "my little men," and slept with them. "[Dickson] never wanted them to do anything but ride over the plantation with him and see what was going on." He "indulged them all." When visitors came to the plantation and were invited to eat, they sometimes asked if they had to eat with Amanda and the children, to which David replied, "By God, yes, if you eat here!"[73]

A former employee, former slaves, and one of David Dickson's nephews observed that a close relationship developed between David Dickson and his grandsons. They called him "Pappy," ate at the table with him, and commonly sat in his lap. W. S. Lozier, one of David Dickson's employees, commented that he acted toward the boys "pretty much like I would towards my children," and James M. Eubanks, David's nephew, observed that he "talked to them kindly as he would his own children." Rebecca Latimer Felton, Georgia's racist suffragist, described the situation in the Dickson household: "I remember well a noted home in Middle Georgia where a rich man lived in open alliance with a colored woman and where Governors and Congressmen were often invited to dine and where they were glad to go. These visitors understood conditions in the Dickson home. They knew there were children there born of a slave mother and the law of Georgia forbade such miscegenation."[74]

By the end of 1870, Amanda America Dickson's son Julian was four and Charles was an infant. Sometime in 1870 or early 1871, David Dickson began construction of a new house for Julia, Amanda America, and the children. The house was approximately three hundred yards from the Dickson home place, on a crest of the sloping land that made up the Dickson plantation. When completed, it was "a very respectable," "comfortable," two-story home, with "a nice room for a parlor." The parlor contained a piano and "had everything that usually constitutes the furniture in that kind of room. . . . Everything was nice and kept in nice order." When one of David Dickson's employees, W. S. Lozier, a carpenter, was asked which was the best of the two houses, the home place or the new house, he replied that the new house was "a good deal the best house. I would rather have had it at the time."[75]

On October 2, 1871, David Dickson drew up a deed selling the new house and 210 acres of land, more or less, with a twenty-foot right-of-way the entire distance between the house lot and the John R. Latimore place. Amanda America Dickson purchased a seven-eighths interest in the property for $1,000 and Julia Frances Dickson purchased one-eighth interest for $125.[76]

After completing the new house and moving his outside family into that comfortable dwelling, David Dickson did something that must have shocked everyone. He married Clara Harris on October 3, 1871. At that time Clara Harris was twenty-five years old, three years older than Amanda America and thirty-seven years younger than David Dickson. She was born in Hancock County in 1846, the second daughter in a prominent family whose history in the county stretched back to 1800. Her mother, Juda Ann Parker Sasnett, was born in the county in 1817; her father, "Colonel" Benjamin Tarpley Harris, was born in 1813. Both of Clara's parents were younger than David Dickson and probably had known his family all their lives.[77]

The Harrises were prominent citizens in Sparta. The "Colonel" had been a member of the secession convention, had been captain of the Hancock Mounted Rifles, and had served on the staff of Governor Joseph E. Brown through the Civil War. By 1871 he and his family were firmly established in Sparta as members of "polite society." [78]

B. H. Sasnett, Clara's first cousin, described her as "a lady of great delicacy and refinement," who "went in the best society." Sasnett also recalled that Clara "had received a very thorough education" and that she was "a fine pianist." Clara was confident enough as a pianist to perform for guests who visited Sparta. In 1865, when the twenty-five-year-old war refugee Eliza Frances Andrews passed through Sparta, the Harris family took her into their home. Eliza Andrews described the Harris home as "a large white house in the midst of a beautiful garden, where roses of all sorts were running riot, filling the air with fragrance and the earth was beautiful." According to Andrews, guests were on the colonnade, "whom the hospitality of our host had brought together. Everyone was treated to supper and then went into the parlor for some music. We tried to sing the old rebel songs, but the words stuck in our throats. Nobody could sing, so Clara Harris [then nineteen], played 'Dixie'; but it sounded like a dirge." Andrews closed her account by stating that the Harris's house was so full of guests sleeping over that "Mrs. Harris was obliged to crowd us a little." [79]

We do not know how David Dickson met Clara or what their courtship was like. Why did David become romantically involved at the age of sixty-two? Why did Clara Harris consent to marry a man who was older than both her parents, who lived out in the country in a simple house surrounded by his tenants? David Dickson was wealthy and famous. He had a reputation for being both generous and hospitable, at least to his good friends and the agricultural community at large. Clara Harris could expect to have a lot of company, but of what sort? And what about David Dickson's outside family?

What did Julia Frances Dickson think about the match? Much later, when she was asked when she ceased to have a sexual relationship with David, she replied, "We separated before he ever married or thought of it, I reckon." Was Julia secure in her new house and in her position of authority as the housekeeper in the Dickson home? This marriage is not mentioned in the African-American Dickson family oral history. Julia Dickson erased it when she retold the family story.[80]

Amanda America Dickson and her sons might also have felt threatened by the arrival of Clara Harris Dickson. The two women were about the same age. In 1871, Amanda America was twenty-two and Clara Dickson was twenty-five. They lived three hundred yards apart. Perhaps Amanda America felt secure enough in her relationship with her father to be civil to Clara at a distance or simply to ignore her. Clara, however, entered a situation with an established set of relationships and consequently was at the greatest disadvantage.

We do not know what the elite white community in Hancock County thought about the marriage, we have no clue to what the remainder of the white community thought, nor do we know what the black community at large or on the Dickson plantation thought. It is clear that those who depended on David Dickson's business enterprises and the management of his farms, as well as his outside family, were placed in a precarious position. If David Dickson died, his young wife might be left in charge.

After their wedding, David and Clara Dickson traveled north for a few weeks and then returned to Sparta. Clara Dickson stayed there a few days with her family and then proceeded to the Dickson home place to settle down as the wife of a country squire, a role that proved to be exceedingly complicated. To take her rightful place on the Dickson plantation, Clara would have to displace Julia Dickson. Before Clara's arrival, Julia held the "keys to the plantation": she controlled the distribution of sugar, meat, and whiskey; paid for the products that were purchased for the kitchen, such as fish; accepted rent payments; managed the production and serving of meals; and did it all, according to some, "like a white wife." Clara Harris had always lived in her mother's home, where, in all probability, her mother remained in charge. The ornamental aspect of being a lady probably appealed more to Clara Dickson than the prospect of taking charge of a complex agricultural household guarded by a formidable older black woman. We do have some insight into how this conflict was sorted out. W. S. Lozier, the carpenter who thought the new house was superior to the home place, described Clara Harris's presence on the Dickson plantation: "I was never there a great many times during the time of Mrs. Dickson; while she was about there, I never saw her take hold of any business, but she seemed to be like someone on a visit."[81]

It appears that Clara Harris Dickson took offense at the presence of David Dickson's outside family and tried to have the offenders removed from the plantation. S. D. Rogers, one of David Dickson's nephews, remembered a conversation that he had with his uncle regarding the situation: "[David Dickson] mentioned to me in the presence of my wife that his wife [Clara] had requested him to send Julia and Amanda away from there, and he told her he wasn't going to do any such thing. He said that Julia and Amanda were there when she came there and that they would have to stay."[82]

After the first year of David and Clara's marriage, Clara went to Sparta to visit her mother more and more often and stayed there for longer periods of time, a reaction that Deborah Gray White has noted was not unusual for plantation mistresses who were caught between the necessity of ignoring outside families and the difficulty of obtaining a divorce. In July 1873, Clara became seriously ill. She died the first day of August, at the age of twenty-seven, at her parents' house in Sparta. David Dickson was not present when she died. B. H. Sasnett, her cousin, described the scene: "I saw [David Dickson] come in when his wife was in her coffin. He was not a demonstrative man; he was a purely unemotional man; and I saw no evidence of any emotion. He seemed embarrassed in company generally—a very awkward man; he showed that awkwardness on that occasion, but I didn't see any emotion."[83]

Clara Harris was not buried with her mother and father in the Sparta cemetery. Legend has it that David Dickson had a rock hollowed out and buried her inside it, but no one remembers where.[84]

Ironically, on July 31, 1873, one day before Clara died, Amanda America's husband, Charles Eubanks, died. In his will Eubanks directed his executors, David Dickson and T. J. Warthen (Dickson's nephew), to keep his estate intact until "my children, Julian Henry Dickson and Charles Green Dickson arrive at years of maturity." Eubanks did not use the legal term "natural children," which would mean that the children were born out of wedlock. Eubanks then charged his executors to maintain and educate his sons and support his mother, Elizabeth Eubanks. Despite the latter provision, Elizabeth and her son, James M. Eubanks, objected to the will on the grounds that it was improperly executed, that it was obtained by fraud, and that the two children were "born of a Negro." They withdrew their objection after David Dickson removed himself as executor.[85]

Shortly after the deaths of Clara Harris Dickson and Charles Eubanks, T. J. Warthen moved into the Dickson household "to look over the plantation and the lots." At the time, Warthen was thirty-five. He too had been a frequent visitor on the Dickson plantation in his youth. From 1867 to 1873 Warthen came to visit his uncle every week "as business required." In 1873 Amanda Dickson was twenty-four years old, a widow with two small children. Sometime during this period, Amanda America Dickson and T. J. Warthen entered into a sexual relationship, which Warthen later described in court as occurring "a few times."[86]

Scholars have described serial sexual relationships between mulatto women and prominent white men—men who were related by blood. Ridgely Torrence, in his biography of John Hope, describes the relationship between John Hope's mother and his uncle after the death of Hope's father. Adele Alexander notes that her great-great-grandmother, Susan Hunt, maintained an intimate relationship with Judge Nathan Sayre and, after the death of Sayre, with his nephew Richard Hunt. These relationships are described by the authors as arrangements between consenting adults that existed within the context of nineteenth-century southern sexism and racism. When Julia Frances Lewis Dickson described her own serial sexual relationships with David Dickson (white), "Doc" Eubanks (white), and Joe Brooken (black), she declared that "I was not a bad woman."[87]

After Clara Harris Dickson's death, David Dickson continued to care for Amanda America and her children. In late 1873, he deeded 1,560 acres of land to Amanda America, "in consideration of the sum of ten dollars to him . . . as well as in further consideration of the good will and kind regard which he, the said David Dickson, has and bears towards the said Amanda A. Dickson and her children, Julian H. Dickson and Charles G. Dickson, the natural children of Charles H. Eubanks late of said county [Hancock] deceased, a long-time and faithful friend of the said David Dickson."[88] Here David Dickson refers to Amanda America's children using the legal term "natural children," or children born out of wedlock.

During this same period, Julia Frances Lewis Dickson "spent most of her time at the meeting house." Indeed, Julia was active in the life of her church and the school it supported. In 1874, as a concession to Julia, David Dickson signed an indenture between himself and John C. Lewis, Julia Frances Dickson's brother, Gilbert Castleberry, Boston Dickson, Washington Warthen, and Julia Dickson, all trustees for the Cherry Hill Church and School of the Methodist Episcopal Church, South. He agreed to sell the Cherry Hill Church three acres of land for five dollars. The trustees were to hold the land as a place of worship and for a schoolhouse and keep the roads in good repair; otherwise, the land would revert back to David Dickson. Through this agreement

Julia Frances secured the future of her church and school against the possibility that David might marry again, and David made sure that the use of the land was limited.[89]

Not long after David Dickson deeded the land surrounding the Cherry Hill Church to its black trustees, an event occurred that illustrates how carefully Dickson maintained the precarious balance between his outside family and his white kin. In August 1874, David Dickson's nieces Mary and Sallie had "some trouble" with their brother and turned to their uncle for help. Dickson sent them to the home of B. F. Riley, his neighbor. Riley explained what happened: "Well, I went down there [to David Dickson's plantation] and he asked me if Mary and Sallie had been to see me. I told him that they had; he asked me if they told me who sent them. He then told me, says he, 'Now, I reckon you think it strange of me for sending those girls to your house when I am their uncle.'" According to Riley, Dickson explained his actions by saying, "Amanda is my child and I want Amanda and her children around me; it might be unpleasant to Mary and Sallie to be there and will be unpleasant to their company." Riley continued: "Therefore he had sent them to my house. He told me that he would see that I got money to pay for their board and to charge them enough to cover all their expenses down at my house. He told me that I shouldn't lose anything by it."[90] Even though David Dickson was sensitive to the needs of nieces, he did not want to change his living arrangement for their benefit, and he knew how to make other acceptable arrangements.

In 1876, although David Dickson wanted Amanda and her children around him, Amanda America Dickson, at the age of twenty-seven, left the security of her father's farm and her children, Julian, who was ten, and Charles, who was six, and enrolled in Atlanta University. Her program, the normal course, consisted of the ordinary grammar school branches and the work of the two higher normal, or high school, courses. No examinations were required, but pupils "were placed according to their attainments." Atlanta University designed this course to "meet the immediate demand for teachers throughout the state." The African-American Dickson family did not remember that Amanda ever taught school. They remembered that she left the university because "she didn't like the discipline." The Atlanta University catalog does not list Amanda America Dickson as a teacher anywhere in Georgia, although she is listed as a onetime alumnae donor of two dollars in 1882.[91]

Julia Frances Dickson is the person who remembered and recounted Amanda America's leaving Atlanta University because "she didn't like the discipline," a statement that seems demeaning. Surely it took courage for Amanda America to leave her place on the Dickson plantation and travel to the largest city in Georgia, enroll in a normal school, and stay there two years, from 1876 to 1878. In the 1870s it may have been flattering to refer to a white "lady" as academically undisciplined, but it would not have been flattering to call a black "lady" academically undisciplined at Atlanta University, or at any other black school in the state, where access to education was a highly valued opportunity. Was Julia Dickson trying to place Amanda in the higher class of white ladies, or was she subtly expressing her regret at the way Amanda America had been raised?

During the 1870s and early 1880s, Julia Frances Dickson continued to be David Dickson's housekeeper and to trade in Sparta. According to an article in the *Sparta Ishmaelite* on August 1, 1885, Julia Dickson was perceived by the people of that town as a "very quiet, inoffensive woman," whose role in the Dickson home was to wait on guests. According to the reporter, she "never put herself forward." When Julia Dickson visited Sparta to trade, she brought "things" to David Dickson's friends, and when they invited her to dinner, "She would always prefer having her dinner sent to the kitchen, where she would eat with the other servants."[92]

During the two decades of Reconstruction and the era of the New South that followed, David Dickson was busily accumulating more and more wealth. By the late 1870s and early 1880s, the local Hancock County newspaper, the *Sparta Ishmaelite and Times Planter*, began to take note of new Dickson money-making enterprises. In 1879 it noted: "Mr. Dickson will apply to the Legislature for an act to promote fish culture in his ponds in this and Washington counties. Such an Act should be passed. Mr. Dickson is a public spirited citizen, and has spent thousands of dollars in developing this industry. If his efforts are seconded by the State, fish will enter largely into the food question in this section." And again in 1881: "Mr. Dickson no doubt has the most extensive fish ponds of any other man in the state and probably the South." Dickson also had a license to sell liquor out of the Dickson home place from 1881 to 1885. In 1881 there were eleven licensed liquor dealers in Hancock County, two of whom were women. By 1885, there were only seven licensed liquor dealers, one of whom was David Dickson.[93]

In 1883, amid all this prosperity, a murder occurred on the Dickson plantation; the ensuing on-the-spot investigation by a jury of inquest gives some insight into David Dickson's style of life. A report of the proceedings appeared in the *Sparta Ishmaelite*. After a "sumptuous dinner with this generous hearted gentleman," the coroner and his jury examined the body, heard the testimony of several witnesses, and declared that, in their judgment, the accused, Wilson Smith, a worker on the Dickson plantation, was guilty of murder. David Dickson then treated the group to a tour of his plantation. They visited Dickson's five-acre scuppernong arbor, where their host provided them with ladders so they could "pick all they wanted." Next the entourage proceeded to the watermelon patch, where "Mr. Dickson" commented, "We will now go through the patch; every man may have one melon of his own choice. He must pull it as he walks through the patch, and no turning back allowed." Despite that admonition, "Bill Culver stopped by the side of a second melon which seemed still larger than a forty pound one which he had picked earlier and looking wistfully at it exclaimed, 'I wish I only had the seed from this one.' " David Dickson "could not withstand the tone of that expressed desire and consented for Bill to pull a second melon." In summary, the author gushed: "The boys were soon on the road, satisfied that they had had the most pleasant time that ever had been experienced by a coroner's jury. The party was full of praise for Mr. Dickson and Jeff Warthen [Dickson's nephew] for their generosity." From the account in the *Sparta Ishmaelite*, we can conclude that in 1883 David Dickson could still entertain in grand style on his "brag farm." Scholars have argued that these demonstrations of hospitality were "the most visible indication of class position, honor, and the ability to run a household."[94]

T. J. Warthen, the other host at this gathering, was forty-five years old at that time and still living in the Dickson home place, sleeping across the hall from his uncle and helping to manage the plantations. Warthen was one of the few people who was acknowledged as someone to whom David Dickson would listen. B. H. Sasnett, who was first cousin to both Clara Harris Dickson and T. J. Warthen, commented, "I don't know that I ever saw anybody exercise any influence over him [David Dickson] except Mr. Warthen; I recollect on one occasion Mr. Warthen differed with him about the erection of a certain building, and Mr. Dickson said to him, 'you can go and do it your own way, then.' "[95]

On November 22, 1884, David Dickson was the victim of another act of arson: "Official information has been received at this Department [Governor's office] that on the night of the 22nd of November, the gin house of David Dickson in the county of Hancock was destroyed by fire, the work of an incendiary." Governor Henry D. McDaniel issued a proclamation of reward ($250) for the "Apprehension and delivery of said incendiary with evidence sufficient to convict, to the Sheriff of said county and State." Of the thirty-three rewards issued in 1884 by Governor McDaniel, seven were for the crime of arson, one for a barn-house burning and six for gin-house burning. According to the Superior Court records of Hancock County, the culprits in this case were not apprehended.[96]

On February 18, 1885, David Dickson died at the age of seventy-six. According to the African-American Dickson family history, Amanda America's reaction was to cling to his body and repeat over and over, "Now I am an orphan; now I am an orphan." Amanda America was an orphan only if she defined herself as a member of a family composed only of herself and her white father. Her mother was alive, her uncle, black John C. Lewis, was alive, and many of her white aunts and uncles were still alive. Nevertheless, Amanda America Dickson defined herself as an orphan with no black relatives and no white relatives, in fact, a kinless "no nation." [97]

Characteristically, David Dickson left a dangerously bizarre set of burial instructions. He instructed his nephew T. J. Warthen to bury his body in the garden of the Dickson home place in a coffin of unpainted pine covered with white alpaca. He ordered Warthen to dress the body in a fine suit of black broadcloth and black silk velvet and to leave the feet bare. The feet were to be crossed with the right leg over the left leg; the right hand clenched with the exception of the index finger, which was to point downward toward the feet; and the left hand placed on the breast holding a beautiful pocket handkerchief. David Dickson instructed T. J. Warthen to place in his right pocket a pocket-knife, a pocket comb, and a gold toothpick. Dickson apparently gave no explanation for these instructions. [98]

David Dickson's burial clothes certainly indicate that he wished to be interred in fine fashion. He had all that he needed to stay tidy, keep order: a comb, a toothpick, and a beautiful pocket handkerchief. But all this class and order were jarred by his instructions to Warthen that his body be placed in a plain pine coffin, barefoot. No one knew what these burial instructions meant to David Dickson, and he did not care to explain, even if they might cast doubt on his sanity.

Dickson's funeral was held in his garden. Both blacks and whites attended. Though David Dickson had not attended church, two ministers of the Methodist Episcopal church, B. H. Sasnett and the Reverend Timmons, officiated. [99]

On March 2, 1885, David Dickson's will entered the public domain when the executors, T. J. Warthen and Dickson's "personal friend" and lawyer, Charles W. Dubose, submitted the document to the Court of Ordinary of Hancock County. Like a clap of thunder this event shattered the silence that had separated David Dickson's private life from his public life. David Dickson made his mulatto daughter and her children the largest property owners in Hancock County, Georgia.

The Dickson Will

We owe it to unborn generations not only to keep up the fertility
of the soil but to increase it . . . I only claim to be a tenant at will,
with the right of appointing my successors.
—David Dickson

SCHOLARS HAVE ARGUED that although the power of the master
constituted the linchpin of slavery as a social system, no one satisfac-
torily defined the limits of that power. Theoretically, this tension was
resolved in favor of the interest of the ruling class; "the collective con-
science of the ruling class must prevail over the individual interests
constituting that class." This does not appear to have been the case with
David Dickson. This master-father both raised his mulatto daughter
inside the boundaries of his family and legally appointed her as his
successor, making her, in some sense, an oxymoronic member of the
ruling class, a wealthy black "lady." Dickson left the administration of
his estate to the "sound judgment and unlimited discretion" of Amanda
America Dickson "without interference from any quarter," including
"any husband which she may have." Before his death, Dickson's community essentially denied the former, and after his death, it endured
the latter.[1]

In bequeathing his estate to Amanda America and bringing his relationship with her into the public domain of the law, David Dickson made it impossible for his community to continue to practice what John Blassingame has labeled "selective inattention," an agreed-upon fiction not to notice this relationship as a political act with, one would assume, dangerous implications. Blassingame argues, "In all probability, then, the most important reason for the lack of violent reactions to interracial sexual contacts was the rather amazing, but psychologically necessary, selective inattention of white males [and one would assume, females] regarding this matter."[2] Everyone knew that everyone else knew.

Realizing that his death would create a new reality, David Dickson made several assumptions. He assumed that he could trust his good friend and lawyer, Charles Dubose, to shepherd the will through the courts. He assumed that his will would eventually be upheld, and he assumed that no one would be so outraged as to resort to violence. In essence, David Dickson assumed that his power to exercise his right to appoint his successor would transcend his own mortality.

As has been demonstrated, David Dickson spent a lifetime accumulating two fortunes and cultivating a web of obligations within his community. Before the Civil War he and Thomas M. Turner had maintained the only banking business in Hancock County through a network of personal loans. Dickson continued to loan money throughout his life. At the time of his death, 147 individuals owed him approximately $75,000. His debtors included lawyers, judges, the ordinary of Hancock County, friends, business associates, relatives, tenants, and former slaves.[3]

Although he loaned money at interest, Dickson literally gave away all that he knew about farming. He wrote articles for the *Southern Cultivator*, the most widely read agricultural journal in the southeastern United States in the nineteenth century, and published a book on farming in 1870. He entertained farmers from Hancock County and their guests in sumptuous style, demonstrating the success of his method of farming with guided tours of his fields and gardens. He sent unusual gifts to his neighbors, things they might not "have on hand," and cartloads of his fish crop to town to be distributed to his friends, including the staff of the *Sparta Ishmaelite*. Citizens of Hancock County could boast of Dickson's wealth and point with pride to his crops, which were more successful than those of James M. Smith in nearby Oglethorpe County, who used convict labor after the Civil War instead of free labor as David Dickson did. Indeed, David Dickson was widely respected. In 1895, the editor of *Memoirs of Georgia* described him as "liberal with his means toward all public enterprises and in matters pertaining to education and religion: and though he favored no particular denomination, his moral character was such as to command the respect of his associates. . . . He never used tobacco or liquor in any form and was very chaste and careful in his language."[4]

Not only was David Dickson respected, but his story was useful. He was described by the *Southern Cultivator* and the *Sparta Ishmaelite* as a self-made man, who started out in life with a small inheritance and worked hard, first as a merchant and then as a farmer, to accumulate enough capital to purchase land no one else wanted. There was no need to migrate west, no need to be discontented because planters owned the bottomlands. Using David Dickson's method of farming, anyone could make a fortune, even on the sandy pine barrens. Ironically, as the *Sparta Ishmaelite* put the case one week before David Dickson's death, using Dickson as an example, "any man can succeed who has the judgment to know how, and the energy to will it and to labor."[5]

David Dickson did not accumulate wealth and create obligations within his community for the sole purpose of taking care of Amanda America. By the time of her birth in 1849, he already ranked among the eight wealthiest slaveholders in Hancock County. As the battle over David Dickson's will reveals, however, his wealth, generosity, and hospitality mitigated the impact of his family arrangements and made it possible for Amanda America Dickson to walk away from her community with a fortune. As the events of the week following the Dickson will case reveal, this community was not above taking the law into its own hands when sufficiently provoked.

On March 2, 1885, T. J. Warthen and Charles W. Dubose, David Dickson's executors, submitted the will to the ordinary of Hancock County for probate in the public sphere. Two days later, the *Sparta Ish-*

maelite listed the beneficiaries of the will. The document bequeathed one thousand acres of land in Rusk County, Texas, between two and three thousand acres of land in Washington County, Georgia, and $20,000 in cash to Dickson's white relatives and friends. The bulk of the estate, valued at $500,000 according to the *Ishmaelite*, went to Amanda A. Dickson, the mother of Julian H. and Charles G. Dickson. Immediately the regional and state newspapers picked up the sensational nature of the will and attempted to goad the *Ishmaelite* into reproducing the document in its entirety. The editor responded that the *Atlanta Constitution* had stated that on March 11, 1885, the *Ishmaelite* would publish Dickson's will in full, but "it will not appear in these columns. First, because it is a private document and the public has no interest in its bequests; second, because it is not possible that any good could grow out of the publication; and third, because its contents are extremely unpleasant to many of his relations and best friends."[6]

What David Dickson's relatives and friends found "unpleasant" was the part of the will that bequeathed the bulk of the estate to Amanda A. Dickson of Hancock County, "now living with her mother near my plantation." The *Atlanta Journal* of August 1, 1885, commented, "It is asserted that Dixon [Dickson] had no right to give this mulatto woman, although she was his child, his landed estate, amounting to 17,000 acres of the best land in middle Georgia, as it will injure those owning lands adjoining." The estate was left to Amanda during her lifetime, "clear and exempt from the marital right, power, control or custody of any husband she may have, with full power to her . . . without the aid or interposition of any court." David Dickson charged Amanda America to support and educate her children, "their support to be ample but not extravagant, their education to be the best that can be procured for them with a proper regard to economy," all of which was left to "the sound judgment and discretion of the said Amanda Dickson." When Amanda America died, her children were to inherit the remains of the estate.[7]

The will warned that if any legatee contested the will, his or her legacy would be revoked "instantly." Undeterred by this threat, seventy-nine of David Dickson's white relatives came forth to object to the will's being admitted to probate. The caveators, or objectors to the will, included sisters and brothers, nieces and nephews, their in-laws and children, and an assortment of cousins. Most of these people resided in Georgia, but several registered their protests from Louisiana, Arkansas, and Alabama. Their number included David Dickson's brother Henry T. Dickson, who received a bequest of two thousand acres of land in Texas.[8]

The disgruntled white relatives brought suit on several grounds. They argued that the will should not be admitted to probate because it was not the "act and will of David Dickson"; that Dickson was not of sound and disposing mind at the time of writing the will; that he was unduly influenced by Amanda and Julia Dickson; that Amanda was not David Dickson's child; and that the will was "in its scheme, its nature and tendencies illegal and immoral, contrary to the policy of the state and of the law" and was "destructive and subversive to the interest and welfare of society."[9]

In accordance with their duties as executors, on May 26, 1885, Dubose and Warthen submitted an appraisal of David Dickson's estate to the probate court. The estate contained $81,000 in bonds and 147 notes and accounts due for approximately $75,000. The executors designated 125 of the notes, for approximately $25,000, as "bad" or "doubtful." Included among the doubtful notes was one for $575 from Judge R. H. Lewis, the ordinary faced with the responsibility of deciding whether the will should be accepted as David Dickson's legal will, that is, admitted to probate. Also included in the estate were crops, livestock, farming equipment, household goods such as silver forks, spoons, and goblets, a bookcase, fifteen thousand acres of land in Hancock County, and forty gallons of whiskey. The executor and appraisers reported that the total value of the estate was $309,543, $281,543 in Hancock County and $28,000 in Washington County.[10]

On July 6, 1885, despite the white relatives' objections, Probate Judge R. H. Lewis ruled in favor of the will. According to the *Ishmaelite*, a large crowd collected to view the spectacle but was disappointed because the lawyers for the excluded white relatives, or caveators, declined to cross-examine witnesses so as not to waste time in the lower court but appealed directly to the Superior Court.[11] And so the stage was set.

The Dickson case was scheduled to be tried in the Superior Court of Hancock County in November 1885 before Judge Samuel Lumpkin, judge of the Northern Circuit of Superior Courts. The white citizens of Hancock County anticipated the trial with excitement. The editor of the *Sparta Ishmaelite* commented that "fur was sure to fly, either from one side or the other." [12] What the black citizens of Hancock County thought about the impending trial is unknown. Perhaps they were pleased that Hancock County's richest and most famous farmer had acknowledged his black family. They may have been proud that a woman of color should become so wealthy. They may have been frightened of what the white community might do. They may have been frightened of what Amanda America Dickson might do. Or they may have assumed that none of this would make any real difference in their lives.

All of this anticipation occurred in a community that was no longer wealthy, no longer the crown jewel of the richest plantation county in middle Georgia. By the 1880s Sparta was the county seat of a farming community that remained in the midst of an agricultural depression from which it never recovered. The *Ishmaelite* lamented that merchants' charges were high, that management of labor was "indolent," that the labor itself was inefficient, and that no one would give credit. "Can any man who has within himself remedies for these evils withhold it from his fellows and be a good citizen?" Before the Civil War, Hancock County led the state in successful agriculture, but times had changed. Even though David Dickson had managed the transition from slave to free agricultural labor, after Dickson's death the wealthiest white citizen of the county was Captain Richard B. Baxter, "a keen businessman," not a farmer.[13]

At the time of the trial of the Dickson will case in 1885, Sparta was an overtly religious community. The white citizens of the town worshiped in the Presbyterian, Baptist, Methodist, and Catholic churches. Black citizens worshiped in at least seven CME churches, including St. Paul's on the Dickson plantation. The county contained a high school for boys and girls and several primary schools for white children. In addition, the Bass Academy enrolled more than one hundred black students, some of whom were candidates for teacher certification. Several black grammar schools, including the Cherry Hill School on the Dickson plantation and the Springfield School established by the Hubert family of former slaves, prospered in Hancock County in 1885.

In the middle 1880s, Sparta had seventeen stores, three "first class soda fountains," one jeweler, two dentists, three doctors, and nine lawyers. The streets were "well laid out" with sidewalks and chinaberry and mulberry trees that provided shade. Cows still roamed the streets, and occasionally someone killed a snake on the square.[14]

Because money was scarce, public entertainments were simple. Speeches for and against the demon liquor attracted crowds. In November 1885, overcome with zeal for reform, the citizens of Hancock voted 393 for and 498 against the sale of "the root of all evil." That same year an excursion train ran from Camak to Devereux for the benefit of the white Sunday School Association, and the ladies of the Presbyterian church held ice cream socials from five to nine in the evenings for the benefit of their church. Black and white citizens organized baseball games with neighboring towns. The white games were umpired by E. A. Rozier, "a most accurate and impartial 'ump.' " The Milledgeville Drama Club came to Sparta to perform, and the Gypsies paid their annual visit to nearby Linton. Even an occasional "professor" came to educate or entertain. Professor Pharyan appeared in 1885 and performed magic tricks and feats of ventriloquism at the courthouse with such skill that the *Sparta Ishmaelite* observed that the basket trick alone was worth the price of admission, fifty cents for adults and twenty-five cents for children.[15]

Into the midst of this quiet community the Dickson will case descended as high drama. David Dickson, the "Prince of Georgia Farmers," had chosen to leave his large estate to his mulatto daughter. Dickson could have avoided the legal conflict over his will if he had transferred all his property to Amanda America during his lifetime, but this would have made the father dependent on the daughter. Dickson did give Amanda America and her children three-fourths interest in thirteen thousand acres of fertile farm land in Rusk County, Texas, and several thousand dollars in bonds before his death.[16] Nevertheless, he controlled most of his property until his death and endeavored to frame the conflict over who would be his successor in terms of the law.

David Dickson chose the actors in this drama with great care. His executors would play a crucial role and therefore had to be individuals whom he could trust without reservation to carry out his wishes after his death. They had to be individuals who would not take advantage of their control over Amanda America's large estate and who could act in an appropriately authoritarian manner toward white debtors to the estate. David Dickson chose T. J. Warthen, his nephew, and Charles Dubose, his lawyer, to play these essential roles. T. J. Warthen was the son of Dickson's older sister Malinda Dickson Warthen. He had been raised close to the Dickson plantation and had known his uncle well all his life. In 1873, Warthen moved into David Dickson's household so that he could assist in the management of the plantations. Charles W. Dubose, a prominent lawyer in Sparta, was chosen to manage the legal confrontation for several reasons. First, he was David Dickson's "personal friend" and could be trusted to carry out Dickson's instructions. Second, Dubose was an excellent lawyer and a respected member of the Georgia bar. He had practiced law in Sparta since 1845, served in the Georgia legislature (1861–66) and the Georgia Senate (1878–81), and been elected clerk of the Georgia Supreme Court (1860–68). Finally, Dubose was a respected member of his community. When Charles Wilds Dubose died in 1891, his obituary in the *Sparta Ishmaelite* described him as a man who had merited "warm affection" and "great admiration." The will charged these executors to see that "Amanda A. Dickson and her children are protected in their person and property under the law as far as they may be able to do so."[17]

David Dickson also chose the witnesses to his will carefully. Judge Frank Lightfoot Little, Lovick "Dock" Pierce, Jr., and Captain Richard B. Baxter were Civil War veterans, longtime residents of Sparta, and respected in the community. Frank Lightfoot Little was the judge of the County Court. Lovick Pierce, Jr., the son of the Methodist bishop George Foster Pierce, was a successful merchant in Sparta and had a reputation as a civic-minded citizen. He was superintendent of the

Methodist Sunday School and president of the board of trustees of the Sparta Academy, on which all three men served. In addition, he had been president of the commission to rewrite the ordinances for the city of Sparta in 1884. Richard B. Baxter was a prominent Presbyterian businessman in Sparta and, after David Dickson, the wealthiest person in the county. Baxter was also well known in Sparta for his "beautiful" Jersey bulls, his imported English shotguns, and his generosity with the game he killed on far-flung hunting trips. David Dickson could not have chosen three more influential citizens.[18]

On July 21, 1884, Charles Dubose called these three men into his law office so that they could witness the signing of David Dickson's will. Dickson was present and informed the gentlemen that the contents of the paper were known to "nobody on earth" except himself and the man who wrote it (Dubose) and that before he signed it, he wished for them to satisfy themselves that he was of sound mind. Judge Little later commented that "his mind, as it has always been since I have known him twenty-five or twenty-six years, was perfectly sound on that day. I regarded him as a man of fine mind, and he seemed to have as good sense on that day as at any time what I have known him." [19] After all three witnesses had satisfied themselves that David Dickson was of sound mind, Dickson signed the will at the end and on each page and placed it in a large envelope, which he sealed and signed across the seal.

David Dickson could not choose the most significant actor in this drama, the judge, Samuel Lumpkin. In 1885 Judge Lumpkin was a young man of thirty-seven. After graduating with first honors from the University of Georgia in 1866, Lumpkin taught school and studied for the bar. Upon passing the bar, the future judge began a meteoric legal career first as solicitor general of the Northern Circuit (1872) and as a member of the Georgia Senate (1877). In 1884 the state legislature elected Lumpkin to serve as judge of the Superior Court of the Northern District, a post to which he was reelected in 1888, after the Dickson will case trial. Turn-of-the-century legal historians have described Judge Lumpkin as accurate and painstaking: "His charges to jurors were models of clearness and were marked by fairness of which the losing side could never justly complain. . . . He took no thought as to the effect of his decision upon friend or foe and was never concerned beyond that inquiry, 'What is the law?' But for that he was always deeply concerned." In anticipation of the trial, the *Sparta Ishmaelite* described Judge Lumpkin as a man "with a high regard for the public interest. And this is the highest test of the worth and accountability in a public official." Again, on November 18, 1885, the *Ishmaelite* stated, "Judge Lumpkin will get 'em straight after awhile. He is a remarkably good straightener." [20]

As the Dickson will case trial approached, more lawyers converged on Sparta than normally lived in the county. Many of those who came had statewide, even national, reputations. The caveators, or excluded white relatives, hired nine lawyers, including U.S. Congressman N. J. Hammond and state representative Nathaniel E. Harris, who later became governor of Georgia. They also hired J. A. Harley and T. M. Hunt of Sparta. Amanda America Dickson hired five lawyers, including Judge E. H. Pottle, Georgia legislator and senator and former judge of the Superior Court of the Northern District; Seaborn Reese, former solicitor general of the Northern District and a former U.S. congressman; Judge Frank Lightfoot Little, a witness to the will and judge of the County Court; and from Sparta, J. T. Jordan and Charles W. Dubose. Of the lawyers whom Amanda America hired, two, Judge E. H. Pottle and Judge Frank Lightfoot Little, owed David Dickson's estate money.[21]

At the special request of C. W. Dubose, who stated that he "felt deeply the responsibility that was upon him as executor" and desired "the aid of the best intelligence of the County," a special slate of grand jurors was drawn. Two of these owed David Dickson's estate money: J. T. Middlebrooks and John Turner. The latter was elected foreman of the grand jury.[22] Although Middlebrooks and Turner were listed as debtors to the Dickson estate in the appraisal that Charles Dubose filed with the Probate Court of Hancock County, a public document, neither man was removed from the grand jury (Appendix 3.1).

The last actors in this drama were the witnesses. Excluding Judge Frank Lightfoot Little and Lovick Pierce, witnesses to the will, the caveators called eleven witnesses, while the propounders, those who would inherit under the will, called twenty-one witnesses. All of these witnesses were men, with the exception of Julia Frances Lewis Dickson. They were David Dickson's kin, his neighbors, his business associates, his doctors, his former slaves, his employees, and his personal friends. Many of them had known David Dickson since childhood.[23] Amanda America Dickson was not called to the witness stand nor is her presence in the courtroom mentioned.

On November 16, 1885, the drama began in the Superior Court room of the recently completed Hancock County Courthouse. The citizens of Hancock County had begun constructing the courthouse in 1880 and completed it in 1883. The stately old building still stands on a ridge that runs through the center of Sparta. Ironically, in 1885, David Dickson's estate still owned $28,000 in Hancock County Courthouse bonds, or 90 percent of the $30,000 that the citizens borrowed to construct this "masterpiece of Victorian architecture."[24]

The Superior Court room still occupies the central sections of the second and third floors of the courthouse. It is a grandiose two-story room with arched windows running from the floor to the ceiling on both the north and south sides of the building. Fluted heart pine columns support the ceiling and a shallow balcony with an elaborately carved balustrade. The floor where the judge and jury still reside is level. It then slopes gently upward to the north, where spectators still sit in pine pews. The high ceilings and windows, sloping floor, and balcony give the room the feeling of a small Victorian opera hall or theater.

On Wednesday morning, November 19, 1885, Judge Samuel Lumpkin called the Superior Court of Hancock County to order. Among the throng of spectators who crowded into the courtroom were a multitude of newspaper reporters, some of them from as far away as New York City, Cleveland, and New Orleans.[25]

The issues before the court were both complex and controversial. The excluded white relatives argued that the court should not sustain the will because Dickson was not of sound and disposing mind when it was written; he had been unduly influenced by Amanda and her mother; Amanda was not David Dickson's child; and the will was "in its scheme, its nature and tendencies illegal and immoral, contrary to the policy of the state and of the law and is destructive and subversive to the interest and welfare of society." [26]

The trial began with testimony by the witnesses to the signing of David Dickson's will, County Court judge Frank Lightfoot Little, Lovick Pierce, Jr., and Richard B. Baxter. Each man testified that he had seen David Dickson sign the will and that Dickson had been in good health and of sound mind at the time. After Judge Little read the will to the court, the document was placed in evidence. Subsequently, the lawyers for the caveators began their efforts to break the will.

In spite of the strange burial instructions that David Dickson had left for his nephew, the first two points at issue, whether Dickson had a sound mind and was able to exercise his own will in the public sphere, were never called into serious question. Uniformly, when pushed if necessary, witnesses for both sides declared that David Dickson was a man with a high level of native intelligence and an effective will. "I think that he had the strongest will of any man I have ever known; I don't know of a man of stronger will or more determined to carry out his own plans and ideas," stated Henry Harris, Clara Harris Dickson's brother. B. F. Riley, who had known David Dickson for forty-five years, declared, "I don't think the man ever lived on earth that could influence him to do something that he didn't want to do." And B. H. Sasnett, one of the Methodist ministers who buried David Dickson and a witness for the excluded white relatives, stated that Dickson was "a man of imperious will; very strong will." [27]

The charge of undue influence exposed the heart of the conflict between Dickson's white kin and his outside kin. The lawyers for the white relatives made no headway in trying to establish, in the abstract, that David Dickson could have been easily influenced by any man. No witness admitted that possibility. Changing tactics, the lawyers for the caveators then asked witnesses if David Dickson could have been influenced by a woman. Two witnesses, W. H. Matthews and James M. Eubanks, testified that Julia did have influence over David Dickson.

Matthews, a crippled Civil War veteran who used to fish in the Dickson ponds just after the war, testified as follows:

> Q. Well, now, did you ever have any transaction with Mr. Dickson which was attended to by Julia?
> A. Yes, sir. I used to do a good deal of fishing during those years [1865–67]; I had just come home from the war and was crippled, and didn't do much work; I didn't have any particular home at that time, and I done a good deal of fishing and Mr. Dickson told me if I would catch fish down at the Hamburg pond he would take them; I would catch the fish and carry them up and he would tell me to deliver them to Julia and she would pay me; he never paid me a nickel in his life, she always paid me. . . . Well, I think this woman had a great deal of influence over Mr. Dickson.[28]

Matthews also stated that Julia was "in charge" of "household matters," that Dickson paid the "most regard" to Julia's suggestions, and that he had seen David Dickson kiss Julia "several times."[29] Upon cross-examination, Matthews admitted that he had never seen Julia Dickson "exercise any control" over David Dickson outside of household matters. Was David Dickson unduly influenced if that influence were exercised only in the domestic sphere?

James M. Eubanks, one of David Dickson's nephews and a business associate who had lived on the Dickson home place from 1855 to 1862, stated that Julia Dickson "exercised more influence over David Dickson than anybody else." Under cross-examination, Eubanks testified that Julia exercised no control over David Dickson's business affairs, but he continued to insist that Julia Dickson did indeed have undue influence over David Dickson because he treated her like a wife, not a servant. "Dickson didn't direct her like a female servant," Eubanks declared, "he directed her like a wife; like a man would direct his wife; he didn't speak harsh to her like a servant."[30]

The other witnesses for the caveators claimed that David Dickson did not treat Julia Dickson like a servant, but they would not conclude that she had undue influence over him. Joe Brooken, one of David Dickson's former slaves and the father of Julia Dickson's second child, stated that Julia had as much control in household matters as any man's wife.

Under cross-examination, however, Brooken admitted that "[Julia] was under [David] and had to obey him; they all had to obey him . . . he had it all in his hands and did as he pleased."[31]

The white relatives endeavored to demonstrate that Julia exercised undue influence over David Dickson because of his affection for her. James M. Dickson, who stated at the trial that he had known David Dickson "ever since childhood," was asked whether, when he visited the Dickson home place as a little boy, he had seen Green Dickson, David's brother, threaten to kill David "because he [David] had put this nigger [Julia] over their mother."[32] Unfortunately, the judge did not allow James to answer. S. D. Rogers, Dickson's nephew, stated that he had known David Dickson since "his first recollection" and that he had lived at the Dickson home place off and on as a boy. Rogers recounted this story from his childhood:

Q. I will ask you whether or not Mr. Dickson ever undertook to oppose Julia in any of her wishes? If you know of any such instance please state it.
A. I never knew of any clashing but once; when I was a boy several years before the war, I was down there on a visit, and he [David Dickson] had a housegirl by the name of Lett, and she made a complaint to him that some articles that he had given her had been destroyed; they were some articles of dress trimming; they all started a search for it, Lett and some other girls he had about the house there, and I think Lett called his attention to the back door where Julia was standing, cutting up this trimming; he asked her what she was doing and she made no reply at all, and he hit her with a cowhide, and I think she hit him, anyway they had a lively little scuffle.
Q. State what she did.
A. She jumped on him.
Q. Tried to whip him? Did he strike her more than one lick?
A. Only one lick. I was satisfied that he regretted that he had struck her.
Q. How long before they made it up?
A. Not before the next morning. I was there and saw her and she seemed to be in a good humor.
Q. What was Julia's condition at that time?
A. She was a slave.
Q. I will ask you to state whether or not the relation between Mr. Dickson

and Julia was that of a master and slave or was it more like the relation between a man and his sweet-heart?

A. It was much more like a man and his sweetheart or a husband and wife, something of that sort.[33]

Other witnesses testified that David Dickson exhibited affection for Julia Frances Dickson. William S. Dickson, another witness for the caveators, stated that he had talked to Tyler Harrison, a black man who worked on the Dickson place after the war, and that Harrison had told him that on one occasion Julia had threatened to leave David Dickson. In response, Dickson had "looked like he was most crazy . . . cried and took on about it." In addition, four hostile witnesses said that they had seen David Dickson kiss Julia. Three of these witnesses were black; Matthew Dickson and Joe Brooken had been Dickson slaves and Washington Printup had worked on the Dickson home place after the war. The fourth was a white person, W. H. Matthews, who traded with David Dickson.[34]

The white relatives claimed that Julia Frances Dickson had exercised undue influence over David Dickson that caused him to mistreat his white wife, Clara Harris Dickson. Julia and Amanda Dickson possessed a "better" house with more elegant furniture. They owned a piano but Clara Dickson, who was an accomplished musician, did not. Clara had a carriage with a pair of "fine, black horses" to draw it but did not always have a proper driver. The caveators also claimed that when Clara Harris died at her family's home in Sparta in 1873, David Dickson had not visited her in her last sickness; indeed, he had not arrived until an embarrassingly long interval after her death. Finally, the white relatives argued that the very presence of Amanda, Julian, and Charles on the Dickson home place was an affront to the legal Mrs. Dickson, even if a sexual relationship between David and Julia no longer existed and the outside family stayed in their new house on the hill.[35]

The white relatives then argued that David Dickson's behavior toward Amanda and her children illustrated that he had been unduly influenced; he treated them as though they were members of a *real*

family. At home Amanda called him "Pappy" and her children called
him "Grandpapa." The boys ate at the table with David Dickson and
hopped up in his lap when white people were present. David Dickson
even allowed his outside grandchildren to raise questions about the
"real" Mrs. Dickson's conduct. S. D. Rogers, one of David Dickson's
nephews, testified that while he and his wife were visiting the Dickson home place, Mrs. Dickson was called away to Sparta. "The older
boy, Julian, came up and took a seat there on the sofa and said, she,
Mrs. Dickson, had gone off that morning in a phaeton and a pair of
horses, 'Pappy, do you reckon she is going to feed your horses while
she is gone?' and David Dickson turned around to me and winked and
smiled."[36]

Finally, the lawyers for the white relatives sought to prove that
the very act of leaving Amanda America and her children his estate
demonstrated that Dickson had been unduly influenced. Under cross-
examination, Richard B. Baxter, a witness for the will, was asked:

> Q. Now, if it be true that some one had induced him to do an act that
> was contrary to his own judgement of propriety and decency, an act that
> tended to bring him into disgrace and disrepute, that would blacken his
> memory, the question that I am asking you is, wouldn't there have to be
> some great and overwhelming influence brought to bear upon him?
> A. I would think so.[37]

Addressing the second objection to the will, the caveators became
vicious. They argued that the will was a result of fraud, that Amanda
America Dickson was not, in fact, David Dickson's child because he was
sterile. W. S. Lozier testified that Dickson "visited" other black women
and, rumor had it, slept with them, and that no children had resulted.
In addition, Clara Harris Dickson had had no children. Therefore, the
lawyers for the caveators reasoned, David Dickson must have been sterile. Amanda America Dickson was not David's child but the child of his
younger brother Green. At the time of Amanda America's conception
in the winter of 1849, Green was a thirty-five-year-old bachelor, living
intermittently on the Dickson home place with his mother, Elizabeth,

David, and his sister Rutha. The lawyers for the caveators argued that
Amanda America was Green's child because she looked like his alleged
mulatto daughter Jane Wilder and because Green had asked Julia to
bring Amanda to see him in his last illness, as a father might ask to see
his child before he died.[38]

Amanda America Dickson's lawyers began their rebuttal by calling
to the stand David Dickson's "personal friend" and attorney, Charles
Dubose. Dubose testified that he had drafted the will "in exact accordance" with Dickson's instruction, that no one had been present when
they had discussed the will, and that no one knew what was in the will
except himself and David Dickson. When asked if Dickson was "a man
who could be influenced by anybody," Dubose replied, "He was a man
of very strong mind, of very strong will, and one who could not be easily
influenced by anybody; indeed, sir, I do not believe in any important
matter that anyone could influence him."[39]

Subsequent rebuttal witnesses reiterated that David Dickson was a
man of "extraordinary intelligence," a "strong native intellect," and
a "decidedly strong native mind." When asked about Dickson's will-
power, rebuttal witnesses uniformly described him as a man with a
strong will. Judge J. C. Simmons, who stated that he had known Dickson for twenty years, reported that Dickson "had the strongest will
power of any man I have ever met with." Samuel A. Pardee, who had
known David Dickson for fifty or sixty years and had been in business
with him as a merchant, described Dickson as a person who, once he
had made up his mind, was "immovable." B. F. Riley, who had known
Dickson for forty-five years and had been a "frequent" visitor at the
Dickson home place for about fifteen years, declared that no man could
make Dickson "do a thing he didn't want to do." When asked, "How
about a woman?" Riley replied, "I don't know about that, but I don't
think they had any more influence on him than a man."[40]

In attacking the charge of undue influence, the lawyers for Amanda
America Dickson asked a series of witnesses to describe how Julia
Frances Dickson and her daughter behaved in the Dickson household.
Augustus E. Eubanks, one of David Dickson's nephews and a minor
beneficiary of the will, described Julia Dickson's role: "Well, she as-

sisted in the house like any other servant's child, and was a great pet
of my grandmother's; and was around her very much; she waited in
the house and minded the table and so on; . . . Like any other slave
would be; this condition of things continued until my grandmother's
death." Other witnesses described Julia Frances's role as housekeeping,
"presiding over the table," "superintending household affairs," and "a
servant." J. T. Barry, who testified that he had known David Dickson
"ever since I was a boy," said Julia Dickson acted "in a very humble
capacity." Dr. E. D. Alfriend, the Dickson family physician from 1875
to 1885, described Julia's work routine: "Julia would come down from
her house in the morning and see to cleaning up the house and give out
the meals, and then she would go away and come back in the evening
and give out the meals an[d] return." When asked if he ever saw any
intimacy between David and Julia, Dr. Alfriend replied, "Not the least
in the world." When Dr. E. W. Alfriend, Dr. E. D.'s father, was asked
to describe Julia's role at the Dickson plantation, he replied: "She was
a very attentive business woman about the house. I became very much
attached to the woman." When the senior Dr. Alfriend was asked if he
had seen any act of intimacy between Julia and David, he replied, "I
never did, sir." [41]

Probably the most difficult issue for the defense to address was that
of sexual intimacy between David and Julia Dickson. For Amanda
America to be David Dickson's daughter, such intimacy had to be acknowledged. If the defense argued that there had been only one act of
intimacy between David and Julia Dickson and that was an act of rape,
then Julia certainly could not be accused of having "undue influence."
Understandably, the lawyers for the propounders did not present this
argument. If Julia Dickson claimed that she was repeatedly forced to
have sex with David, she could not be labeled as having undue influence. Joe Brooken testified that "[Julia] was under him [David] and
had to obey him." The lawyers for the propounders did not present this
argument either. If the defense had claimed that David Dickson felt
affection, or even love, for Julia, would that have been equivalent to
undue influence?

When asked about their relationship, Julia replied that they had "separated before he ever married or thought of it, I reckon." She also stated that she had never threatened to leave "Mr. Dickson" and that she had never seen him "take on like a maniac." Finally, Julia Dickson admitted that she had kissed "Mr. Dickson" but added "that has been a long time ago. . . . Long before the war—during the war" (Appendix A.2).[42]

In defense of David Dickson's conduct toward Julia Frances Dickson, the lawyers for the will argued that if his behavior had been improper, no one would have gone to visit the Dickson plantation. In fact, many of the "best people in the county" went there. Judge Simmons, one of David Dickson's business associates, testified that he visited the Dickson plantation frequently and that he had seen Judge Little's, Mr. Harris's, and Colonel Lane's families there, along with "a great many others of the best people in this community." T. J. Warthen stated that there was "more or less company all the time: Judge Simmons and family; John Culver's daughters; Louis Culver and family; Bishop Pierce, Lovick Pierce, and many others." Wryly, T. J. Warthen added that he had seen the lawyer who was questioning him, Seaborn Reese, visiting at the Dickson plantation.[43]

Under cross-examination by the lawyers for the caveators, Judge J. C. Simmons was asked, "Had you known that David Dickson was living with a negro strumpet who not only permitted him to have access to her person but negroes and white men, that he was in the habit of kissing and hugging this negro strumpet, and that he was in the habit of hugging and kissing those negro children, would you have carried your wife to visit his house if you had known these things?" Judge Simmons replied, "Well, sir, I don't think I would." When asked the same question under cross-examination, J. L. Garner, a witness for the will, replied, "I don't know as I would." B. F. Riley was asked, "If you had known that David Dickson was living in an open state of adultery with a negro woman, that he had a child by her, that he was hugging and kissing this negro woman and that he was hugging and kissing her negro children; if you had known all that would you have carried your wife and daughters to visit there?" Riley replied, "If I had seen it with my own eyes I would not have; I would have to see it with my own eyes to believe it." When B. H. Sasnett, a Methodist minister and witness against the will, was asked essentially the same question, he replied, "I don't think that I would sir, . . . but, Colonel, I have known people in this county to have been visited under those facts; and I do not know that I could make a positive statement."[44]

Rev. Sasnett appears to have been trapped in a dilemma. The question put to him implies that he ought to have been shocked by David Dickson's open affection for his outside family, so shocked that he should have protected his family from such a spectacle. But Rev. Sasnett refused to state positively that he would not have taken his wife and children to visit David Dickson. W. S. Lozier, the lead-off witness against the will, responded similarly when he was asked to "state the facts within your knowledge giving to show the intimacy existing between David Dickson and this girl Julia, which would lead one to suppose that there was sexual intercourse going on between them." Lozier replied, "Well, at that time that was a matter that never seemed to trouble us much; it was generally understood." These two statements present a before-and-after dilemma. Before David Dickson left his estate to his outside family, his behavior was sometimes censured but more frequently, judging from this testimony, ignored, tolerated, or accepted. After Dickson left his fortune to his outside kin, his heirs-at-law portrayed his behavior as illegal, immoral, and even shocking so that they could gain control of his estate.[45]

Returning to the charge of undue influence, the lawyers for the will addressed the accusation that David Dickson had been induced by Julia and Amanda Dickson to mistreat his white wife. In rebuttal, they called Clara Harris Dickson's brother Henry Harris to the stand. Harris testified: "I never heard of any instance in which he treated her unkindly; he was not a demonstrative man, he did not pet her but he was a man that would provide for her needs." Harris declared that Dickson gave Clara ample money, that she had a phaeton and a fine pair of black horses at her disposal, and that Dickson had had plans for a $30,000 house for Clara drawn up by an architect in Augusta. When asked why the house was never built, Harris replied that Clara "was afraid that it was inappropriate to have so fine a house down there so far in the country." In cross-examining Henry Harris, the lawyers for the caveators asked why he had not "remonstrated" against David Dickson for keeping "this bastard nigger . . . right close to his house?" Harris replied that he thought "it was none of my business."[46] Finally, Henry Harris declared:

> If I have left the impression that my sister was happily married, I want it understood that I don't think so; but I swear positively that I do not know of any unkindness; I still stand to that, but I know that in her condition of health, and from want of congeniality between the two that she was never happy; their residence was way out in the country, and she was born [and] raised in town and accustomed to society and, together with her state of health, she could not have been happy.[47]

Moving from the question of undue influence to the accusation that David Dickson was not Amanda America's father, the lawyers for the will relied on two counterarguments: that Amanda America resembled David in her appearance and in her manner and that David had openly acknowledged his paternity.[48]

Several witnesses for the propounders claimed that they thought that Amanda America physically resembled David Dickson.[49] Dr. E. W. Alfriend stated that he believed that Amanda was David's daughter because of the likeness and because Julia Dickson had told him so:

> This child Amanda was in the room on one occasion when I was there. I asked Julia whose it was; I thought I had discovered some traces of resemblance to Mr. Dickson, and rather thought that it presented Mr. Dickson's features; she told me that it was her child; I told her I supposed it was, but asked if she didn't have any assistance in getting it; she asked me if I could see any favor, and that I might judge from the favor; I told her I wouldn't risk my judgement on the favor, and asked her why she declined to tell; she then told me, I thought at the time, rather reluctantly, that it was "Massa David's."[50]

In addition to noting a physical resemblance, Judge J. C. Simmons, who collected coupons, or interest payments, for Amanda America Dickson, commented that he thought that "[Amanda] favored Mr.

Dickson in her personal appearance, her manner of speech and general management of business."[51]

After establishing that Amanda America Dickson resembled her father, the lawyers for the will called to the stand B. F. Riley, Augustus E. Eubanks, and T. J. Warthen. All testified that David Dickson had acknowledged that Amanda America was his child. In addition, when J. L. Garner, one of David Dickson's neighbors, was asked if Dickson recognized Amanda as his child, Garner replied, "He recognized her all his life—all her life . . . we got to talking about children that were born a little outside; he said he had one, Amanda, who he recognized as his child."[52]

The most revealing testimony regarding David Dickson's paternity of Amanda America was given by Clara Harris Dickson's brother Henry Harris. Harris testified that on one occasion he and David Dickson had been riding across Dickson's farm and they stopped near the house that had been built for Julia and Amanda America Dickson on a hill. Dickson spoke of Amanda's living there and his "taking care of her." According to Harris, David Dickson said that he had no doubt that Amanda America was his "natural child" and that he felt that it was his "duty" to care for her, even though "some people censured him very much for doing so." Dickson then stated that he had been relatively young at the time of the child's conception and was "of course endowed with all the passions of a young man; that this girl [Julia] was his mother's house servant, that she slept in the house and I think his expression was that he 'let his foot slip.' "[53]

Finally, Julia Frances Lewis Dickson testified that David Dickson was Amanda America's father. When asked how David found out that Amanda was his child, Julia replied, "Very likely a man would know; because he was at the getting of her and because he knew nobody wasn't having anything to do with me but him; nobody there but him."[54]

The last legal objection presented by the caveators, that the will was "in its nature and tendencies illegal and immoral contrary to the public policy of the state and of the law and is destructive and subversive to the interest and welfare of society," was not addressed directly during this trial.

Unfortunately, the closing arguments were not included in the official trial transcripts. According to the *Sparta Ishmaelite*, each side was
allocated four and a half hours, and the speeches "on both sides were
earnest and in some cases, eloquent." If the lawyers for the excluded
white relatives reiterated their argument that David Dickson had been
unduly influenced, the lawyers for Amanda Dickson were faced with a
dilemma. If David Dickson was of sound mind and had not been unduly influenced, why would he do something that "was contrary to his
own judgment of propriety and decency, an act that tended to bring
him into disgrace and disrepute, that would blacken his memory"? The
lawyers for the will had to argue that the act of bequeathing a fortune
to an illegitimate mulatto daughter did not, in and of itself, prove that
David Dickson either was of unsound mind or had been unduly influenced. They could have argued that David Dickson did not give a fig
what other people thought; that he was doing what he thought was his
duty, regardless of public opinion; or that he acted out of affection. According to the *Sparta Ishmaelite*, the central theme that the proponents
of the will endeavored to establish was that David Dickson had acted
out of "natural affection." [55]

On the last objection, the issue of public policy, the lawyers for the
will could have argued that the law was clear in that private property
rights overrode the vague issue of public policy. There was no law in
Georgia, as there was in Louisiana, prohibiting a concubine or her
illegitimate mulatto children from inheriting property under a will.
On this point the lawyers for the caveators presented their counterarguments of law in a written request to Judge Lumpkin to charge
the jury that "under the constitution and laws of the State of Georgia,
marriages between white persons and Negroes are forbidden, and the
public policy of the State is against the mingling of the blood of these
races, and if you believe this will is against said policy, it is absolutely
void." By 1885, Georgia law forbade illicit sex, that is, sex outside of
marriage, without mentioning race. A separate law forbade interracial
marriage. Consequently, all interracial sex acts were acts of fornication. According to the excluded white relatives, David Dickson's will,
which gave his property to his illegitimate mulatto daughter, would en-

courage the "mingling of the blood" and was, they argued, much more dangerous than ignoring the sanctity of property rights.[56]

The *Sparta Ishmaelite* described Judge Samuel Lumpkin's charge to the jury as "clear and fair to both sides." According to the legal records, Lumpkin instructed the jury on what constituted a legal will and described the mental capacity required to draw up such an instrument. He pointed out that "anything which destroys [the] freedom of volition invalidates a will; such as fraudulent practices upon [a] testator's fears; affections or sympathies; duress or any undue influence whereby the will of another is substituted for the wishes of the testator invalidates a will." Judge Lumpkin cautioned the jury to bear in mind the primacy of property rights: "To set aside a will because it is capricious or unreasonable, or because the testator may have selected an unworthy object for the bestowal of his bounty would be to deprive him of the right secured by law to dispose of his estate by will in such a way as may seem good in his own eyes." The judge stated explicitly that "every man in this state has the right to will his property to whom he pleases." This reference to the sanctity of private property is not surprising if we remember that the 1880s witnessed a flowering of farmers' alliances against the property interest of bankers, railroad tycoons, and other middlemen, culminating in the radical Ocala Platform of 1890. This platform demanded the prohibition of absentee landownership and the reclamation of this land and unearned portions of railroad grants by settlers. It advocated the nationalization of banks and strong government control or, if necessary, outright ownership of communications systems. These threats to the sanctity of property echo in Judge Lumpkin's charge.[57]

In conclusion, Judge Lumpkin reminded the jurors to do their duty: "Take the case, gentlemen, with an honest purpose to do justice to all concerned. You should permit nothing to influence your findings but the law and the testimony. As you shall believe from the evidence and under the law as given you in charge, let your verdict be made."[58]

After "about twenty minutes" of deliberation, John Turner, the foreman of the jury, returned to the court a verdict for the will. Immediately the lawyers for the excluded white relatives filed a motion to grant a stay on all proceedings for sixty days so that they might file an appeal to the Georgia Supreme Court for a new trial. The *Sparta Ishmaelite*'s only editorial comment on the verdict was remarkably detached: "Thus closed the first chapter in the most interesting will case ever brought to trial in the Hancock Court." The editor then mused, "How many more chapters there will be and what will be their length and character is beyond human ken."[59] David Dickson had won the first round in his battle to bequeath his worldly goods to his mulatto daughter. In addition, if the comments of the *Sparta Ishmaelite* reflected the general attitude of the community, the people of Hancock County were willing to let the law function. As the events of the next week illustrate, this was not always the case. The citizens of Hancock County were perfectly capable of taking the law into their own hands if they were sufficiently provoked.

On Wednesday night of the week after the Superior Court decision, a vigilante execution occurred in Hancock County. According to the *Sparta Ishmaelite*, Ike Etheridge, a white person, had escaped from the state mental institution in Baldwin County and returned to Hancock County to wreak havoc in the community. He had been captured by the sheriff and was being held in jail until he could be returned to the insane asylum rather than stand trial for his crimes. At midnight, fifty men appeared at the jail house and "forced" the sheriff to turn over the culprit, "whether and to what end are conjecture." The *Ishmaelite* declared that "the act was a lawless one" but added that the "circumstances leading up to it were of a mitigating character. The people who had felt the weight of [Etheridge's] stealing and murderous hand simply stood upon their own defense and took the law into their own hands." The *Ishmaelite* "regretted" the affair because of its lawlessness but observed, "If it shall have the effect of teaching the authorities that extra effort and diligence in the protection of communities from midnight marauders, constitute the very last measure of protection with which communities will be content, then some good will be the unavoidable result from the violent and unlawful methods of last Wednesday night's proceedings." In summary, the editor of the *Ishmaelite* "hoped that Hancock County will never again be the scene of such an affair." [60] This event illustrates that the citizens of Hancock County, at least some of the males, were willing to step outside the law and resort to violence in dealing with a perceived threat to the safety of their community.

In March 1886, the Georgia Supreme Court recorded an appeal for a new trial of the Dickson will that listed thirty objections by the excluded white relatives.[61] On October 11, 1886, Chief Justice James Jackson and Associate Justices Samuel Hall and Mark Blanford heard the case on appeal. A smaller number of lawyers journeyed to Atlanta to argue for their clients: for the white relatives, Captain John C. Rutherford and Nathaniel Harris;[62] for the defendants, Colonel Charles Dubose, Milton Reese, and Judge Seab Reese. On the first day of the hearing, Justices Hall and Blanford asked questions that led the attorneys for the white relatives to believe that the justices were prepared to rule against the motion for a new trial. At noon, Hall and Blanford called Harris into their chambers and warned him to settle with Amanda America Dickson's lawyers, a proposition that her attorneys refused that afternoon. On the second day of the hearing, Captain John C. Rutherford, realizing that his clients were likely to lose the appeal, delivered one last impassioned plea for the caveators. Lawyer Harris, for the caveators, described the scene:

> The eloquence of [Rutherford's] words, the fire in his eye, and the deep feeling of his soul stirred to the utmost, made a terrible impression upon me, and I knew must have affected the court. One after another he took up the points; showed that the future of the Anglo-Saxon, the traditions of the past, the hopes of the future were all concerned in the questions he was discussing. The appeal grew fiercer and stronger as he spoke.[63]

According to Harris, after Rutherford had finished speaking, Chief Justice Jackson "brought his hand down upon the book in front of him with a resounding crash and said: 'I would rather die in my place than uphold the will.'" That afternoon the counsel for the will proposed a settlement that the attorneys for the caveators refused. A few days later, Judge Jackson contracted pneumonia and died, leaving a vacancy on the court that was filled by Logan E. Bleckley. Bleckley ruled that he would not hear a reargument of the case. Thus Judges Hall and Blanford remained to render a ruling on whether the caveators should be granted a new trial.[64]

On December 17, 1886, the *Sparta Ishmaelite* drolly commented: "The Dickson will case has not been decided. The decision will not likely be unanimous. Flipping nickels would be as good a way as any for forecasting the outcome." On June 13, 1887, eight months after the Supreme Court hearing, Judge Hall finally rendered an opinion upholding the ruling of the lower court. Judge Hall's opinion was lengthy, thirty-two pages long, and precise in its argument that lawyers should "look to your law books for the law, and not to your brain." Above all, lawyers "should not give themselves up to the guidance and direction of their feelings and sentiments, for this would unquestionably lead to excessive irregularities, fluctuations and doubt." Justice Hall believed that the law was clear. The jury had ruled that David Dickson was of sound mind, that he had not been improperly influenced, and that Amanda was David Dickson's "natural" child. Under the Fourteenth Amendment of the Constitution of the United States, the Supreme Court of the United States had ruled that all "colored" persons born in the United States were subject to its jurisdiction and were citizens of the United States and of the state in which they resided and that the Georgia constitution declared that all citizens of the United States residing in the state were citizens. Therefore, "all distinctions as to the rights pertaining to citizenship between the two races are abolished, and as to their civil rights, they stand upon the same footing." Justice Hall summed up his opinion with what must have been a startling judgment: "Therefore, whatever rights and privileges belong to a white concubine or to a bastard white woman and her children, under the laws of Georgia, belong also to a colored woman and her children, under like circumstances, and the rights of each race are controlled and governed by the same enactments on principles of law."[65]

Justice Hall's reference to the Fourteenth Amendment constituted the most important and unexpected part of the decision. The justices could have ruled against the will because Georgia state law was unclear concerning bequests to bastard children and used Louisiana law, which prohibited illegitimate black children from inheriting under a will, as a precedent. By refusing to rule against the will on public policy grounds and by resorting to the Fourteenth Amendment as justification, the Georgia Supreme Court had ruled that no state interest had primacy over property rights, not even the issue of "racial purity." Ironically, this clear statement of the equality of black and white citizens before the law was never used in a civil rights decision in Georgia.[66]

Local newspapers in the region and newspapers as far distant as the *Cleveland Gazette* printed news of the verdict. The *Gazette* commented that the case had been decided by the state supreme court in favor of Amanda Eubanks, "the colored legatee," holding that whites and blacks are "on an equality so far as inheritance goes." The *Atlanta Constitution* reprinted the "facts" of the case. Its article described David Dickson as a farmer who had accumulated a "handsome fortune," a man who lived in a "comfortable manner" and who was held in "high esteem by his neighbors." The editor described Amanda America Dickson as a "mulatto woman" of about thirty who was the daughter of Julia Dickson, "a colored woman who had lived with Mr. Dickson for many years." The verdict of the court, the editor argued, was based on the Constitution of the United States, decisions of the United States Supreme Court, and the constitution and laws of the state of Georgia, all of which prohibited discrimination on the grounds of color in claiming a legacy. The editor of the *Constitution* then commented, "It appears that Amanda A. Dickson and her two children are fully in possession of the magnificent property, and cannot be legally disturbed hereinafter in the enjoyment of the same."[67]

While local white newspapers in Sandersville, Macon, and Augusta reprinted the *Atlanta Constitution* article in its entirety, the *Sparta Ishmaelite* editorialized that there was a lesson to be learned by "unreconstructed Republicans" from this verdict. First, the *Ishmaelite* condemned David Dickson's "methods of life" as "abhorrent to race instincts and the proprieties of decent living." Then it took the opportunity to call the attention of "unreconstructed Republicans" to the case, which the *Ishmaelite* claimed demonstrated that "colored" people in Georgia had "equal rights" with all other people before the law and that these rights would be enforced by courts and juries. The editor then used the outcome of the Dickson will case to rebuke the North: "It is doubtful if so much can be truthfully said of Maine, Ohio, New Hampshire and others of the 'ga-lorious' states where devotion to 'equal rights' is nine parts lip service to one part sincerity."[68]

The black *Savannah Tribune* reported the verdict of the Georgia Supreme Court with a clear sense of pride that some white fathers were recognizing their outside families by making them wealthy. "Dickson, of Georgia, one of the richest men in the state, died not long ago and left his colored wife (the White papers and folks say 'concubine' but not so [actually daughter]) and children [grandchildren] something over $400,000, and now as if to keep the ball moving and add new inspiration to the Negro's progress, one Reynolds, of South Carolina, has died and left a fortune even more princely to his colored wife and children, estimated to be near $600,000." The editor closed his comments with a prayer: "God grant that the good work may go on. Nothing can stop it. It is bound to go forward," signed "Defiance."[69]

With the legal proceedings completed, Amanda America offered a final gesture of appeasement to the community of Hancock County, black and white. Early in the Dickson trial, Charles Dubose testified that he had told Lovick Pierce and William and Hal Culver, debtors under the Dickson will, that if the will was upheld, Amanda America Dickson would not need the money owed to her. On the first Tuesday in November 1887, Amanda America Dickson appeared on the courthouse steps in Sparta and bought up approximately $21,000 in doubtful notes for one dollar, thus forgiving all the debts. Those who were legally beholden to a wealthy mulatto woman were formally released from their obligations.[70]

The drama was over. The Superior Court in Hancock County and the Georgia Supreme Court had ruled in favor of David Dickson's will—his right to leave his private property to whomever he pleased. In the process, Dickson's community had to acknowledge that one of its most prominent members had maintained a family outside the category of race, a family to whom he was willing to leave his vast fortune even though doing so might "bring him into disrepute and blacken his memory forever."

The Death of a Lady

Then tell us gentlemen, which are you really for: the color line,
or the line of character, intelligence, and property that divides those
who have and those who have not the "right to rule?"
—George Washington Cable

DAVID DICKSON'S DEATH created a change of a cosmic order for
Amanda America Dickson. She was no longer protected by her white
father or controlled by his powerful presence. What choices faced this
thirty-six-year-old woman who described herself as an orphan? Her
first concern was to address the legal implications of her father's will.
Would the excluded white relatives, or caveators, be able to overthrow
the will? A second concern must have been for her own safety on
the Dickson plantation. David Dickson's gin houses had been burned
twice, once in 1871 and once shortly before his death, in October 1884.
Would she be safe living nine miles from town, among David Dickson's
former slaves and tenants? If she chose to remain, would the white
community allow her to take control of the Dickson empire? Would the
black community allow her to remain? Should she leave the county,
the state, or the country? How could she create a safe place for herself?

Amanda America Dickson could have remained on the Dickson
home place and managed the plantations with the aid of T. J. Warthen,

or she could have remained there and managed the estates herself. If she chose the latter alternative, she would have faced a double jeopardy. She was a woman, and she was not white. How could she control a large labor force of black and white tenants?

Amanda America Dickson and her mother owned a comfortable home on the largest Dickson plantation. Their extended black family lived nearby, including Amanda America's half-sister, Julianna Dickson Youngblood and her five children. John C. Lewis, Julia's brother, also lived in Hancock County. Many members of David Dickson's white family also lived nearby, some of whom had not been disinherited by the will. If we remember that after David Dickson's death Amanda America defined herself as an orphan, however, we can reasonably conclude that family ties were not a decisive factor in her thoughts about the future.

Amanda America Dickson's racial classification may have been an important consideration as she faced the question of whether to move away from the Dickson home place. If Amanda Dickson chose to accept a public definition as black, she could have moved to a nearby southern city or to a larger southern metropolis such as New Orleans or Charleston, where an established community existed for elite people of color. If Amanda America chose to "pass" in the white world, she could have discarded her notoriety as David Dickson's daughter and moved north, to Europe, to South America, or even to Africa. Life would have been more difficult in some of these locations than in others, but in any of them Amanda America Dickson not only could have changed her place but she could have changed her racial identity and lived discreetly as a white person.[1]

If she chose to leave Sparta but to stay in the urban South as Amanda America Dickson, the notoriety of being David Dickson's illegitimate mulatto daughter would travel with her. She would be labeled as both wealthy and black. Given that labeling, Amanda Dickson then faced another choice: to be an active member of the black community and use her wealth for racial uplift, a perfectly ladylike alternative in that community, or to use her wealth and manners to endeavor to shield herself from the consequences of being identified as black, to retreat into a make-believe world. Elsa Barkley Brown has described the choice for urban blacks in Richmond, Virginia, in this era: elite African-Americans could retreat into "possessive individualism" or join the black community, where "resources, and troubles, were more likely to be shared."[2]

Immediately after David Dickson's death, Amanda America Dickson began to make choices. First, she took control of her legal affairs. On July 6, 1885, she personally appeared in court to petition the ordinary to be appointed the legal guardian of her two children and was granted letters of guardianship after she posted an $800 bond with T. J. Warthen.[3] That same day, David Dickson's excluded white relatives filed their objections to admitting the Dickson will to probate and, after losing their case, appealed to the Superior Court of Hancock County.

After the Superior Court ruled in favor of David Dickson's will in November 1885, and before the Georgia Supreme Court upheld that ruling on June 13, 1887, Amanda America Dickson began preparing to leave Hancock County for good. On July 15, 1886, she purchased a large brick house at 452 Telfair Street in Augusta, Georgia, for $6,098. An *Atlanta Constitution* reporter described the house as "quite a large, double brick house, three stories high, containing some twelve to fifteen rooms, shaded in front by three mammoth oaks, surrounded by a large yard; all in all, a most desirable residence." Because of the attention the Dickson will case had received in the newspapers of the state, we can safely assume that Amanda A. Dickson's fame preceded her to the city of Augusta. As Dr. W. H. Foster, a prominent physician in Augusta, later observed, "Her surroundings were altogether superior to the average colored person and I had always understood for years past that she was very wealthy." The *Atlanta Constitution* also noted: "Amanda A. Dickson, the $400,000.00 heiress from Hancock went to Augusta last Friday. Everybody on the train was anxious to see the richest colored woman in the United States. She created about as much of a sensation as did Henry Ward Beecher when he traveled through the South. She was dressed in deep mourning and had her mother and youngest boy with her." The general populace in Augusta would know that Amanda America Dickson was wealthy, illegitimate, and a woman of color.[4]

Why did Amanda Dickson choose to move to Augusta? In 1886

Augusta was a relatively cosmopolitan southern city. Gas lights lit the main thoroughfares, and as many as four rows of trees on the main streets provided both relief from the heat and a grand promenade. Citizens could purchase ice from the Arctic Ice Company, ready-made clothes, cut flowers, fine French wine and pastry, a newspaper edited by a black editor or a newspaper edited by a white editor. They could also take a ride on a streetcar.[5]

In addition to appreciating these attractive manifestations of civilization, Amanda America Dickson was familiar with the city of Augusta. She had traveled there before and after her father's death and stayed at his house on Greene Street. W. H. Howard, her factor, lived seven blocks from the house that she purchased on Telfair and could act as a white male emissary for her. African-American schools, including Ware High School, Georgia's only publicly supported high school for blacks, and Paine College were located in the city. Other wealthy African-Americans lived in Augusta, citizens with whom Amanda America could associate if she chose to do so and they were agreeable. Most important, however, Amanda America Dickson could buy a large and expensive house in the most fashionable section of the city and live there comfortably despite the notoriety of being the illegitimate mulatto daughter of David Dickson and consequently the "richest black woman in the South." This status as an exotic afforded her limited protection in the white community. As her health failed, this status also made it possible for Amanda America to obtain medical care from distinguished professors at the Medical College of Georgia.[6]

Sherman and his marauding troops had spared both the downtown business district of Augusta and the industries that had flourished there during the war. These resources, coupled with Augusta's location at the headwaters of the Savannah River and at the crossroads of the railroads, resulted in a postwar boom. Augusta became "a gateway through which passed most of the agricultural products of several southern states." Its population increased from 12,000 in 1860 to approximately 40,000 in 1900. By 1890, Augusta was the third largest city in the state after Atlanta, with a population of 65,533, and Savannah, with a population of 43,189, and the second largest exporting point for cotton in the country.[7]

In 1886 Augusta could boast of six banks, including the Georgia Railroad and Banking Company with assets of $4.2 million, a canal, which had cost the city $1 million to build in 1873, a trolley car system, and "enough water to turn a million spindles." Indeed, the city was succeeding in "bringing the factory to the field." The factory consisted of six cotton mills, which employed 5,264 workers who operated 89,464 spindles. Among those workers were 3,381 males over the age of sixteen, 1,340 females over the age of sixteen, and 543 children, a total of 30 percent of the white population of the city in 1890.[8]

The rapid urbanization and industrialization that Augusta experienced during the postwar period also produced tensions within the city's population. City services were archaic and deteriorating in the 1880s and 1890s, especially in the white factory settlements and in the poor black section south of Gwinnett Street known as "the Territories." In these sections water pipes were constructed from hollow logs, and septic fields bubbled to the surface producing green scum and foul odors about which the citizens complained to no avail. From 1880 to 1890 factory wages declined. At the Sibley mill, workers' annual wages dropped from $216 in 1880 to $181 in 1900. The same trend prevailed in the King mill, where annual wages dropped from $242 to $225 in the same period.[9]

Five days before Amanda America Dickson purchased her house on Telfair Street, these tensions erupted into the Knights of Labor strike of 1886. This strike was the first large confrontation between capitalists and workers in Augusta and the first attempt by the Knights of Labor to unionize in a southern mill town. The struggle was bitter and ultimately futile for the workers. Early in the strike, mill owners, in a concerted effort, posted eviction notices, and on September 17, 1886, the authorities evicted the workers, leaving them to stand "stunned, shocked and bewildered" in the streets while new mill hands and their families moved into their homes. By 1890, the Knights of Labor had disappeared from Augusta, leaving the capitalists, many of whom were Amanda America Dickson's neighbors, to rule. Richard German described the consequences: "Victory for the capitalists meant that the owners, investors, directors and supervisors would continue to increase their personal fortunes, assure their privileged positions in the middle

and upper class society and perpetuate their wealth . . . all factors which
tended to tighten social solidarity among the top strata and widen distinctions between upper and lower white society." The white upper
class remained in control, a circumstance that contributed to the safety
of Amanda America Dickson as an exotic in their midst.[10]

When Amanda America Dickson arrived in Augusta in 1886, race
relations in the public sphere were in flux. The city was partially segregated. Two hospitals served the city's chronically ill, the City Hospital
for whites and the Freedmen's Hospital for blacks. The city directory
listed the majority of the community's churches and cemeteries as
either white or "colored." Of the fifteen Baptist churches listed, four
were designated as white and eleven as colored. The Christian, Jewish,
Lutheran, and Catholic churches were listed as single congregations
with no racial designation, as were the Presbyterian[11] and Episcopal
churches. The Methodist Episcopal church had ten congregations of
which five were white and five were colored. Black and white children
in Augusta attended both public and private segregated schools. In
1886, the means of public transportation were not yet legally segregated
nor were other public accommodations.

In this era Augusta still housed colored military units. Of the seven
military organizations, two were colored: the Douglas Infantry and the
Augusta Light Infantry. Of the social organizations in Augusta in 1886,
the relief and benevolent societies did not advertise with racial desig-
nations, but the secret societies did. Six Masonic societies were white,
while the A. Y. M. Benneker Lodge No. 3 was colored. The Independent
Order of Odd Fellows lists two white lodges and two colored lodges, the
B.U.O.F. Boaz Lodge and the Star of Bethlehem Lodge. The Woman's
Christian Temperance Union (WCTU) lists three chapters with no
racial designation, which probably means they were exclusively white.
Separate unions were characteristic of the WCTU in Georgia from its
inception in the 1880s because "our colored people wish to do their
work as an independent organization, and not auxiliary to our state
W.C.T.U."[12]

A small number of black citizens of Augusta worked as artisans and
in the professions. They dominated the trades of barbering (83 percent

of twenty-nine listed), blacksmithing (60 percent of fifteen), carpentering (80 percent of five), huckstering (83 percent of twelve), junk dealing (100 percent of four), and restauranteering (85 percent of seven), and they controlled half the undertaking establishments (three of six). Several of these African-Americans dealt only with white clients. George Walton, for example, practiced the trade of barbering at the fashionable Augusta Hotel on Broad Street, and John C. Ladeveze sold art supplies at 315 Reynolds Street. John C. Ladeveze's cousin Robert A. Harper, the only African-American piano tuner in the state of Georgia at the time, also sold pianos in the art store. One black lawyer, Judson W. Lyons, a graduate of Howard Law School, practiced in Augusta in 1886, and one black physician, Dr. E. H. Mayer, practiced medicine at 928 Walker Street, one street south of Telfair and five blocks from Amanda Dickson's house.[13]

In 1886 several of Augusta's black citizens were wealthy. By 1890 six of them owned property worth $6,000 or more: Nora Butterfield ($16,000); L. Henson, a restaurateur ($18,500); Mary Butts ($11,800); Mary J. Ladeveze and Mary F. Harper ($17,500); Henry Osborne, a merchant ($8,650); and Mary Skinfield, a mortician ($7,850). These estates are particularly impressive compared to the per capita worth of other African-American ($1.65) and white ($6.85) Georgians in 1890.[14] Forty percent of these extraordinarily large estates were controlled by women.

In the elite black community of Augusta, status was based on more than wealth, either earned or inherited. Community position was more likely to depend on a constellation of attributes, including color, status before the Civil War, education, manners, family connections, and wealth. According to these standards, Amanda America Dickson's status in the elite black community of Augusta would have been enviable. She was a mulatto, specifically a quadroon. Although she had not been legally free before the Civil War, or at least she was not listed in the Register of Free Persons of Color in Hancock County, Amanda Dickson enjoyed material advantages that the individuals who were listed as free in the Hancock County register could never have afforded. She was literate and had attended Atlanta University for two years. She could play the piano and dress with impeccable taste, as was expected of any proper lady, black or white. Before Amanda America Dickson came to Augusta, her African-American family connections were not impressive; shortly thereafter, however, her children married into the city's most prominent black families. Finally, Amanda America Dickson was the wealthiest black person in the state of Georgia. That wealth was put on display in Augusta in the place in which she chose to live and in the way she chose to furnish her residence, in the most elite section of the city.[15]

Amanda America Dickson's home at 452 Telfair was in a multiracial neighborhood. Elite whites lived on the streets that ran east and west, and African-Americans and whites of meager means lived in homes on the numbered avenues, which ran north and south. There were, however, exceptions to this general rule. George Walton lived at 831 Telfair, and Nora Butterfield lived at 307 Walker Street. Mary J. Ladeveze, Mary F. Harper, John C. Ladeveze, and Henry Osborne all lived in the 300 block of Reynolds Street, which was located on the other side of Broad Street, beyond the main business district. All of the residences in the 400 blocks of Greene, Telfair, and Walker streets were headed by whites, except for two on Telfair Street: 452 Telfair Street, owned by Amanda America, and 464 Telfair Street, home of Green Proffet. Other houses on the three streets were inhabited by people of color, but the households were headed by whites. On Fourth Street, between Greene and Telfair, there were five houses that were headed by whites. Between Telfair and Walker streets only one house was occupied by a black family, and between Walker and the next street south were seven houses, of which four were headed by African-Americans.[16]

If we assume that Amanda Dickson's neighborhood was bounded by Third Avenue on the east, Broad Street on the north, Ninth Street on the west, and Walker Street on the south, it becomes clear that this area was the hub of Augusta's civic, social, and business life for both black and white citizens. The city hall, city jail, and the main post office were located here, as well as all six of the city's banks. Forty of Augusta's forty-two lawyers practiced in this area, including Judson W. Lyons, Augusta's only African-American lawyer, who practiced at 633 Ellis Street. All of the public halls were in this area: the Masonic Temple, the Odd Fellows Hall, and the Young Men's Library Association Building. The First Baptist Church, the Thankful Church (black), the First Christian Church, the Congregation Children of Israel (Augusta's only synagogue), the German Evangelical Lutheran Church, St. James Episcopal Church, St. John's Episcopal Church, the First Presbyterian Church (integrated), and St. Patrick's Roman Catholic Church were also in this neighborhood.[17]

Amanda America Dickson's immediate neighbors included two bank presidents: C. H. Phinizy, president of the Georgia Railroad and Banking Company, Augusta's largest bank, at 519 Greene Street, and Z. McCord, president of the National Bank of Augusta, at 444 Greene Street. William McCoy, president of Riverside Mills, lived at 304 Greene Street, and Augusta's richest citizen, W. C. Sibley, president of Sibley Manufacturing, who owned $1 million in assets, lived one block away, at 502 Telfair Street. In 1892, 452 Telfair Street was within two blocks of the homes of three officials of the white WCTU: Mrs. W. C. Sibley, president, at 502 Telfair; Mrs. E. F. Kinchley, recording secretary, at 609 Telfair Street; and Mrs. E. F. Kimbrough, treasurer, at 443 Telfair Street.[18]

According to one of Amanda America Dickson's white neighbors, John M. Crowley, manager of the Western Union Telegraph, the Dickson family was held in high regard in this elite neighborhood. When asked to describe the wealth, refinement, intelligence, and comforts of Amanda Dickson, Mr. Crowley replied: "It was common report that she was worth one-hundred-thousand dollars. My family held her family in very high esteem and would exchange little neighborly acts. I have never heard a word of slander or anything of that nature against them." Crowley continued in a matter-of-fact tone: "The general reputation of the Dickson family in the neighborhood [was] very good. From the reported wealth of the Dickson family they made no ostentatious show nor did they push themselves forward or out of their way. Whilst they had every comfort, I never observed any excess of comfort." Amanda America Dickson displayed what William S. McFeely described in his biography of Frederick Douglass as "bourgeois values maintained with the staunchest respectability."[19]

Amanda America Dickson furnished her residence handsomely. The house contained seven bedrooms, including one for a live-in servant, a library, a hall, a dining room, a parlor, and a kitchen. The furniture in these rooms included beds, one of fine walnut, cane-bottom chairs, rockers, marble-top dressers and washstands, wardrobes, two sideboards and one tin safe, one walnut dining room table with twelve chairs, a walnut bookcase with glass doors containing "various books," eighteen oil paintings (six of which were in the hall), one Brussels carpet, one corner ornamental table, one ottoman, and one suite of parlor plush furniture, consisting of twelve chairs and two sofas, one organ, and one piano. The house was also equipped with linen and silver, including two dozen silver goblets marked D.D., two dozen solid silver spoons marked D.D., one dozen solid silver forks marked D.D., one dozen silver-plated knives, one solid silver water pitcher with a tray, two other solid silver water pitchers, one dozen cups and saucers of fine china, and glass tumblers. Thus by 1887 Amanda America Dickson had purchased a comfortable home and had furnished it with luxury and taste. She had created a comfortable, safe place for herself in the midst of Augusta's white elite.[20]

On June 13, 1887, the Dickson will case was settled in Amanda's favor and the Dickson family story again appeared in the newspapers. A reporter from the *Atlanta Constitution* made an attempt to interview Amanda by contacting the firm in Augusta that was "attending to" her business affairs, Messrs. Howard and Company, David and Amanda's cotton factors. Howard and Company informed the reporter that Amanda Dickson had been advised not to talk to members of the press. Nevertheless, when the reporter knocked on the door at 452 Telfair Street, Amanda America Dickson answered the door. "She was," he said, "an unassuming, intelligent mulatto and does not seem at all 'set up' by her singular good fortune. She would not be noticed in the streets from hundreds of other colored women by any display or show of dress." He continued, "She states that as yet she has no idea what she will do or where she will live in [the] future, but I understand that she has been advised to move north."[21] Amanda America Dickson may have told the *Atlanta Constitution* reporter that she did not know where she would go or what she would do, but the manner

Portrait of Amanda

David Dickson

Julia Frances Lewis Dickson

David Dickson's house in the early nineteenth century

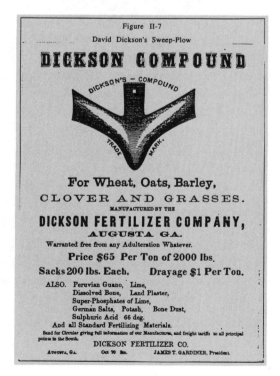

Figure II-7

David Dickson's Sweep-Plow

DICKSON COMPOUND

DICKSON'S — COMPOUND

TRADE MARK.

For Wheat, Oats, Barley,

CLOVER AND GRASSES.

MANUFACTURED BY THE

DICKSON FERTILIZER COMPANY,

AUGUSTA GA.

Warranted free from any Adulteration Whatever.

Price $65 Per Ton of 2000 lbs.

Sacks 200 lbs. Each.   Drayage $1 Per Ton.

ALSO. Peruvian Guano, Lime,
Dissolved Bone, Land Plaster,
Super-Phosphates of Lime,
German Salts, Potash, Bone Dust,
Sulphuric Acid 66 deg.
And all Standard Fertilizing Materials.

Send for Circular giving full information of our Manufactures, and freight tariffs to all principal points in the South.

DICKSON FERTILIZER CO.

AUGUSTA, GA.   Oct 70 3m.   JAMES T. GARDINER, President.

The Dickson Sweep-Plow

Charles Eubanks,
Amanda's first husband

Julian Henry Dickson,
elder son of Amanda
and Charles

Amanda in mourning after the death of her father

Charles Green Eubanks, younger son of Amanda
and Charles, and his wife, Kate Holsey Dickson

Hancock County courtroom

Amanda's house at 452 Telfair Street, Augusta, Georgia

in which she settled herself into a large, expensive, and well-furnished house does not suggest that she intended to remain at 452 Telfair Street temporarily.

Amanda's life changed dramatically after she moved to Augusta. On September 17, 1887, she gave the new house on the Dickson home place to her mother, acknowledging the "natural love and affection which she has and bears to her mother." Six days later, on September 23, 1887, T. J. Warthen gave up his position as manager of the Dickson plantations and moved onto the three thousand acres of land in Washington County that David Dickson had given him in the will. In October of the same year, Amanda Dickson's younger son, Charles, married Kate Holsey, the mulatto daughter of Bishop Lucius Henry and Harriet Holsey of Augusta. Charles was seventeen at the time of his marriage and Kate was eighteen. Kate had graduated from Paine College, from the normal, or teachers' training course, in 1886. Charles would graduate from the same department at Paine College in 1891. On December 10, 1885, shortly after the Hancock County Superior Court ruled in favor of the will, Julian Dickson married Eva Walton, the mulatto daughter of George and Isabella Walton of Augusta.[22]

During these early years in Augusta, Amanda America Dickson transferred some of her real estate directly to Julian but not to Charles. In 1889 she gave the house at 921 Greene Street to Julian, and in 1891 she gave a city lot on West Boundary Street, which she had purchased from the Holsey family, to Charles Dickson's family, placing limits on what Charles could do with the property. By 1892, Julian owned $21,637 in taxable property, including 1,646 acres of land in Hancock County, while Charles owned $13,745 worth of taxable property, including 2,500 acres of land in Hancock.[23]

Between 1886 and 1892, Charles entered school and Julian and Eva started a family. Julia Frances II was born in November 1887, and David II was born in December 1889. In May 1891, Charles and Kate had their first child, Amanda America II.[24]

These were not peaceful years for black Georgians who lived outside the world of private privilege. After the Civil War, a legal code based on the segregation of the races began to evolve in Georgia, moving race relations from a postwar period of measured hope, to an era of inconsistency (1872–91), to a system of apartheid by 1908.

Immediately after the Civil War, Georgia's most prominent African-American leaders, Tunis Campbell and the Reverend Henry McNeal Turner, articulated a vision among freemen of a world based on racial equality. Reverend Turner went so far as to advise those "on freedom's shore" to "love whites" and "soon their prejudice would melt away." By 1872 this faith in the possibility of "reconstruction" had vanished in Georgia, leaving these and other African-Americans to enter the realm of a public struggle for equal rights. Horace Wingo has described the era in race relations from 1872 to 1891 as characterized by inconsistency: "Alternatives clearly existed, and Negroes and whites alike exercised them on occasion without incident. . . . From 1872 to 1891, white Georgians frequently spoke on behalf of the Negro, protected him against violent racism, and promised him a better day." By the 1890s, the federal government had begun to abandon its African-American citizens to states' rights, and the states had taken their cue to "ostracize, segregate and disfranchise" all "negroes regardless of individual achievement and worth." With the repeal of the Civil Rights Act of 1875 and the withdrawal of federal troops in 1877, black Georgians lost their legal right to equal accommodations in public transportation, in public accommodations, in places of entertainment, in churches, in cemeteries, and in the public schools for all citizens regardless of race, color, or previous state of servitude. The defeat of the Lodge Bill in 1890, which would have put federal troops back in the South to supervise federal elections, left black citizens with no government protection of their civil rights.[25]

Following the lead of the federal government, Georgia began the process of establishing legal apartheid by segregating all schools. In 1887, the Glenn bill was introduced in the Georgia legislature making it a crime for any teacher to educate white and colored children together in the same institution in the state. Glenn argued: "It is the settled policy of this State, as inherited from our fathers, and as imbedded in our constitution, that the two races shall run parallel, but separate courses. They shall be as two streams, which flow alongside of each other, each with equal privileges, and equal rights, but inexorably forbidden to commingle." Why? Because "social chaos" would result from commingling of the races, and the author threatened, "If the co-education of the races is permitted in Georgia, all the intelligence of this State cannot save the public school system from instant destruction." In 1891 the Georgia legislature passed a statute segregating all railroad passenger cars except Pullman sleeping cars. The law also urged streetcar conductors to separate the races "as far as possible." By 1898, white Georgians had succeeded in segregating first-class sleeping cars as well.[26]

While white southerners were encoding the rules of segregation into the law, they were also resorting to the most violent form of extralegal social control. The peak years for lynching in the United States were during the same period, from 1889 to 1893, the nadir for black citizens, the Gilded Age and the Age of Innocence for others.[27]

During the decade of the 1890s, the white citizens of Georgia created a legal caste system that did not recognize class distinctions among African Americans in the public sphere. At the end of this era, Bishop Lucius Henry Holsey lamented: "We are now confronted by conditions where merit in the black man does not weigh one iota in human rights and very little in human life, if that life and character is under a black or brown skin." The bishop continued: "Learning, personal accomplishment, the achievement of wealth, the reign of morality and skilled handicraft amount to nothing whatever in the black man. Merit and fitness for the high and holy functions of civil life cannot win for him the rights and safety that is the national and God-given inheritance of all. Black men and women, though cultured and refined, are treated as serfs and subjected to every imaginable insult and degradation that can be invented or discovered by an ill-plighted and perverse ingenuity."[28] By 1908 black citizens of Georgia would be effectively denied the right to vote through that very "perverse ingenuity."

While white Georgians were establishing apartheid as the ruling social order, Amanda America Dickson and her family went on about their private lives. On July 14, 1892, Amanda America married Nathan Toomer of Perry, Georgia. Toomer was also a "wealthy and highly educated" mulatto. The *Houston Home Journal*, Toomer's hometown newspaper, stated at the time that Toomer, "the esteemed colored farmer," had married the "richest Negress in Georgia" and that he "has many white friends in Houston County who will cordially congratulate him."[29]

Nathan Toomer was born in 1839 near the Haw River in Chatham County, North Carolina, the slave of Richard Pilkinson. While still a child, he was sold to John Toomer, who subsequently moved from North Carolina to Houston County, Georgia. John Toomer died in 1859, and his brother, "Colonel" Henry Toomer, purchased Nathan's mother, Kit, and seven of her children from the estate. Nathan became Henry Toomer's body servant and in that position had the opportunity to learn the manners of gentility. Sometime before 1869, Nathan married a mulatto woman named Harriet, and eventually they had four daughters: Theodosia, born in 1869; Fannie, born in 1871; Martha, born in 1872; and Mary, or "Mamie," born in 1879 (Appendix B.3). Harriet died on August 17, 1891, without a will, and the Toomer plantation, which she had purchased and mortgaged in her own name, reverted to the grantor.[30]

The public sources that describe Nathan Toomer's personal wealth are abundant. The tax digest of 1869 lists Toomer as living in Houston County as a freedman employed by Henry Toomer and worth $13,300. All the freedmen in Houston County together had assets worth only $37,592 in that year. The census of 1870 lists Toomer as living near Henry Toomer and married to Harriet. Nathan Toomer is described by the census taker as a thirty-one-year-old mulatto male from North Carolina, with real estate worth $20,000, personal property worth $10,000, and two live-in "domestic servants," Ellen Goodwin and Reese Jones, both mulatto females. In the same census, Henry Toomer is listed as worth only $26,000. The census of 1880 for Georgia lists Nathan Toomer, a forty-one-year-old mulatto male, married to Harriet, with four daughters. The agricultural census of the same year lists him as a farmer who "rents and shares 800 tilled acres, 100 acres in meadows, and 700 unimproved acres with a value of $5000. In 1879, Toomer hired five colored laborers and produced $3,500 worth of farm products." In the tax and census records, a picture emerges of Toomer as a wealthy freedman, slowly accumulating capital, mostly in livestock, and eventually purchasing land.[31]

Eleven months after his first wife died, Nathan Toomer married Amanda America Dickson at her home in Augusta, with the Reverend R. S. Williams of the colored Methodist church presiding. Nathan was at that time fifty-three years old, over six feet tall, and "well nourished," weighing over two hundred pounds. Years later he was described by his son from another marriage, Jean Toomer, the Harlem Renaissance author of Cane, as a handsome, elegant man who had the "air of a Southern Aristocrat of the old stamp."[32]

After their marriage, Nathan took up residence in Amanda America's house in Augusta. There the Toomers lived amid all the luxury money could buy, including a live-in maid. But Amanda's health was frail, and she was afflicted with an assortment of ailments that required the constant attention of her family physician, Dr. Thomas D. Coleman, a neighbor. Dr. Coleman was a prominent doctor in Augusta. He had graduated from the University of the City of New York and retained a position as professor of physiology at the Medical College of Georgia. Dr. Coleman described Amanda as "a woman of delicate constitution" who suffered from chronic bronchitis, uterine trouble, premature menopause, wandering pains, catarrh of the stomach, and muscular rheumatism.[33]

By May 1893, Amanda America's health had improved to the point that her symptoms had "practically disappeared." Unfortunately, at about the same time a family tragedy erupted. Charles Dickson, age twenty-three and married to Kate Holsey, became infatuated with his fourteen-year-old stepsister Mamie Toomer. Nathan and Amanda were so disturbed by the ensuing events that on March 10, 1893, they placed Mamie in the care of the mother superior of the Oblate Sisters of Providence, who ran the St. Francis School and Convent in Baltimore, Maryland, an order of black nuns. They warned the mother superior that Charles might try to kidnap the child.

The St. Francis School and Convent was founded on June 5, 1829, by the Oblate Sisters of Providence. The nuns purchased a three-story

brick building on Richmond Street in Baltimore and conducted a free
school and the convent at that location. Before the Civil War, free
women of color could board at the convent and receive an education
in English, French, writing, reading, spelling, arithmetic, music (gui-
tar and piano), sewing, embroidery, washing and ironing, drawing,
and other fields of art, just as young white women did in their genteel
boarding schools. Before the Civil War, the African-American boarders from southern states at the Oblate Sisters of Providence Convent
were "in most instances [the] daughters of wealthy planters."[34]

As Nathan and Amanda Toomer had expected, Charles Dickson attempted to kidnap Mamie from the convent. Charles convinced his
brother-in-law Dunbar Walton and his sister-in-law Carrie Walton
Wilson to go to Baltimore and retrieve Mamie. On Friday, April 23,
1893, they called at the convent and asked that she be released into
their custody. This attempt failed because the mother superior became
so suspicious that she warned Amanda America and Nathan, who left
immediately for Baltimore.

On Saturday, April 24, the conspirators hired a hackman, Louis E.
Frank, to appear in court under the pretense of suing Dunbar Walton,
who used the alias of Jacob Calhoun. Their plan was to call Mamie as
a witness and abduct her from the courtroom. During the proceedings,
the judge became suspicious and postponed the hearing. At a subsequent hearing, Mamie did not appear and Dunbar Walton became
so frustrated that he offered the court officials $150 to require her to
attend.

In the meantime Nathan and Amanda America arrived in Baltimore
and went to the magistrate to explain the situation. The conspirators
were subsequently arrested. Charles arrived and complicated the situation even further by asking that the court assume custody of Mamie
until he could get a divorce and marry her. The court refused and
placed Mamie back in the care of the mother superior. On June 6, 1893,
the Waltons, Frank, and their lawyer, E. J. Waring, were indicted by
the grand jury of the city of Baltimore for conspiracy to kidnap Mamie
Toomer. Charles was not indicted.[35]

In June 1893 Nathan and Amanda America came to Baltimore for the presentments and immediately thereafter made arrangements to return to Augusta. They purchased two first-class tickets from the Pullman Palace Car Company's representative in Baltimore, which entitled them to a space in a "vestibuled" sleeping car, with a drawing room and porter. The car, "The Salem," left Baltimore at 9:20 P.M. on June 7 and was to arrive in Augusta on June 8 at 4:25 P.M. Unknown to the Toomers and the ticket agent in Baltimore, William H. Green, the general manager of the Richmond and Danville Railroad, had sent out a directive on June 4, 1893, informing all conductors that all Pullman cars on the New York to Augusta line would thereafter be terminated at Columbia, South Carolina, for "economy's sake." [36]

As the Toomers traveled down the Richmond and Danville tracks in private luxury, they came closer and closer to tragedy. They reached Columbia at 1:20 P.M. on Thursday, June 8. The train slowed to a stop and, on the directions of the yardmaster, "The Salem" was disconnected from the train, which continued on to Augusta. The Toomers, ensconced in their Pullman car, were switched off onto side track number one, next to the end of Lady Street, in the broiling hot summer sun. Nathan Toomer immediately sought out the conductor and asked what had happened. Mr. Newman, the conductor, apologized and offered to send the Toomers on the next day, June 9. Toomer then returned to "The Salem" to explain the situation to his distraught wife. [37]

As the afternoon passed, freight trains moved noisily about the yard. The temperature rose, and Amanda America Dickson Toomer became more and more overwrought. How could such a thing happen? They had first-class tickets. At 2:00 P.M. a cleaning crew asked Nathan for permission to clean the car, which he granted. The crew "quietly" cleaned the car inside and out, washing the glasses, changing the "plush sheets," dusting the furniture, and removing the carpets, leaving undisturbed only the drawing room, where Amanda lay. During this time, according to L. E. Stant, foreman of the cleaning crew, Amanda America was lying in the drawing room with a blanket covering her body and appeared to be "a very sick woman," who "seemed to have no strength." [38]

During the night, Amanda America was intermittently unconscious, and at dawn Nathan sent a messenger for a doctor. Dr. F. D. Kendall arrived between 7 and 8 A.M. and found Amanda "exceedingly ill and very much excited." According to Dr. Kendall, she was "suffering apparently more from nervous shock than anything else; she was highly nervous; and when the train would pass . . . she would start from her couch, and her bowels would start running off, and her husband would have to take her and sit her on the chamber." Dr. Kendall found no evidence of "functional disease." "I examined her carefully—her heart and lungs and they were in good condition, excepting she was very nervous and very much excited, and very anxious to get home. That seemed to be her object, to be at home; and she complained bitterly about being left off in the place she was." Dr. Kendall reported to Nathan that Amanda was very ill and that if they insisted on leaving— as she did—he would accompany them. During the course of the morning Dr. Kendall visited "The Salem" several times and on one of these visits began to administer anodyne, a class of pain-relieving medicine which includes opium, morphine, codeine, and aspirin, to Amanda America.[39]

That afternoon, between one and two o'clock, the yard crew attached "The Salem" to a train bound for Augusta and the Pullman car proceeded on its journey with Dr. Kendall, the porter, and the Toomers inside. They arrived in Augusta between four and five on Friday afternoon, June 9, and Amanda was immediately taken home. Dr. Kendall then returned to Columbia, and the family sent for Amanda's personal physician, Dr. Thomas D. Coleman. Dr. Coleman was out of town and Dr. Eugene Foster arrived in his stead. Dr. Foster was also a prominent doctor in Augusta. He served as president of the Board of Health of Augusta, as professor of the practice of medicine and hygiene at the Medical College, and as a member of the board of directors of the State Lunatic Asylum. Dr. Foster examined Amanda and found her "in a state of general exhaustion, asthenia—that is, general exhaustion of the nervous system," or "neurasthenia." He left "minute instructions" with Nathan and Julia for Amanda America's care during the night and advised Nathan and the family that if they wished to call in a consulting physician, they should do so at once because Amanda was "on the brink of death." At about 3:00 P.M. on Saturday, June 10, Dr. William H. Foster, Dr. Eugene Foster's brother, was called to 452 Telfair. He too examined Amanda America. Dr. William Foster concurred in the diagnosis of "general asthenia-nervous depression" and agreed with his brother that the case was "beyond hope." At the request of Nathan, Dr. W. H. Foster remained through the night.[40]

Nineteenth-century physicians defined neurasthenia as a disease characterized by profound physical and nervous exhaustion. It was first described in 1869 by Dr. George M. Beard, a pioneering specialist in neurology in New York City, as a "functional nervous disorder for which no gross pathological symptoms could be found." The symptoms of neurasthenia, sometimes called Beard's disease, included sick headache, noises in the ear, atonic voice, deficient mental control, bad dreams, insomnia, nervous dyspepsia (disturbed digestion), heaviness of the loin and limb, flushing and fidgetiness, palpitations, vague pains and flying neuralgia (pain along a nerve), spinal irritation, uterine irritability, impotence, hopelessness, claustrophobia, and dread of contamination. The persistence and severity of this motley group of symptoms and, more important, the patient's wealth, separated the neurasthenic from the insane.[41]

Amanda America Dickson Toomer died at 5:00 on June 11, 1893. Her death certificate listed the cause of death as "complications of diseases." [42]

Haggie Brothers Funeral Home was called to 452 Telfair Street to prepare Amanda America Dickson for burial. They embalmed her body and dressed it in the wedding gown she had worn when she married Nathan. The body was then placed in an expensive copper-lined casket with rose-colored plush cushioning. It was described by the *Milledgeville Union Recorder* as the "handsomest casket ever brought into that city [Augusta]." Nathan and the family ordered one hearse and six carriages from Haggie Brothers for the funeral.[43]

Amanda America Dickson Toomer's funeral was held in the Trinity Colored Methodist Episcopal Church. According to a tribute written for the *Augusta Chronicle* by "a friend," the funeral was attended by "a very large and respectful gathering of friends and acquaintances."

Three ministers of the gospel "officiated," and they paid tribute to Amanda America's "Christian life and character, her exemplary worth, her unostentatious charities, and the beauty of her home life." Scripture passages that she had marked in her own Bible were read, and the service ended with a song that Amanda had requested to be sung on that occasion, "Shall We Meet Beyond the River," which "moved to tears almost the entire audience." The body was buried in Augusta, in the Toomer plot, in the Colored Cedar Grove Cemetery, behind the Magnolia Cemetery for whites. The tombstone that was later erected is the largest in the Cedar Grove cemetery and bears the inscription:

> Sacred to the Memory
> of
> Amanda Dickson Toomer
> Wife of Nathan Toomer
> Born November 20, 1849
> Died June 11, 1893
> A True Christian a Loving
> Wife a Devoted Mother
> and Daughter
> May her Soul Be at Rest[44]

Amanda America Dickson's obituaries in white newspapers described her as the "wealthiest colored woman in the world," "the wealthiest Negro in the United States," and "one of the wealthiest, if not the wealthiest negro woman in the state." Without exception, these obituaries mentioned that Amanda America inherited her wealth from her father, David Dickson, one of the wealthiest planters in Hancock County. The black *Savannah Tribune*'s obituary described Amanda America Toomer "née Dickson," with no mention of David, as "one of the richest persons in the state." Nathan Toomer was mentioned in the newspaper obituaries as a lawyer from Perry, who was also wealthy and highly educated or who was "immensely rich." In the *Augusta Chronicle* obituary the Dickson family connection to the Holseys was mentioned and the Holseys were described as one of the best-known and most respected black families in the state. Amanda America Dickson Toomer's only claim to fame and respect in these obituaries seems to be that she was David Dickson's daughter and that she was wealthy by any standard of the day.[45]

The *Sparta Ishmaelite* did not mention Amanda America Dickson Toomer's death until 1895. In an article titled "Her Last Resting Place," the editor noted that a tombstone was being prepared in Augusta for her grave site. "There are very few of our readers who are not perfectly familiar with the name, Amanda Eubanks, the colored woman who was so liberally remembered in the distribution of the immense fortune of the late David Dickson, of Hancock County." After establishing these facts, the *Ishmaelite* continued: "A short time after the death of Mr. Dickson, she married Nathan Toomer and they moved to Augusta where they lived together until her death, which occurred a few years ago. She was the richest colored woman in the South, her portion of the estate being about $400,000." In a consoling tone, the editor wrote: "In the marble yard of Theo. Markwalter, Augusta, Georgia, stands a beautiful monument cut from Georgia granite which will soon be placed in position to mark her last resting place. It is a fine piece of art, and speaks well for the affectionate remembrance of her people."[46]

Amanda America's obituaries and the tribute by "a friend" reveal something about the way she was perceived by the black and white communities in which she lived. She was described in the *Atlanta Constitution* as "modest, generous, and benevolent, a woman who enjoyed her fortune," and "others shared her pleasure." The article continued: "She was kind-hearted and in no way pompous or assuming on account of her wealth."[47] In the tribute by "a friend" we learn a great deal about this author's perception of Amanda:

> The subject of this notice was well known to the writer as a most amiable, gentle woman. To everyone with whom she came in contact she was always kind, considerate, respectful. Although for years she was very feeble of health, and endured great suffering, she was very patient, submissive, uncomplaining. Possessed of great wealth, she made no display of it, nor did it affect her, as it has so many others. She fully appreciated the true value of riches. She felt that they were given her not only for her own use, but for the use of others. No narrow selfishness marked her posses-

sion of her means. While she gave them liberally to procure the comforts and many of the luxuries for herself and those of her own household, she never forgot the needy—as was said most tenderly at her funeral services today. She was a devoted and loyal wife, and the tender affection between herself and her husband, Mr. Nathan Toomer, late of Houston County, Georgia, evidenced a union of mutual happiness. For her two children, Mr. Julian H. Dickson and Mr. Charles G. Dickson, the former of Hancock County, Georgia, the latter of Augusta, Georgia, she always felt the most intense and anxious solicitude and motherly love. To her mother she was all that a dutiful, loving child should be. As she lived, so she died, a gentle, sweet spirit.[48]

The Amanda America Dickson of these obituaries is a fiction not unlike the myths of true womanhood and of the southern lady that were articulated in the nineteenth century for white ladies. In this era, ladies were socialized to accept purity, piety, domesticity, and submissiveness as ideal behavior patterns. Southern ladies were also described as physically weak, timid, modest, beautiful, graceful, innocent, and self-denying. Amanda was not described as beautiful, graceful, innocent, or self-denying in her possession of physical luxury, but she was described as physically weak, respectful, and uncomplaining: a devoted and loyal wife, a loving mother, and a dutiful child.[49]

The Amanda America of the obituaries does not fit the myths of the white lady in several ways. Purity (innocence) and beauty (grace) are not missing by accident. When applied to white ladies, these attributes created the essential symbol used to justify racism. It would have been ideologically untenable, perhaps even dangerous, for whites to describe Amanda America Dickson as beautiful and pure.

If we compare the idealized Amanda America Dickson Toomer of these obituaries with expressed ideals for the behavior of African-American ladies of the late nineteenth century, another important imperative is missing: racial uplift. It was not unusual for African-American women to aspire to the cult of true womanhood. But they were also encouraged by the ideals of their community to step outside the domestic sphere and engage in community building and racial uplift. The Amanda America Dickson Toomer of these obituaries, with her quiet charities and attention to the needy, appears to have no racial identification, no influence outside the limited sphere of an attractively disabled "lady."[50]

The real Amanda America Dickson Toomer left one husband and refused to return to him; left the security of her father's empire to attend Atlanta University at the age of twenty-seven; endured her father's death; used the legal system to fight for control of a vast fortune; left the security of her own plantation and moved to the city of Augusta; and remarried while retaining control of her estate, giving Nathan Toomer "gifts." The real Amanda Toomer also died of nervous exhaustion, of "something which profoundly shocked her nervous system." Perhaps that shock was the private chaos and shame of having her son Charles Dickson try to kidnap his fourteen-year-old stepsister Mamie. Perhaps the shock was produced by the turmoil of having to wait on a side track in Columbia, South Carolina, because of an error on the part of a railroad manager, a simple but inconvenient error. Perhaps the public humiliation that faced other African-Americans and that was beginning to invade her own privileged sphere shocked Amanda America Dickson's system to death. Perhaps these shocks plus her "delicate health" combined to kill her. The behaviors that she so carefully practiced in the public sphere, to be unassuming, amiable, gentle, kind, considerate, respectful, patient, submissive, and uncomplaining, were a prescription for self-destruction in her time and place. The last thing in the world Amanda America Dickson needed to be in an increasingly racist public space was a "gentle, sweet spirit." Amanda America may have escaped the prevailing white myths about being a degraded female African-American described by Drew Gilpin Faust only to become trapped by a myth of the proper role of an elite white lady.[51]

Because Amanda America died without a will, a battle began immediately after her death for control of her estate. Julian Dickson and Nathan Toomer both appeared before the ordinary of Richmond County on June 12 and petitioned to be designated as the temporary administrator of the estate. The ordinary ruled in favor of Nathan as Amanda America's husband and consequently first entitled under the law. The ordinary fixed the amount of assured bond, by agreement, at $50,000 and appointed Toomer temporary administrator on June 17, 1893. He was not approved as permanent administrator until August 9, 1898, when he was required to make a complete inventory of the Dickson estate, a task which, regrettably, he never performed. In 1893 Nathan posted a bond of $700 in cash and $50,000, which was guaranteed by the American Security Company of New York. Thus Nathan Toomer gained some control over the estate as the administrator. David Dickson's will, however, directed: "Upon the death of said Amanda A. Dickson I give, bequeath and devise what may remain of the property embraced in this item of my will to the children of the said Amanda A. Dickson and the representatives of any deceased child share and share alike." [52]

In an effort to settle the estate "amiably, without reference to any court," Nathan, Julian, and Charles agreed to a legal settlement on June 27, 1893. Nathan gave up all claim to $22,000 in bonds, $13,969 in notes payable to either Amanda or David Dickson, about $2,100 in cash, Julian's personal note to his mother for $1,500 and Charles's personal note to her for $200, and all claims to the crops on the plantations. Toomer also agreed not to seek repayment of the money he had spent to have David Dickson's body moved from the Dickson home place to the Sparta cemetery and for the erection of a monument there or for the expenses of Amanda America's funeral. He agreed to give two-thirds interest in the house at 452 Telfair Street to Charles and Julian and to pay the estate's debts to the estates of Charles W. Dubose, A. M. Dubose (Charles's son, who was also a lawyer), and M. P. Reese and M. A. Foster, Amanda and Nathan's attorneys. In return, the sons agreed not to lay claim to anything that Amanda owned outright. Herein lay a Gordian knot. David Dickson had given Amanda property before he died, including three-fourths interest in thirteen thousand acres of land in Rusk County, Texas. The agreement ends with the statement that "all other property of said estate of said Amanda A. Toomer than that herein agreed to be received by J. H. and C. G. Dickson is to be the property of the said Nathan Toomer." [53]

Even though it was obvious to Nathan Toomer that Amanda America Dickson had been ill for at least eighteen months before her death and that she had suffered severe emotional stress during the Mamie Toomer kidnapping episode, Nathan sued the Pullman Palace Car Company for $100,000. The Toomers had been able to buy a first-class ticket on a Pullman car in 1893 because George Pullman had refused to segregate his sleeping cars in response to the Georgia law of 1891. On July 27, 1893, Nathan Toomer filed suit in the Court of Common Pleas of the city of Baltimore, claiming that "he was caused to suffer great pain and discomfort and anguish of body and mind and was deprived of and lost the services of his said wife and was put to great expense and caused to lay out and expend large sums of money in and about her care, nursing and attention and was otherwise greatly injured and damaged." Toomer argued that Amanda America "was accustomed to attend and serve him with great care and devotion" and that she "constantly" made "very considerable gifts of money and valuables" to him. Nathan claimed that Amanda had intended to will to him certain "lands, goods, chattels and effects of very great value" as soon as they reached Augusta. Consequently, Toomer argued, he had suffered "great pecuniary loss" as a result of her death.[54]

As the case progressed, lawyers for both sides took depositions from several employees of the Richmond and Danville Railroad on whose tracks "The Salem" ran from Washington to Augusta. These included all of Amanda America Dickson's doctors and one of her neighbors. A trial date was set for January 10, 1894.

In the meantime, Nathan Toomer began traveling to Washington, D.C., and courting Nina Pinchback, the twenty-six-year-old daughter of P. B. S. Pinchback. The Pinchbacks were a prominent family of color in Washington. The citizens of Louisiana elected Pinchback Reconstruction governor, and he served as acting governor of that state for a short period. In 1873 he was elected to the United States Senate. Although Pinchback never took his seat in the Senate, that august body granted him the satisfaction of being compensated with a salary of $16,000 as though he had served one term. The family stayed on in Washington, and the Pinchbacks continued to be prominent figures in politics and the society of the "aristocrats of color."[55]

As Nina Pinchback and Nathan began to see more and more of

each other, P. B. S. Pinchback became suspicious. Nathan was fifty-four years old, twenty-eight years older than Nina and only a few years younger than her father. Nathan had no recognized family connection and was evasive about his business affairs. Nevertheless, Nathan and Nina became engaged, and Nathan gave Nina $12,000 in cash to buy whatever house she pleased. Nathan and Nina married on March 29, 1894, nine months after Amanda America died. Nine months and three days later, Jean Toomer was born. During the months of Nina's pregnancy, Nathan came and went, attending to his mysterious business affairs.

One of those items of business was Toomer's suit against the Pullman Palace Car Company, which was heard in the Court of Common Pleas of Baltimore on January 10, 1894. Nathan's lawyers argued that the Pullman Company was responsible for Amanda America's death because it had broken its contract to "safely and continuously and without delay and interruption, carry the plaintiff and his said wife from said city of Baltimore to said city of Augusta, by schedule time, to-wit within the twenty-four hours." The Pullman Company argued that the contract that Nathan claimed existed was "beyond the corporate powers of the defendant." [56]

During the course of the trial, a witness for the defendant, the manager and general passenger agent of the Richmond and Danville Railroad, stated that a directive had been sent to the Pullman Palace Car Company informing it that the Baltimore-to-Augusta Pullman car service would be terminated in Columbia, South Carolina, after June 4, 1893, but that he had no way of knowing if the notice had been received. The yardmaster in Columbia testified that he had been directed to disconnect the car, and he did so.

Nathan Toomer's lawyers argued that Amanda Toomer had become more and more emotionally distraught and physically ill because the Pullman car was sidetracked in the hot sun in a noisy train yard and that no one would take charge and remedy the situation. The lawyers for the Pullman Car Company retorted that their employees had done all they could for the Toomers and raised the issue of why Amanda America had not been taken off the Pullman car via Lady Street, which was next to the track where "The Salem" had been placed. Nathan's lawyer, through the testimony of Dr. Kendall, replied that Amanda was too sick to be moved, which raises an interesting question. Where would Nathan have taken Amanda America if she had been well enough to be moved—to a hotel?

During the deposition of Dr. William H. Foster of Augusta, Nathan's lawyer asked the doctor about the "custom" of hotels in the South regarding receiving or excluding "colored" guests. Dr. Foster replied that in Augusta, "they are universally refused admittance to hotels as guests." Under cross-examination, the railroad company's lawyers asked in disbelief if Dr. Foster knew for a fact that no hotel or boarding-house in Augusta would take "a person of Mrs. Toomer's respectability as a guest if they were informed that she was extremely ill and that it would be cruel and inhumane to refuse her shelter." Dr. Foster replied, "From my knowledge of the sentiment of our people on that subject, she would have been refused admission to a hotel conducted for white guests in the expectation and belief that she would receive shelter and care in the house and at the hands of some responsible colored family in the city."[57]

The lawyers for the defendant maintained that Amanda had been sick before the accident and had been treated for many ailments over the past eighteen months. They argued that Amanda Dickson Toomer was going through a premature "change of life," and was it not true that "at the time of a change in life all women are more irritable and high strung and nervous than at other periods of their [lives]?" Wasn't it true that "many women become insane?" They argued that because Amanda Dickson Toomer was "a colored woman of the more educated and refined class," with "evidences of education, wealth, comfort and refinement in her home," was it not "reasonable to suppose that she was a person of more refinement of feelings and sensibility than the average female of her race?" In essence, they argued, Amanda Dickson Toomer's sex, class, and age made her vulnerable to nervous exhaustion. The court ruled in the Pullman Palace Car Company's favor, and Nathan was forced to pay the court cost of $38.70.[58]

Nathan returned to Nina intermittently during the next few months, and tension began to develop between them. Nathan would not give Nina money to carpet the house or, after Jean's birth, to hire anyone to help her. Nina became desperate. In November 1895 she pawned her wedding ring and rented out her house. In September 1898 she petitioned the courts in Washington for a divorce and alimony, and on January 27, 1899, a divorce was granted. Because Nathan refused to pay alimony of $60 a month, he could not return to Washington without risking arrest. Consequently, he saw his son Jean only once when Jean was a small child. Many years later, after Nathan's death, Jean Toomer journeyed to Sparta, Georgia, to teach and try to locate his father's family. There he probably discovered the source of his father's wealth—Amanda America Dickson Toomer's estate.[59]

By August 1899, Nathan had returned to Sparta to sue Julian, Charles, and Julia for the contents of Amanda's house in Augusta, which he argued were worth $3,000. According to the depositions taken before the trial, on or about August 15, 1895, Julia Dickson, her grandson Wil Youngblood, and a woman named Mariah Nunn, who had been living with Julia, spent several days packing up the contents of the house at 452 Telfair Street. They sewed up the bedding in croaker sacks and packed the pictures in boxes. The furniture was not packed in crates. Julia then made arrangements with Thomas McNair, a public drayman, to take the contents of the house to the Georgia Railroad office in Augusta, which he did in four two-horse cartloads. Everything was removed from the house except one wardrobe, one trunk, and a picture that Julia left for Nathan Toomer. Julia and Mariah Nunn then "swept the house out from top to bottom" and finished all the other cleaning, and Julia locked the door. When Nunn asked Julia why she was leaving, she replied that "Julian Dickson had written that he had secured a house for her in Sparta, Georgia, and urged her to come home at once and bring all that was in the house with her."[60]

On the same day that the house was locked, the goods were sent by Julia Dickson via the Georgia Railroad to Julian Dickson in Sparta. The shipment arrived and was taken off the railroad car, loaded into one of Julian Dickson's wagons, and moved to Julia's new house on the corner of Elm and Hamilton streets.[61]

Nathan Toomer's case was heard in the August term of 1899. The court rendered a verdict on August 6, 1901, in favor of the defendants, again forcing Nathan Toomer to pay court costs.[62]

By 1900 Nathan Toomer was living with his daughter Martha and son-in-law Seymore Glover in Macon, Georgia. The census taker listed Toomer as a black male whose occupation was farming. On March 4, 1901, the court granted Nathan letters of dismissal as the administrator of Amanda America Dickson's estate. Toomer died in Macon in 1906, leaving no will and no obituary.

By 1900 Charles and Kate Holsey Dickson had separated, and she had sued for divorce. According to the Dickson family oral history, Charles moved to Stockton, California, and passed into the white world as Fred V. Carlyle. He died there of Bright's disease in his early forties.[63] About the turn of the century, Eva and Julian Dickson moved to Beaufort, South Carolina, to a community that was predominantly African-American. Julian died there on February 1, 1937, leaving no will and no obituary.

Julia Frances Dickson died some time after January 7, 1914. On that day she deeded 102 acres, more or less, to her grandson, William Youngblood, "in consideration of the sum of my love and affection." The land was described as "deeded to myself, the said Julia F. Dickson, by Amanda A. Dickson."[64]

Julian Dickson retained control of the Dickson plantation until 1912. In the last decade, the property, once so famous for its productivity, has been considered by the Georgia Department of Natural Resources and by the Hancock County Board of Commissioners as a possible site for a toxic waste dump.

Appendix A
DOCUMENTS

1. The African-American Dickson Family Oral History

THIS APPENDIX relates Amanda America Dickson's story from the point of view of the Dickson family's oral history as told to me by Amanda America's granddaughter Kate Louise Dickson McCoy-Lee. Kate Dickson McCoy-Lee was born in 1894, the year after Amanda Dickson died. She was the third child of Amanda America's son Charles Green Dickson and his wife, Kate Holsey Dickson. McCoy-Lee's sources of information on the Dickson family history include her great-grandmother, Julia Frances Lewis Dickson, who lived in Sparta until 1914; her mother, Kate Holsey Dickson, and other members of the Holsey family, who raised Kate after her mother and father separated; and Aunt Mary Long, Amanda America Dickson's lifelong personal servant, who later worked for McCoy-Lee "until she got too old and had to go to Kentucky." The following story was distilled from a series of three interviews with McCoy-Lee, in November 1981. I have also relied on the notes of two other scholars who interviewed McCoy-Lee in the course of their own work: Adele Alexander, for her master's thesis, "Ambiguous Lives: Free Women of Color in Middle Georgia, 1787–

1879," and John Rozier for his book *Black Boss: Political Revolution in a Georgia County*. McCoy-Lee died in 1985.

Amanda was born on the Dickson plantation. Her mother was Julia, one of the slaves. One day David Dickson saw Julia playing in a field and rode up beside her and slung her up behind him on his horse, and that was the end of that. Julia was very tiny and only thirteen years old at the time. She had not had her first period. She never forgave him. She ruled David Dickson with an iron hand, had the keys to the plantation, and controlled everything.

Amanda was the darling of David Dickson's heart. He adored her and gave her everything in the world. He had her bathed in sweet milk to lighten her skin. He allowed her to claim newborn slaves as her own and name them whatever she liked. She named one of them Ambrose, and the other slaves thought that his name was Ambrosia. Later he bought her a house on Greene Street in Augusta so that she and Granny Julia could go shopping. Amanda traveled to Augusta on the train with her pet parrot and monkey. Women also came down to the plantation to make clothes for them. Everybody on the plantation called Amanda "Miss Mandy," including David Dickson. She was his pampered darling.

Granny Julia had another daughter, Juan, by a young slave in 1853. She was not related to David, who was her master. She married Raibun Youngblood and had several children, one of whom, Wil, lived with Granny Julia and took care of her when she moved to Sparta.

Amanda went to school in Paris, and professors would come out to the plantation to teach her, including old Dr. Porter and Rev. Ambrose Long. She read a lot, including *Camille*. She also attended Atlanta University for a while but she didn't like the discipline. David Dickson had a fireplace built in the north hall for her because she liked an open fireplace and not a stove.

David Dickson arranged a marriage between Amanda and his white cousin Charles Eubanks. In 1862 he took them to Baltimore, and they were married there. After their marriage he gave them a plantation on the Ooustanaula, near Rome, Georgia. Aunt Mary Long used to tell a story about watching Charles and Amanda and their two boys, when they still had nurses, crossing a river on a ferry, going to their plantation.

Not long after the birth of their second son, Amanda left Charles Eubanks and went back home to live with her father. She said, "I want to live with you, 'Papie.'" Charles came up one day in a buggy and tried to get her to come back with him. She put her hands on her hips and stormed at him, and he never came back. The boys stayed close to the Eubanks family. They used to visit their white grandmother.

The boys' names were changed back to Dickson, and David Dickson took them to New Orleans, Louisiana, and had them declared white. He loved the little boys, called them "my little men," and slept with them. He never wanted them to do anything but ride over the plantation with him and see what was going on. David Dickson indulged them all.

Dickson built a schoolhouse on the place for his grandchildren and imported tutors, including old Dr. Porter, to teach them. Charles Dickson went to Amherst, but he only stayed one year. His mother took him to school and bought a house in the area.

When David Dickson died, Amanda clung to his body, repeating over and over, "Now I am an orphan, now I am an orphan." Dickson left everything to Amanda and paid all the lawyers in the county $10,000 not to contest the will. Thomas Warthen did contest the will in the Macon Superior Court.

After the will was settled, Amanda handled everything herself. She and Granny would ride out and check the work. She also had legal advice. They had so much money they didn't know what to do with it.

In the will, each of Amanda's children was given a plantation. The property was left to the children of their grandfather's friend Charles Eubanks.

The oldest son, Julian Henry Dickson, married Eva Walton from Augusta. She was the granddaughter of George Walton, who signed the Declaration of Independence for Georgia. Julian and Eva left Georgia after a fire burned up all their carriages and stock. He sued an insurance company in Lake Toxaway, North Carolina, and won. They went to Beaufort, South Carolina, and set up a place called Dickson Village. Julian later became an alderman in Beaufort. A relative found some of the family in recent years at Dickson Village. They were rich. Julian's children were scattered.

Charles Green Dickson married Kate Holsey of Sparta, the daughter of Bishop Lucius Henry Holsey, who was the first black bishop of the CME church. My great-grandfather Holsey was a Scotsman. He gave my grandfather to Richard M. Johnston. Bishop Holsey was Rev. Johnston's driver. He supplied him with books. There were books about Bishop Holsey, *The Incomparable Holsey*, and his own poems, *Little Gems*. He had blue-gray eyes and red hair. His hair was mixed brown and gray by the time I knew him. His skin was like an Egyptian's from staying out in the sun so much. My mother had red hair.

Kate Holsey Dickson divorced Charles because he was spending his fortune on fast horses, white friends, and women. He went to live in the Drummers' Hotel in Sparta. We stayed out on the plantation, at the Lockhart Place, until my mother built a rather large house on the edge of town and moved there, taking her servants with her. When I was about five years old, we moved to Atlanta near my mother's parents, Bishop and Mrs. Lucius Henry Holsey, on Auburn Avenue. Grandfather owned a block in the rear of the house. He was a fabulous gardener. He had TB when he was seventeen and was told to work outdoors as a cure. He had a wonderful garden, where I sat and ate his beautiful strawberries. Dr. Martin Luther King, Jr., is buried right where that garden was.

After my father left my mother, he moved to Stockton, California, and passed. He changed his name to Fred D. Carlyle. He died in his forties of Bright's disease. He lost one fortune in Georgia only to make another one in California.

Both Julian and Charles had to get permission to marry black women. David Dickson lived in an unorthodox way. When guests came, Julia entertained them. People came from all over the country to see him. His favorite expression was "By God!" White visitors would look at Amanda and the boys and say, "Have I got to eat with them?" He would say, "By God, yes, if you eat here!"

My great-grandmother [Julia] always let us use the family silver. She
said that when Sherman came through they hid the silver in bags and
buried them under a locust tree. She wasn't sure they ever dug it all up.
David Dickson gave her diamonds when the children were born. I have
some of the old family silver. I have David Dickson's silver pitcher. The
pitcher has an English patent, 1829. David Dickson had a big safe from
Augusta brought to his plantation and a big hole dug to put it in. It had
"David Dickson" on the dial. They say that he had barrels of gold in
there. Granny kept the keys to everything on the plantation.

After David Dickson died, Amanda lived on there at the home place.
She died of pneumonia in 1893. After Amanda died, granny moved to
town and lived across from the Harris place on Elm Street. She owned
everything from her house down to Broad Street. The property was
covered with pecan trees. She moved Mr. Dickson's body to town to the
Sparta Cemetery and put up a monument.

Her house in Sparta was full of beautiful things. The furniture was
covered with mohair. Granny died after she got burned in a fire. Everybody in Sparta came to her house and took everything they wanted.
There was nobody to stay [stop] them. Granny died in 1912.

Granny always said that she was Portuguese, said that she didn't
have any black blood in her. She was copper-colored and had soft hair.
She was small, and she had beautiful teeth. She had a twig in her
mouth, polishing her teeth all the time. She was very temperamental
and high-strung.

Some of the facts in the census were wrong. They listed Amanda's
house servants as boarders. The census also said that my mother had
seven children. She had four, not seven. My older brother was named
Miller Dubose after the big Sparta lawyer, but he changed it to Charles
Green Eubanks, Jr. My father took him hunting; he drank water and
died of typhoid. Mama and my older sister Amanda America II, and
then me, and then my younger brother Thomas. He died at eleven. He
loved the Bible. His favorite character was Jehosaphat. He had mama
tack a Bible verse about Jehosaphat over his bed. I don't even remember
where he was buried. I am all that is left now.

2. Julia Frances Lewis Dickson's Testimony

Direct Examination

Mr. Reese: What is your name?

A– Julia Frances Dickson.

Q– Are you the mother of Amanda?

A– Yes, sir.

Q– Who is the father of Amanda?

A– Mr. David Dickson.

Q– How old were you when Amanda was born?

A– I was just thirteen years old.

Q– When were you thirteen?

A– I was 13 that July, I had just turned in my 14th year; I would have been 14 the next July, and she was born in November.

Q– What time in November?

A– The 20th.

Q– What year?

A– '49.

Q– By whom were you raised?

A– By Mrs. Elizabeth Dickson.

Q– State what you did there, if anything.

A– I assisted in making up the beds, swept the yards and did anything else about the house and garden.

Q– State whether or not you continued to do that during the life of Mrs. Dickson.

A– Yes, sir, I worked that way all the time.

Q– Who did you belong to?

A– I belonged to the old lady.

Q– After Amanda's birth where did she stay?

A– After they took her from the breast she stayed in the house all the time.

Q– Where abouts?

A– In Mrs. Dickson's room.

Q– Did she stay there day and night?

A– Yes, sir, she stayed there day and night.

Q– Where did she sleep?

A– She had a little trundle bed.

Q– Who had it made?

A– Mrs. Dickson.

Q– Where was that bed?

A– It run under another bed she had there.

Q– Who slept in that room?

A– Mistress.

Q– How long did Amanda live that way?

A– She lived till emancipation.

Q– When did Mrs. Dickson die?

A– She died the 6th of August; I don't know the year; it was the same year that the raid come; the raid was in the fall; she died in August.

Q– What did Amanda do then?

A– Well, she didn't do much because she wasn't old enough; never done much but study her books; done whatever they told her.

Q– Where did Green Dickson die?

A– He died at home down at his mother's place.

Q– Where was Green Dickson when Amanda was born?

A– He was at home I reckon, but he wasn't there when she was got; he was in Texas when she was got.

Q– What time did he go to Texas?

A– He went in the fall; I don't know when.

Q– Was that after or before Amanda was born?

A– He went there before she was born—he went in 48, I think, sir.

Q– Julia, when did you move from Dickson's there to where you lived at the time of his death?

A– I don't know what year it was; it was the year he married, though.

Q– Was it before or after the marriage of Dickson?

A– Before.

Q– During the life of his wife did you continue to live up there?

A– Up at the house? Yes, sir. I lived there all the time.

Q– Did you go down to the house at all during Mrs. Dickson's life?

A– No, sir. I never went down there at all.

Q– Julia, I will ask you if Dickson ever had anything to do with you after his marriage up to the time of his death?

A– No, sir. Never had a thing; we separated before he ever married or thought of it, I reckon.

Q– Julia, I will ask you to state to the court and jury whether you ever said anything to him about making a will or how he should dispose of his property?

A– No, sir. I never said a thing to him in my life; never did say a word to him. I didn't know that he had a will.

Cross-Examination

Mr. Rutherford: Q– Did you know William P. Seymour?

A– Yes, sir, I knew him when he was there. He was there such a short time; I knew him while he was there.

Q– I will ask you to state if you didn't say to Mr. Seymour that David Dickson was not the father of Amanda?

A– I never told him so. I never told him anything about that; no, sir, I never told him so.

Q– I will ask you to state whether or not you knew Mr. T. Dickson?

A– Yes, sir, I knew him.

Q– Didn't you tell him that David Dickson was not the father of Amanda?

A– No, sir, I never told him so. I never told anybody so.

Q– I will ask you to state if you didn't always deny that David Dickson was the father of Amanda?

A– No, sir, I never denied it.

Q– Didn't you always deny that David Dickson was the father of Amanda until she got to be a big sized girl?

A– No, sir, I always said he was her Dad, because I knew no one else ever got her but him.

Q– Julia, did you know Mr. Lozier?

A– Yes, sir, I know him.

Q– Didn't you say to Mr. Lozier that Green Dickson requested you while he was sick to bring Amanda to see him?

A– No, sir, I never told him so.

Q— And you have never denied at any time to any one that David Dickson was the father of Amanda?

A— I always said that he was her father.

Q— Didn't you carry Amanda to see Green Dickson?

A— No, sir.

Q— And you never told Mr. Lozier so?

A— No, sir, I never told him so.

Q— How did David Dickson find out that Amanda was his own child?

A— Very likely a man would know; because he was at the getting of her and because he knew nobody wasn't having anything to do with me but him; nobody there but him.

Q— Nobody had any chances with you except him?

A— No, sir.

Q— Didn't you tell him, David Dickson, that he was not the father of your child?

A— No, sir, I never told him so in my life.

Q— Did you always tell him that he was the father of your child, Amanda?

A— Yes, sir, I told him so; I always told him he was her father when he asked me anything about her.

Q— You told him that he was the father of Amanda?

A— Yes, sir, I told him, he was her father.

Q— And you say that you never denied it to anybody else that he was the father of Amanda, and you never denied it to him?

A— No, sir, I never denied that he was her father.

Q— Julia, have you ever had other children?

A— Yes, sir, I have had other children.

Q— Before those other children were born, didn't you say that David Dickson was the father of them?

A— No, sir, I never.

Q— Joe Brooken was the father of one of them, wasn't he?

A— I never told anyone about the father of it.

Q— It was the child of a black man, wasn't it?

A— A dark man.

Q— Wasn't he a nigger?

A– I reckon they call him a nigger; but I never laid it on to Mr. Dickson.

Q– Never laid a nigger to Mr. Dickson?

A– No, sir.

Q– Didn't you try to do it before it was born?

A– No, sir.

Q– And then tried to take it back after it was born?

A– No, sir, I never took it back; I never laid it on him.

Q– Who was the father of Lola?

A– The man they called Doc.

Q– Doc Eubanks?

A– Yes, sir.

Q– Wasn't Joe Brooken the father of the other one? Or can't you tell?

A– Certainly I can tell you; I know very well; yes, sir, I do know.

Q– Was it Joe?

A– Make Joe tell you who was her daddy.

Q– Joe won't tell, and we want you to tell us; wasn't Joe the father of that child?

A– Yes, sir, Joe was the father.

Q– [Were] you married to him?

A– No, sir, I was not married to him.

Q– Did you ever hear of Joe's being whipped on account of it?

A– No, sir, I never heard of his being whipped.

Q– Now you said that Green Dickson went to Texas in 1848, what time in 1848?

A– I said in the fall somewhere; I don't know whether it was in October or November; it was somewhere along there.

Q– About what time was Amanda gotten?

A– She was gotten between January and February somewheres.

Q– Did it take a month to get her?

A– It might have taken one minute for all I know; it didn't take a month to get one child.

Q– What year was that?

A– She was got in 1849, somewhere along in 1849, in the early portion.

Q– Now, Julia, which do you remember the most distinctly, the raid that passed here in 1865 or the time that Green Dickson went to Texas?

A– I probably remember the time he went to Texas more distinctly.

Q– Now, why do you?

A– Because I know what he went for.

Q– What did he go for?

A– Because he was a drinking man, and he thought that if he went there it would stop him from drinking.

Q– How old were you when he went to Texas?

A– I don't know exactly. I was thirteen somewhere along there.

Q– When were you born?

A– I was born in '36.

Q– How do you know when you were born?

A– They always told me so; the white folks told me so, and I reckon they knew; they said I was born in 1836.

Q– What part of it?

A– The fourth of July.

Q– Did you know Charles Eubanks?

A– Yes, sir.

Q– How often did he have to do with you?

A– Charles Eubanks? He never had nothing to do with me.

Q– Did anybody else have anything to do with you except the men who were the father[s] of these children?

A– No, sir.

Q– You say it mighty weak? Julia?

A– I can say it strong.

Q– You just confined your favors to those three?

A– To those three.

Q– And to Joe Brooken?

A– I don't know anything about confining myself; I was not a bad woman.

Q– You said that you had separated from Mr. Dickson, when was that?

A– I told you I didn't know what year it was, all of fifteen years.

Q– Was it after the war?

A– Yes, sir.

Q– How long after the war?

A– I don't know how long after the war.

Q– What do you mean by separating?

A– Well, I never had nothing to do with him any more.

Q– You mean he never went to bed with you anymore?

A– He never went to bed with me.

Q– Well, how did he get Amanda then?

A– He just laid down and got her like anyone else would get her.

Q– You mean he stopped laying down with you about fifteen years ago?

A– Yes, sir.

Q– When was Juan born?

A– She was born in 1853.

Q– What month?

A– March.

Q– What day of the month?

A– The 31st.

Q– When was Lola born?

A– She was born the second day of December. Just a month and a day older than Juan; I forget what year it was exactly.

Q– Who was your father?

A– Joe Lewis.

Q– Was he a white man or a negro?

A– He was considered white, he was a Spaniard, but very dark though.

Julia Dickson, Called by Propounders in Rerebuttal

Mr. Reese: Q– State to the jury whether you ever threatened to leave Mr. Dickson at any time.

A– No, sir.

Q– State whether or not you ever saw Mr. Dickson cry?

A– No, sir, never saw him cry for nothing.

Q– Did you ever see him take on like a maniac?

A– I never seen him take on.

Q– I will ask you whether or not you ever threatened to leave Mr. Dickson or ever purposed leaving there?

A– No, sir, I never purposed to leave and never said I was going to leave.

Mr. Rutherford: Q– Did you ever kiss Mr. Dickson?

A– That has been a long time ago.

Mr. Reese: Q– How long ago?

A– Long before the war—during the war.

Appendix B

GENEALOGICAL CHARTS

1. The African-American Dickson Genealogy

David Dickson ⊤ Julia Frances Lewis Dickson
(1809–1885) | (1836–1914?)

Amanda America Dickson ⊤ Charles Eubanks
(1849–1893) | (1836–1873)

Julian Henry Dickson ⊤ Eva Walton   Charles Green Dickson ⊤ Kate Holsey
(1866–1937) | (1868–1935)   (1870–?) | (1868–1938)

| Julia Frances II b. 1887 | David II b. 1889 | Henry b. 1893 | William b. 1899 | Isabel b. 1904 | Charles | Amanda America II b. 1891 | Kate Louise b. 1894 | Thomas W. b. 1898 |

2. The Anglo Dickson Genealogy

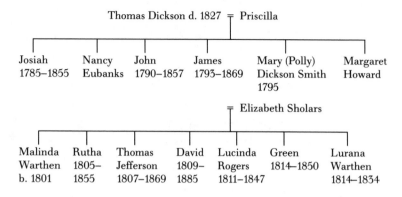

I am grateful to Gordon Smith for this genealogical information, letter, May 13, 1982, p. 4.

3. Nathan Toomer's Genealogy

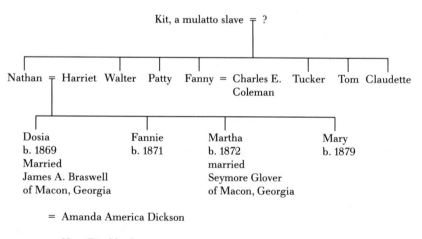

Appendix C

TABLES

1. Land Values and Productivity in Hancock and Adjacent Counties

County	Area (sq. miles)	Population White	Population Black	Cotton (acres)	Corn (bar. or bu/acre)	Wheat (bu/acre)
Taliaferro	176	2,130	2,671	450	2 bar.	8 bu.
Greene	374	4,515	7,458	500	3.5 bar.	10 bu.
Putnam	360	3,756	7,183	600	3 bar.	10 bu.
Baldwin	244	2,579	4,871	400	6–8 bu.	NA
Washington		NA	NA	NA	NA	NA
Warren	416	5,975	5,443	350	10 bu.	5 bu.
Hancock	440	4,210	7,306	550	12 bu.	5–6 bu.

Source: George White, *Statistics of the State of Georgia* (Savannah: W. Thorne Williams, 1849).

NA = not available; bu. = bushels; bar. = barrels.

2. Black and White Church Membership
in Hancock County, 1851 and 1860

Church	Membership 1851		Membership 1860	
	White	Colored	White	Colored
Bethel	108	49	66	22
Powelton	108	43	103	54
Beulah	68	36	44	39
Island Creek	NR	NR	160	57
Mount Zion	38	13	NR	NR
Horeb	64	36	60	76
Sparta	49	41	38	25
Darien	157	90	90	114
Shoulderbone				

Source: Minutes of the Washington Association in the library of Mercer University, in Forrest Shivers, *The Land Between: A History of Hancock County, Georgia, to 1940* (Spartanburg, S.C.: Reprint Company, 1990), 103.

N.R. = not reported.

3. The Founding Members of the Hancock
County Planters' Club, 1837

Name of member	Number of slaves	Taxes paid in 1837 (dollars)
I. Wheaton		
A. Dickson	17	3.08
N. C. Sayre	11	6.36
Robert S. Sayre	5	15.50
J. B. Ransom	3	2.12
Dr. Charles Ridley	24	6.37
R. S. Hardwick	36	8.20
Burwell S. Winn	63	18.80
Tully Vinson	16	4.24
D. Gilbert	8	2.16
Richard P. Sasnett		
L. A. Paron		
William Terrell (first president)	160	29.81
Henry Rogers		
Eli H. Baxter		
Wilkins Smith		
Joel Crawford	64	14.16
Allen Gilbert	25	4.25
David Dickson (not a member)	2	.48

Total tax return for Hancock County in 1837 = $1,566.15.

Source: The almost unreadable 1837 tax return for Hancock County, Hancock County Courthouse, Sparta, Ga.

4. David Dickson's Wealth

Year	Slaves	Individuals with more slaves	Total aggregate value	Acres
1837	2			40
1840	6			40
1841	10	159		40
1842	26	55		40
1843	32	42		40
1844	37	29		266
1845	45	18		1,000
1846	49	19		961
1847	48	16		956
1848	46	14		960
1849	53	7		2,010
1851	61	9		5,000
1853	66	11		7,000
1854	80	5		7,000
1855	91	6		7,500
1860	150	0		
1862	156	0		
1863	160	0		
1867	93 (hands)		$72,000	8,000
1870	12–65 (hands)		$72,920	10,000
1874			$170,000	18,000
1875			$151,275	19,000
1876			$122,630	17,400
1877			$93,450	10,000
1878			$92,325	10,000
1879			$126,945	17,000
1880			$134,250	18,000
1881	100		$124,650	17,000
1882			$161,550	17,000
1883			$176,600	17,000
1884			$216,000	19,500
1885			$276,030	17,750

5. A Selected List of Debtors to the Estate of David Dickson

Name	Description
John Turner	Foreman of the Hancock County Superior Court grand jury that ruled to uphold the will
J. T. Middlebrooks	A member of the same grand jury
Frank Lightfoot Little	Judge of the Hancock County Court; one of the witnesses to David Dickson's will; one of the lawyers who shepherded the will through the Georgia Supreme Court
Judge Lewis	The ordinary of Hancock County, who admitted the will to probate
Lovick Pierce	One of the witnesses to the will
L. Culver	Lovick Pierce's business associate; testified for the will
Henry Harris	Clara Harris Dickson's brother, who testified for the will
A. E. Eubanks	A nephew who testified for the will
Joe Brooken	The wagoner, a former slave, who testified against the will
John C. Lewis	A former slave, Julia's brother; Amanda America Dickson's uncle
W. H. Howard	David Dickson's cotton factor in Augusta
W. H. Jewel	David Dickson's friend who was rescued from insolvency by an anonymous person acting through Charles Dubose; the assignment of Jewel's debts was made without the slightest reservation
Henry T. Dickson	David Dickson's relative, to whom he left 2,000 acres in Texas; a caveator against the will
James B. Redfern	A citizen of Hancock County, who testified for the will

6. Occupations of African-American Citizens of Augusta, 1886

Occupation	Total	White	Colored	Percent colored in each occupation	Women
Bakers	11	10	1	17	3
Barbers[a]	29	5	24	83	0
Blacksmiths	15	6	99	60	1
Boardinghouses	20	19	1	5	13
Boot and shoe	56	36	20	36	0
Butchers	22	19	3	14	0
Carpenters	5	1	3	80	0
Dentists	5	5	0	0	0
Dressmakers	16	15	1	6	16
Fish and game	9	6	3	33	0
Furniture repair	2	0	2	100	0
Grocers	208[b]	193	15	7	20
Hucksters	12	2	10	83	0
Junk dealers	4	0	4	100	0
Lawyers	42	41	1	2	0
Milliners	11	11	0	0	9
Music teachers	5	5	0	0	0
Painters	6	6	0	0	0
Physicians and surgeons	35	34	1	3	0
Restaurants	7	1	6	86	1
Saloons	41	37	5	12	0
Stables	9	9	0	0	0
Tailors and repairers	7	5	2	29	0
Undertakers	6	3	3	50	0
Wagon makers	9	9	0	0	0
Wood dealers	15	10	5	33	0

[a] Including Eva Walton's father, George Walton, who practiced at the Augusta Hotel.
[b] Eight have recognizably Oriental names.

Notes

Introduction

1. Elizabeth Fox-Genovese, *Within the Plantation Household: Black and White Women of the Old South* (Chapel Hill: University of North Carolina Press, 1988), 62.

2. For a more complete discussion of Amanda America Dickson's story from the perspective of the black Dickson family oral history see Kent Anderson Leslie, "An Elite Mulatto Lady in Nineteenth Century Georgia: Amanda America Dickson," in *Southern Women, Culture and Identity*, ed. Virginia H. Bernhard, Betty Brandon, Elizabeth Fox-Genovese, and Theda Perdue (Columbia: University of Missouri Press, 1992), 71–86.

3. James C. Bonner, *A History of Georgia Agriculture, 1732–1860* (Athens: University of Georgia Press, 1964); Ralph B. Flanders, *Plantation Slavery in Georgia* (Chapel Hill: University of North Carolina Press, 1933); Willard Range, "The Prince of Southern Farmers," *Georgia Review* 2 (Spring 1948): 92–97.

4. Flanders, *Plantation Slavery*, 272.

5. Judge C. J. Lumpkin of the Georgia Supreme Court in *Bryan* v. *Walton*, 33 Georgia 11, March 1864; William Harper, "Harper's Memoir on Slavery," in Chancellor Harper, Governor Hammond, Dr. Simms, and Professor Dew, *The Proslavery Argument as Maintained by the Most Distinguished Writers of the Southern States . . .* (Philadelphia: Lippincott, Grambo, 1853), 40; Louis Wirth and Herbert Goldhamer, "The Hybrid and the Problem of Miscegenation," in Otto Klineberg, ed., *Characteristics of the American Negro* (New York: Harper

and Brothers, 1944), 249–365; Robert Brent Toplin, "Between Black and White: Attitudes Toward Southern Mulattoes, 1830–1861," *Journal of Southern History* 45 (May 1979): 179–80; E. Franklin Frazier, *The Negro Family in the United States* (Chicago: University of Chicago Press, 1966), 69.

6. Eugene Genovese, *Roll Jordan Roll: The World the Slaves Made* (New York: Vintage, 1976), 415–19; Wirth and Goldhamer, "The Hybrid and the Problem of Miscegenation"; Carl N. Degler, "Slavery and the Genesis of American Race Prejudice," in Donald L. Noel, ed., *The Origins of American Slavery and Racism* (Columbus, Ohio: Charles E. Merrill, 1972), 70–71.

7. Edmund S. Morgan, *American Slavery, American Freedom: The Ordeal of Colonial Virginia* (New York: Norton, 1975), 158–79; Helen Tunncliff Catterall, *Judicial Cases Concerning American Slavery and the Negro*, 5 vols. (Washington, D.C.: Carnegie Institution, 1932), vol. 1, *Cases from the Courts of England, Virginia, West Virginia, and Kentucky*, 53–54; Degler, "Slavery and the Genesis of American Race Prejudice."

8. Carl Degler, *Neither Black nor White: Slavery and Race Relations in Brazil and the United States* (New York: Macmillan, 1971); Joel Williamson, *The Crucible of Race* (New York: Oxford University Press, 1984) and *New People: Miscegenation and Mulattoes in the United States* (New York: Free Press, 1980).

9. Lat. *miscere*, to mix + *genus*, race. Allen D. Candler, comp., *The Colonial Records of the State of Georgia* (Atlanta: Franklin Printing and Publishing, 1904), 1:59–60; *Acts of the Georgia Legislature, 1979*, 948–49, effective July 1, 1979.

10. *Scott* v. *Georgia*, 39 Ga. 321 (1869); *State* v. *Tutty*, 41 Fed. 753 (S.D. Ga., 1890).

11. By an agreed-upon will not to notice I mean to imply an agreed-upon fiction within a family or community not to notice the transgression of a taboo, in Foucault's words, "the will to non knowledge" (Michel Foucault, *The History of Sexuality*, vol. 1, *An Introduction* [New York: Vantage, 1980]).

12. Kathleen Mary Brown, "Gender and the Genesis of a Race and Class System in Virginia, 1630–1750" (Ph.D. dissertation, University of Wisconsin, Madison, 1990), 355; Melton A. McLaurin, *Celia, A Slave: A True Story of Violence and Retribution in Antebellum Missouri* (Athens: University of Georgia Press, 1991); Bertram Wyatt-Brown, *Southern Honor: Ethics and Behavior in the Old South* (New York: Oxford University Press, 1982); Steven M. Stowe, *Intimacy and Power in the Old South: Ritual in the Lives of the Planters* (Baltimore: Johns Hopkins University Press, 1987).

13. Drew Gilpin Faust, *James Henry Hammond and the Old South: A Design for Mastery* (Baton Rouge: Louisiana State University Press, 1982), 87.

14. Herbert G. Gutman, *The Black Family in Slavery and Freedom, 1750–1925* (New York: Vintage Books, 1976), 419; Sylvia D. Hoffert, "This One Great Evil," *American History Illustrated* 12 (May 1977), 38; Martin Yant, "Father Healy: A Negro, a Building, a Dream," *Georgetown Today,* September 1971, 4–9; Ridgely Torrence, *The Story of John Hope* (New York: Macmillan, 1948); Ella Gertrude Clanton Thomas, *The Secret Eye: The Journal of Ella Gertrude Clanton Thomas, 1848–1889,* ed. Virginia Ingraham Burr (Chapel Hill: University of North Carolina Press, 1990), 320; Fawn M. Brodie, *Thomas Jefferson: An Intimate History* (New York: Norton, 1974).

15. It is probably impossible to determine whether "meaningful relationships" between blacks and whites in the nineteenth-century South were rare. Wirth believes that there were "many instances," while Gutman states that "meaningful affairs" were "not rare" (Wirth and Goldhamer, "The Hybrid and the Problem of Miscegenation," 264; Gutman, *Black Family,* 419). Interview with Doris Tanner, a descendant of the Durham family, June 1985; Will of Stephen Griffith, Probate Court for Pickens County, Jasper, Ga.

16. Catterall, *Judicial Cases;* Caroline Bond Day, *A Study of Some Negro-White Families in the United States* (Westport, Conn.: Negro University Press, 1932).

17. Catterall, *Judicial Cases,* vol. 3, *Cases from the Courts of Georgia, Florida, Alabama, Mississippi, and Louisiana: Hunter v. Shaffer,* 12; *David, guardian of Erasmus, claiming his freedom,* 16; *Allen (a slave) v. State,* 26; *Cooper v. Blakey,* 28; *Bryan v. Walton,* 33, 50–51; *Cleland v. Waters,* 38; *Knight as pro. ami of Margaret (a free woman of color) v. Hardeman,* 40–41; *Thornton v. Chisholm,* 50; *Smithwick v. Evans,* 60; *Walker v. Walker,* 62; *Carrie v. Cumming,* 68; *Ingram v. Fraley,* 75; *Myrick v. Vineburgh,* 75; *Cone v. Force,* 79–80; *Hughes v. Allen,* 80; *Sullivan v. Hugly,* 81; *Miller v. Lewis,* 88; *Cobb v. Battle,* 92; *Odum v. Odum,* 95; *Green v. Anderson,* 98–99.

18. *Bryan v. Walton,* 20 Ga. 480, June 1856, ibid., 50–51.

19. Ibid.; and *Bryan v. Walton,* Suppl. to 33 Ga. 11, March 1864, ibid., 87–88.

20. Day, *Study of Some Negro-White Families,* 108.

21. Ibid.

22. Sister Frances Jerome Woods, *Marginality and Identity: A Colored Creole Family Through Ten Generations* (Baton Rouge: Louisiana State University

Press, 1972); Gary M. Mills, *The Forgotten People: Cane River's Creoles of Color* (Baton Rouge: Louisiana State University Press, 1977), 191.

23. Michael P. Johnson and James L. Roark, *Black Masters: A Free Family of Color in the Old South* (New York: Norton, 1984).

24. Thomas O. Madden and Anne Miller, *We Were Always Free: The Maddens of Culpepper County, Virginia, A 200-Year Family History* (New York: Norton, 1992); Kathryn L. Morgan, *Children of Strangers: The Stories of a Black Family* (Philadelphia: Temple University Press, 1980); Pauli Murray, *Proud Shoes: The Story of an American Family* (1956; reprint, New York: Harper & Row, 1978); Adele Alexander, *Ambiguous Lives: Free Women of Color in Rural Georgia, 1787–1879* (Fayetteville: University of Arkansas Press, 1991).

25. Morgan, *Children of Strangers*, 27; Murray, *Proud Shoes*, 276.

26. Elsa Barkley Brown, "Weaving Threads of Community: Richmond Example," paper presented at the Southern Historical Association Convention, Norfolk, Virginia, November 12, 1988, p. 17.

27. Williamson, *New People*.

Chapter 1   Exceptions to the Rules

1. Edward Byron Reuter, *The American Race Problem: A Study of the Negro* (New York: Thomas Y. Crowell, 1927), 129–30. According to Sidney Kaplan and the *Oxford English Dictionary*, the word *miscegenation* was coined by David Goodman Croly, managing editor of the *New York World*, and his friend George Wakeman, a reporter on the staff of the same newspaper. In 1863–64, these two enterprising souls composed a pamphlet titled *Miscegenation: The Theory of the Blending of the Races. Applied to the American White Man and Negro*," which purported to be an argument for miscegenation. See Kaplan, "The Miscegenation Issue in the Election of 1864," *Journal of Negro History* 34 (July 1949): 274–343.

2. A line connecting the waterfalls of two nearly parallel rivers that marks a drop in land level.

3. Forrest Shivers, *The Land Between: A History of Hancock County, Georgia, to 1940* (Spartanburg, S.C.: Reprint Company, 1990), 3–4.

4. Ibid., 5, 7–8.

5. John Rozier, *Black Boss: Political Revolution in a Georgia County* (Athens: University of Georgia Press, 1982), 197.

6. Shivers, *Land Between*, 73.

7. Rozier, *Black Boss*, 200, n. 17; James C. Bonner, "Profile of a Late Ante-Bellum Community," *American Historical Review* 49 (July 1944): 663–80.

8. Ibid., 671.

9. Ibid.; Daniel R. Hundley, *Social Relations in Our Southern States* (1860; reprint, Baton Rouge: Louisiana State University Press, 1979), 250–83.

10. George White, *Statistics of the State of Georgia Including an Account of Its Natural, Civil, and Ecclesiastical History; Together with a Particular Description of Each County, Notices of the Manners and Customs of Its Aboriginal Tribes and a Correct Map of the State* (Savannah: W. Thorne Williams, 1849), 310–16.

11. Ibid.

12. Using the 1850 U.S. census for the total white population and White's estimates of the number of people who lived in Sparta (700), Powelton (150), and Mount Zion (200) in 1849 (White, *Statistics*, 311; Shivers, *Land Between*, 131).

13. Bonner, "Profile," 665–66, quoting *Soil of the South* 5 (1855): 321; *Southern Countryman* 1 (1859): 27; *Southern Cultivator* 18 (1860): 262; White, *Statistics*, 311–12; Shivers, *Land Between*, 81.

14. *Bulletin of the Sparta Female Academy*, December 13, 1838, Georgia Department of Archives and History, Atlanta.

15. Richard Malcolm Johnston, "Early Educational Life in Middle Georgia," in *Report of the Secretary of the Interior*, Fifty-fourth Cong., 1st sess. House Document 5, vol. 5, pt. 2; Fifty-fourth Cong., 2d sess., House Document 5, pt. 1, 862.

16. Alexander, *Ambiguous Lives*.

17. Mary E. Moragne, *The Neglected Thread: A Journal from Calhoun Community, 1836–1842*, ed. Delle M. Craven (Columbia: University of South Carolina Press, 1951), 148–49.

18. U.S. Census for Hancock County, Ga., 1850; Register of Free Persons of Color, Hancock County, Ga., Georgia Department of Archives and History.

19. U.S. Census for Hancock County, Ga., 1860.

20. Michael P. Johnson and James L. Roark, "'A Middle Ground': Free Mulattoes and the Friendly Moralist Society of Antebellum Charleston," *Southern Studies: An Interdisciplinary Journal* 21 (Fall 1982): 246–65.

21. Act of December 22, 1829, in *Acts of the General Assembly*, 1829, 171; Bishop Lucius Henry Holsey, *Autobiography, Sermons, Addresses and Essays* (Atlanta: Franklin Printing Co., 1899), 1.

22. Holsey, *Autobiography*, 16–17.

23. U.S. Census for Hancock County, Ga., 1850, 1860; for the Hubert family,

Lester F. Russell, *Profile of a Black Heritage* (N.p.: Published by Lester F. Russell, 1977); for the Hunt family, Alexander, *Ambiguous Lives;* for the Barneses and the Harrisons, Edmund L. Drago, *Black Politicians and Reconstruction in Georgia: A Splendid Failure* (Baton Rouge: Louisiana State University Press, 1982).

24. The original records of the Hancock County Planters' Club are in the possession of the clerk of the Superior Court of Hancock County. Microfilm copies are in the Southern Historical Collection of the University of North Carolina at Chapel Hill and the Manuscript Collections of the Georgia Department of Archives and History.

25. James C. Bonner, "Genesis of Agricultural Reform in the Cotton Belt," *Journal of Southern History* 9 (November 1943): 476.

26. Mrs. Martha Lewis to Tuttle H. Audas, January 6, 1845, in Hancock County Planters' Club Records, Manuscript Collections, Georgia Department of Archives and History, Atlanta.

27. David M. Potter, *People of Plenty: Economic Abundance and the American Character* (Chicago: University of Chicago Press, 1954); Dickson Will Case Transcript, Appealed September 1, 1886, Superior Court of Hancock County, Ga., Records of the Georgia Supreme Court, Box 219, Location 246–10; case 14443, Georgia Department of Archives and History.

28. Wyatt-Brown, *Southern Honor*, xv, xii.

29. Mary Douglas, *Purity and Danger: An Analysis of the Concepts of Pollution and Taboo* (Boston: Routledge Kegan & Paul, 1966), describes how cultures resort to the idea of pollution, here racial contamination, to resolve internal contradictions. "Four kinds of social pollution seem worth distinguishing. The first is danger pressing in external boundaries; the second, danger from transgressing internal lines of the system; the third, danger in the margins of the lines. The fourth is danger from internal contradictions, when some of the basic postulates are denied by other postulates, so that at certain points the system seems at war with itself" (122).

Chapter 2   A Story

1. Article by "L," *Augusta Chronicle*, February 19, 1885, 8, col. 1.

2. *Sparta Ishmaelite*, February 25, 1885, 3, col. 3.

3. The white population of Hancock County in 1800 was 9,605, or 20 white people per square mile (the total area was 485 square miles); the density of

whites in 1810 was 14 individuals per square mile; in 1820, 12; in 1830, 9; and in 1840, 8.

4. Will of Thomas Dickson (1827), Will Book L, 104, Probate Court, Hancock County Courthouse, Sparta, Ga.; Inventory of Thomas Dickson's Estate, 186, lists forty-eight slaves worth $12,617 on December 25, 1827. In 1825 eighty-six individuals in Hancock County owned from twenty to forty-nine slaves, while thirteen owned from fifty to ninety-nine slaves.

5. Range, "Prince of Georgia Farmers," 95; *Sparta Ishmaelite*, February 25, 1885, 3, col. 3. The *Ishmaelite* lamented, "Had [Dickson] been a man of liberal educational advantages he would have been fitted for eminence in any profession or calling." *Southern Cultivator* 18 (January 1860): 16–18, 338–40; David Dickson, *A Practical Treatise on Agriculture to Which Is Added the Author's Published Letters* (Macon, Ga.: Burke, 1870), 3, 57–62, 92, 113–17.

6. Dickson Will Case Transcript, testimony of Dr. E. W. Alfriend, November 16, 1885, 131.

7. Dickson, *Practical Treatise*, 235.

8. Will of Thomas Dickson, Probate Court, Hancock County Courthouse.

9. U.S. Census of 1840 for the state of Georgia, District 114, p. 226; Tax Digest for Hancock County, 1840, Tax Records, Georgia Department of Archives and History; Dickson Will Case Transcript, testimony of S. D. Rogers, for the caveators, 61.

10. Tax Digest for Hancock County, 1849, Georgia Department of Archives and History.

11. Dickson, *Practical Treatise*, 145.

12. Slave Census for Hancock County, 1850.

13. A Dickson family oral history was collected from the granddaughter of Amanda America Dickson (Eubanks Toomer). Her name was Kate Louise Dickson McCoy-Lee. Kate Dickson McCoy-Lee was born in 1894, the year after Amanda America Dickson died. She was the third child of Amanda America's son Charles Green Dickson and his wife, Kate Holsey Dickson (see Dickson family tree, Appendix Int. 1). Kate Dickson's sources of information on the Dickson family history included her great-grandmother Julia Frances Lewis Dickson, who lived in Sparta until at least 1914, her mother, Kate Holsey Dickson, other family members, and Aunt Mary Long, Amanda America Dickson's lifelong personal servant, who later worked for Kate Dickson, "until she got too old and had to move to Kentucky."

14. Dickson Will Case Transcript, testimony of Henry Harris, for the propounders, 90; testimony of Augustus E. Eubanks, for the propounders, 147;

Deborah Gray White, *"Ar'n't I a Woman?" Female Slaves in the Plantation South* (New York: Norton, 1985), 54; Lucius Henry Holsey, "Amalgamation and Miscegenation," *CME Church Bulletin* (1899): 233.

15. Dickson Will Case Transcript, testimony of Julia Frances Dickson, 160–88; U.S. Census, 1840, Hancock County, District 114, 226.

16. Dickson Will Case Transcript, Henry Harris, for the propounders, 90; Augustus E. Eubanks, for the propounders, 147.

17. Mary Boykin Chesnut, *A Diary from Dixie* (Boston: Houghton Mifflin, 1961), 58; Fox-Genovese, *Within the Plantation Household*, 163; Thomas, *Secret Eye*, 268.

18. Dickson Will Case Transcript, W. S. Lozier, for the caveators, 26; B. F. Riley, for the propounders, 99. The question was asked by lawyer Rutherford of James M. Dickson, for the caveators, 50.

19. Ibid., J. M. Dickson, for the caveators, 51; Will of Green Dickson (1850), Probate Court, Hancock County Courthouse.

20. Will of Rutha Dickson (1855), Probate Court, Hancock County Courthouse.

21. Deed by Elizabeth Dickson, Book R, 394–95 (1855–70), Hancock County Courthouse.

22. "Section I. From and After the passing of this Act, it shall not be lawful for any person or persons to manumit or set free any Negro slaves, any mulatto, mustizoe, or any other person or persons of color, who may be deemed slaves at the time of the passing of this Act, in any other manner or form, than by an application to the legislature for that purpose. Section II. If any person or persons shall, after the passing of this Act, set free any slave or slaves, in any other manner or form than the one prescribed herein, he shall forfeit for every such offense, $100.00, to be recovered by action of debt, or indictment, the one-half of the said sum to be applied to the use of the county in which the offence may have been committed, the other half to the use of the informer or informers; and the said slave or slaves so manumitted and set free, contrary to the true meaning and intent of this Act, shall be still to all intents and purposes, as much in a state of slavery as before they were manumitted and set free, by the party or parties offending" (Oliver H. Prince, ed., *A Digest of Laws of the State of Georgia* [Athens: Privately published, 1837], 787). See also Lucius Q. C. Lamar, ed., *A Compilation of the Laws of the State of Georgia, 1810–1819* (Augusta: W. S. Hannon, 1821), 811–12.

23. Deed, John Dickson to David Dickson, registered 1857, John Dickson

Estate Records, Hancock County Courthouse, Will of Green Dickson, Probate Court, Hancock County Courthouse.

24. Dickson Will Case Transcript, testimony of Julia Frances Dickson, for the propounders, 161; testimony of Dr. E. W. Alfriend, for the propounders, 129.

25. Ibid., testimony of A. E. Eubanks, for the propounders, 148.

26. Jane Turner Censer, *North Carolina Planters and Their Children, 1800–1860* (Baton Rouge: Louisiana State University Press, 1984), 135; W. E. B. Du Bois, "Princess of the Hinter Isles," in *Darkwater: Voices from Within the Veil* (New York: Schocken Books, 1969), 75–80; African-American Dickson Family Oral History, Appendix 2.1.

27. Fox-Genovese, *Within the Plantation Household*, 111.

28. U.S. Census, 1840; David Dickson's signature, *Practical Treatise;* Amanda America Dickson's signature, Hancock County, Probate Court, records of the Probate of David Dickson's Will, Acknowledgement that Melinda Warthen was Melinda Johnson, May 10, 1888.

29. Dickson Will Case Transcript, testimony of Judge J. C. Simmons, for the propounders, 156; African-American Dickson Family Oral History, Appendix 2.1.

30. Dickson Will Case Transcript, testimony of J. M. Eubanks, for the caveators, 57–58.

31. Ibid., testimony of Augustus E. Eubanks for the propounders, 147, Julia Frances Dickson, for the propounders, 160.

32. Ibid., testimony of Dr. E. W. Alfriend, 130.

33. Ibid., testimony of Julia Frances Dickson, for the propounders, 160–66, 173; W. H. Matthews, for the caveators, 37; Washington Printup, for the caveators, 40; Joe Brooken, for the caveators, 32. Matthews was an employee, and the other two men had been David Dickson's slaves.

34. Ibid., Matthews, for the caveators, 36; Printup, for the caveators; James M. Dickson, David's nephew, for the caveators, 49.

35. Ibid., testimony of Julia Frances Dickson, for the propounders, 165.

36. Lucy Dickson is listed in the U.S. Census of 1880 as a mulatto female, twenty-seven years old, living in the house with David Dickson and T. J. Warthen (David's nephew) as a servant. Lucy Dickson is mentioned in the Dickson Will Case Transcript as "the most important servant" (Henry Harris, 91). Lucy Dickson died on June 19, 1884. John C. Lewis, Julia's brother, was the administrator of the estate. Dickson Will Case Transcript, testimony of Lozier, for the caveators, 20, 29; Printup, for the caveators, 41; Barry for

the propounders, 85; Harris for the propounders, 91; testimony of Dr. E. W. Alfriend, for the propounders, 130.

37. Anne Goodwyn Jones, *Tomorrow Is Another Day: The Woman Writer in the South, 1859–1939* (Baton Rouge: Louisiana State University Press, 1981), 12; White, *"Ar'n't I a Woman?"* 29, 49; Douglas, *Purity and Danger*, 162.

38. Bonner, *History of Georgia Agriculture*, 432; *Southern Recorder*, July 10, 1860, 4.

39. Willard Range, *A Century of Georgia Agriculture, 1850–1950* (Athens: University of Georgia Press, 1954), 24; *Southern Cultivator* 17 (December 1852): 367; 18 (April 1861): 113.

40. *Southern Cultivator* 18 (October 1860): 400–404.

41. Dickson, *Practical Treatise*, 30.

42. Ibid., 253, 89.

43. *Southern Cultivator* 18 (June 1860): 175–76; 17 (September 1859): 261–62.

44. *Southern Cultivator* 18 (October 1860): 300; Dickson, *Practical Treatise*, 89.

45. Bonner, "Genesis of Agricultural Reform"; Chester M. Destler, "David Dickson's 'System of Farming' and the Agricultural Revolution in the Deep South, 1850–1885," *Journal of Agricultural History* 31 (1957): 30–39; Flanders, *Plantation Slavery*, 142, n. 31; Ulrich B. Phillips, *Life and Labor in the Old South* (Boston: Little, Brown, 1930), 132; Range, "Prince of Southern Farmers," 92–97; Dickson Will Case Transcript, testimony of Matthew Dickson, for the caveators, 73, Joe Brooken, for the caveators, 47; Amanda America Dickson's half-sister, the child of Julia Frances Dickson and Joe Brooken; Interview with Peaches Armstrong of Warthen, Georgia, March 1, 1987. Peaches Armstrong is the granddaughter of Julianna Dickson Youngblood. Her father was Ferdinand Youngblood, the youngest child of Raibun and Julianna; Interview with Eula Youngblood of Decatur, Georgia, October 26, 1989.

46. Bonner, *History of Georgia Agriculture*, 113–89; Destler, "David Dickson's 'System of Farming,'" 39; Flanders, *Plantation Slavery*, 272; *Southern Recorder*, November 11, 1857, 3, col. 4; *Southern Cultivator* 17 (September, 1859): 4; David Dickson, quoted by Range in "Prince of Georgia Farmers," 95.

47. *Southern Cultivator* 17 (1859): 368.

48. David Dickson to James Thomas, April 8, 1865, in Box 1, Folder 1, Location 2135-10C, James Thomas Collection, Georgia Department of Archives and History.

49. Dickson, *Practical Treatise*, 241–42; Tax Digest, Hancock County, Ga., 1863.

50. Quoted in Shivers, *Land Between*, 160; James Waddell, *Biographical Sketch of Linton Stephens* (Atlanta: Dobson and Scott, 1877), 244.

51. Deposition of Carey Stevens, Hancock County Superior Court Minutes, 1858–70, 399–414.

52. Mary Roxie Edwards, "The Lost Dinner," *In Daddy Jesse's Kingdom* (Macon, Ga.: J. W. Burke, 1922), 81.

53. Ibid., 82.

54. Ibid., 85.

55. Dickson, *Practical Treatise*, 141.

56. African-American Dickson Family Oral History, Appendix 2.2.

57. Ibid.; Fox-Genovese, *Within the Plantation Household*, 64.

58. Gutman, *Black Family*, 88; Censer, *North Carolina Planters*, 7; Lillian Henderson, comp., *Roster of the Confederate Soldiers of Georgia, 1861–1865*, 7 vols. (Hapeville, Ga.: Longino and Porter, 1959), 2:476.

59. African-American Dickson Family Oral History, Appendix 2.2, Marriage Records, Maryland State Archives, Annapolis, Md.; Marriage Records, Massachusetts State Archives, Boston.

60. African-American Dickson Family Oral History, Appendix 2.2, Deeds between S. C. Johnson and Charles H. Eubanks, Floyd County Courthouse, Rome, Ga.

61. Dickson, *Practical Treatise*, 242; Pardon, a "Special Pardon" by Andrew Johnson, petitioned for on August 9, 1865, National Archives, Washington, D.C.

62. Shivers, *Land Between*, 180, 188.

63. Ibid., 183.

64. *American Union* (Macon, Ga.), October 29, 1869, quoted in Edmund L. Drago, "Militancy and Black Women in Reconstruction Georgia," *Journal of American Culture* 1 (Winter 1978): 841. Cooperative communities were set up after the Civil War in various parts of the South. Wilkes Flagg organized such an enterprise on a thousand acres of land in middle Georgia.

65. Dickson, *Practical Treatise*, 86.

66. Destler, "David Dickson's 'System of Farming,'" 36; Tax Digest for Hancock County, 1860; Dickson, *Practical Treatise*, 86–87.

67. Dickson, *Practical Treatise*, 171.

68. *Southern Recorder*, December 1, 1868, 5, col. 5; January 5, 1869, 3, col. 1.

69. *Southern Cultivator* 18 (February 1860): 44; 19 (May 1861): 298; *Sparta Ishmaelite and Times Planter,* July 11, 1863, 3, col. 2; Dickson Fertilizer Company, November 10, 1870, in R. G. Dun Collection, volume for Georgia, Baker Library, Harvard University.

70. Tax Digest for Hancock County, 1870–85.

71. Dickson, *Practical Treatise,* 182, 89, 153, 67, 117,158, 203.

72. *Savannah Morning News,* October 1, 1870, 4, col. 1; Superior Court Records of Hancock County, "C Bundle," Georgia Department of Archives and History.

73. African-American Dickson Family Oral History, Appendix 2.1.

74. Dickson Will Case Transcript, testimony of Lozier, for the caveators, 19–20; Brooken, for the caveators, 44; J. M. Eubanks, for the caveators, 57; Rebecca Latimer Felton quoted in Hoffert, "This One Great Evil," 38.

75. Dickson Will Case Transcript, testimony of Lozier, for the caveators, 18–19.

76. This deed was not recorded until June 11, 1885, Deed Book W, 298–99, Clerk of the Superior Court, Hancock County Courthouse.

77. Marriage Certificate, Marriage Records, no. 106, 1871, Hancock County Courthouse; Elizabeth Wiley Smith, *The History of Hancock County, Georgia,* 2 vols. (Washington, Ga.: Wilkes, 1974), 1:128; Historical Activities Committee of the National Society of Colonial Dames of America in the State of Georgia, comp., *Early Georgia Portraits, 1718–1870* (Athens: University of Georgia Press, 1975), 92–93.

78. Smith, *History of Hancock County,* 1:69, 70, 83, 85, 128; Historical Activities Committee, comp., *Early Georgia Portraits,* 92–93.

79. Dickson Will Case Transcript, testimony of B. H. Sasnett, for the caveators, 67; Eliza Frances Andrews, *The War-Time Journal of a Georgia Girl, 1864–1865* (New York: D. Appleton, 1908), 32, 167–69.

80. Dickson Will Case Transcript, testimony of Julia Frances Dickson, for the propounders, 162.

81. Ibid., B. H. Sasnett, for the caveators, 67; Washington Printup, for the caveators, 41; Lozier, for the caveators, 37, 16, 20; James M. Dickson, for the caveators, 48; J. M. Eubanks, for the caveators, 55.

82. Ibid., testimony of S. C. Rogers, for the caveators, 66.

83. White, *"Ar'n't I a Woman?"* 41; Milledgeville *Union Recorder,* August 6, 1873, 2, col. 6; Dickson Will Case Transcript, testimony of B. H. Sasnett, for the caveators, 68–69.

84. Interview with the owner of the Exxon filling station on the road to Hamburg that runs by David Dickson's plantation.

85. Estate records and will of Charles H. Eubanks, Judge of Probate Office, Hancock County Courthouse.

86. Dickson Will Case Transcript, testimony of T. J. Warthen, for the propounders, 154–58.

87. Ibid., testimony of Julia Frances Dickson, cross examination, 160–66; Torrence, *Story of John Hope*; Alexander, *Ambiguous Lives.* John Hope's grandmother, Althea, was from Hancock County.

88. Book of Deeds, "U," 137–38, Hancock County Courthouse.

89. Dickson Will Case Transcript, Lozier, for the caveators, 17; Book of Deeds, "U," 595–96, registered July 31, 1877.

90. Ibid., testimony of B. F. Riley, for the propounders, 101.

91. *Atlanta University Catalogue,* 1876–77, 19, Special Collections, Woodruff Library, Atlanta University.

92. *Sparta Ishmaelite and Times Planter,* August 1, 1885, 1, col. 6.

93. Ibid., May 23, 1879, 3, col. 2; ibid., July 1, 1881, 3, col. 2.

94. Ibid., September 5, 1883, 3, col. 3; Brown, "Gender and the Genesis of a Race and Class System in Virginia," 496.

95. Dickson Will Case Transcript, testimony of B. H. Sasnett for the caveators, 70–71.

96. Executive Department, Book of Rewards and Proclamations, 1878–88, 283, Georgia Department of Archives and History.

97. Dickson Family Oral History, Appendix 2.1; James Kinney, *Amalgamation! Race, Sex, and Rhetoric in the Nineteenth-Century American Novel* (Westport, Conn.: Greenwood Press, 1970), 100.

98. *Savannah Morning News,* February 23, 1885, 1, col. 2.

99. Ibid.

Chapter 3   The Dickson Will

1. Fox-Genovese, *Within the Plantation Household,* 326; Eugene Genovese, *The World the Slaveholders Made* (New York: Vintage Books, 1971), 213; David Dickson's will, March 2, 1885, Probate Court Records, Drawer "D," Hancock County Courthouse.

2. John W. Blassingame, *Black New Orleans, 1860–1880* (Chicago: University of Chicago Press, 1973), 209.

3. Smith, *History of Hancock County*, 1:122; Inventory of David Dickson's Estate, May 26, 1885, 66–70, Hancock County Probate Court Records, Inventory of Estates, 1885, Drawer "D," Hancock County Courthouse.

4. "Mr. Dickson's Farm," *Sparta Ishmaelite*, February 11, 1885, 2, col. 1; *Memoirs of Georgia* (Atlanta: Atlanta Southern Historical Society, 1895), 1034.

5. *Sparta Ishmaelite*, February 11, 1885, 2, col. 1.

6. Ibid., March 4, 1885, 3, col. 3, March 11, 1884, 3, col. 3.

7. *Atlanta Journal*, August 1, 1885, 1, col. 6; David Dickson's will, item 7.

8. David Dickson's will, Hancock County, Ga., Index to Wills, 40–41, 60–61, 63; Records of the Supreme Court of Georgia; Georgia Department of Archives and History, Case Number 14443, Box 219, Location 246–10, 92-2-2.

9. Dickson Will Case, Legal Records, 117, Objection to the Probating of the Will in Solemn Form addressed to the Ordinary, R. H. Lewis, July Term, 1885.

10. David Dickson's Estate Records, Office of the Ordinary, Hancock County, 65–73, the Appraisal of David Dickson's Estate; *Sparta Ishmaelite*, June 10, 1885, 3, col. 2.

11. *Sparta Ishmaelite*, July 14, 1885, 3, col. 4.

12. Ibid., July 15, 1885, 3, col. 4.

13. Ibid., January 28, 1885, 3, col. 4; December 23, 1885, 3, col. 5; Smith, *History of Hancock County*, 2:71.

14. *Sparta Ishmaelite*, March 5, 1886, 3, col. 4; July 2, 1886, 3, col. 3; August 19, 1885, 3, col. 1.

15. Ibid., November 18, 1885, 2, col. 3; August 5, 1885, 3, col. 1; August 12, 1885, 3, col. 3; December 10, 1886, 3, col. 4; January 28, 1885, 3, col. 4; August 18, 1885, 3, col. 2; February 4, 1885, 3.

16. Dickson Will Case Transcript, T. J. Warthen, for the propounders, 155–58.

17. Dickson Will Case Records, Index to Wills, 251, Hancock County Courthouse.

18. *Sparta Ishmaelite*, January 21, 1885, 3, col. 3; February 6, 1884, 1, cols. 2–7; May 3, 1883, 3, col. 2; January 9, 1884, 3, col. 2; January 23, 1884, 3, col. 5.

19. Dickson Will Case Transcript, Charles W. Dubose, for the propounders, 74–84; Judge Frank Lightfoot Little, for the propounders, 4–6.

20. Allen D. Candler and Clement A. Evans, eds., *Georgia: Comprising Sketches of Counties, Towns, Events and Institutions and Persons Arranged in Cyclopedic Form*, 3 vols. (Athens: State Historical Association, 1906), 2:502–3; *Sparta Ishmaelite*, October 14, 1885, 2, col. 3; November 18, 1885, 2, col. 3.

21. Candler and Evans, *Georgia*, 2:188–89, 272–73, 1:404–6. Nathaniel Har-

ris was Clara Harris Dickson's first cousin (Candler and Evans, eds., *Georgia*, 3:116, 166–67). See Inventory of David Dickson's Estate, Office of the Ordinary, Hancock County, 66–67. E. H. Pottle owed David Dickson's estate $2,180, and Frank Lightfoot Little owed the estate $147.25.

22. Inventory of David Dickson's Estate, 66. J. T. Middlebrooks owed David Dickson's estate $1,500 and Turner owed $5,012.68 (*Supreme Court of Georgia Reports*, 78 Ga. 446).

23. Dickson Will Case Transcript.

24. *Sparta Ishmaelite*, March 5, 1886, 3, col. 4; Inventory of David Dickson's Estate, 65–66; John Linley, *Architecture of Middle Georgia: The Oconee Area* (Athens: University of Georgia Press, 1972), 144. The courthouse was begun in 1881 and finished in 1883. The stately old building still stands on a hill in the center of Sparta.

25. *New York Times*, November 16, 1885, 1, col. 6; *Cleveland Gazette*, November 28, 1885.

26. Dickson Will Case Records, Supreme Court of Georgia, 122, 125–26, 137–38.

27. Dickson Will Case Transcript, Henry Harris, for the propounders, 91; B. F. Riley, for the propounders, 99; B. H. Sasnett, for the caveators, 70.

28. Ibid., W. H. Matthews, for the caveators, 37–38.

29. Ibid.

30. Ibid., James M. Eubanks, for the caveators, 57, 59.

31. Ibid., Joe Brooken, for the caveators, 47.

32. Ibid., James M. Dickson, for the caveators, 50.

33. Ibid., S. D. Rogers, for the caveators, 62–63.

34. Ibid., W. S. Dickson, for the caveators, 53; Matthews, for the caveators, 37; Washington Printup, for the caveators, 40; Brooken, for the caveators, 44; Matthew Dickson, for the caveators, 72.

35. Ibid., W. L. Lozier, for the caveators, 19; J. M. Eubanks, for the caveators, 56; Henry Harris, for the propounders, 88, 113; Rogers, for the caveators, 65.

36. Ibid., Brooken, for the caveators, 44; Lozier, for the caveators, 19–20; Rogers, for the caveators, 63–64.

37. Ibid., Richard B. Baxter, for the propounders, 126.

38. Ibid., Lozier, for the caveators, 24–26; Green Dickson's will, Probate Court Records, Hancock County Courthouse; Dickson Will Case Transcript, Lozier, for the caveators, 26, 24–25; James M. Eubanks, for the caveators, 55.

39. Dickson Will Case Transcript, Charles W. Dubose, for the propounders, 77.

40. Ibid., John L. Culver, for the propounders, 94; Dr. E. D. Alfriend, for the propounders, 134; Augustus E. Eubanks, for the propounders, 149; J. C. Simmons, for the propounders, 104; Samuel A. Pardee, for the propounders, 121; Riley, for the propounders, 99.

41. Ibid., A. E. Eubanks, for the propounders, 147; Harris, for the propounders, 91; E. W. Alfriend, for the propounders, 128, 130–31; Simmons, for the propounders, 104; J. T. Barry, for the propounders, 85; E. D. Alfriend, for the propounders, 133.

42. Ibid., Julia Frances Dickson, for the propounders, 162, 165, 174.

43. Ibid., Simmons, for the propounders, 106; T. J. Warthen, for the propounders, 155.

44. Ibid., Simmons, for the propounders, 107. The lawyers for the excluded white relatives were referring to the fact that Julia Frances Dickson had three daughters, each with a different father. Amanda America Dickson's father was David Dickson. Julianna Dickson Youngblood's father was Joe Brooken (the wagoner), who was black; she was born in 1843. Lola's father was "Doc Eubanks" (not Charles), who was white. When asked if she confined her "favors" to those three men, Julia Dickson replied, "I don't know anything about confining myself; I was not a bad woman" (ibid., 164–65). Ibid., J. L. Garner, for the propounders, 112; Riley, for the propounders, 102; B. H. Sasnett, for the caveators, 71.

45. Ibid., Lozier, for the caveators, 16–17.

46. Ibid., Harris, for the propounders, 88, 69, 117.

47. Ibid., 119–20.

48. Ibid., James Redfern, for the propounders, 141; Mark Clay, for the propounders, 142; Augustus E. Eubanks, for the propounders, 147; Julia Frances Dickson, for the propounders, 165. James Redfern ($335.37), Mark Clay ($487.60), and Augustus E. Eubanks ($291.76) all owed David Dickson's estate money.

49. Ibid., J. L. Culver, for the propounders, 95; B. F. Riley, for the propounders, 98; Dr. E. W. Eubanks, for the propounders, 130.

50. Ibid., Dr. E. W. Alfriend, for the propounders, 130.

51. Ibid., J. C. Simmons, for the propounders, 104.

52. Ibid., Riley, for the propounders, 10; Augustus E. Eubanks, for the propounders, 148; T. J. Warthen, for the propounders, 156; J. L. Garner, for the propounders, 112.

53. Ibid., Harris, for the propounders, 90. In the Old Testament of the Christian Bible the word foot/feet is used as a euphemism for genitals. As in the

story of Ruth and Boaz, Ruth uncovers Boaz's "feet" and lies down next to him on the threshing floor (Ruth 3:6–7).

54. Dickson Will Case Transcript, Julia Frances Dickson, for the propounders, 163.

55. *Sparta Ishmaelite*, November 25, 1885, 2, col. 2; Dickson Will Case Transcript, Richard B. Baxter, for the propounders, 124.

56. Is there no male equivalent of a concubine? See 78 Ga. 430, objection #24; 78 Ga. 414; 78 Ga. 430.

57. *Sparta Ishmaelite*, November 25, 1885, 2, col. 2; Dickson Will Case Records, Box 219, Location 256–10, case no. 14443. Judge Lumpkin's charge to the jury, 8, Dickson Will Case Records; Dickson Will Case Transcript, 11, 22.

58. Dickson Will Case Transcript, 23.

59. *Sparta Ishmaelite*, November 25, 1885, 2, col. 2.

60. *Sparta Ishmaelite*, December 2, 1885, 3, col. 3.

61. Dickson Will Case Records, 8.

62. Nathaniel E. Harris, *Autobiography: The Story of an Old Man's Life and Reminiscences of Seventy-five Years* (Macon: J. W. Burke, 1925), 488.

63. Ibid., 491.

64. Ibid.

65. *Sparta Ishmaelite*, December 17, 1887, 3, col. 3; *Georgia Supreme Court Reports*, 78 Georgia, 442, 414.

66. Jonathan M. Bryant, "Race, Class and Law in Bourbon Georgia: The Case of David Dickson's Will," *Georgia Historical Quarterly* 71 (Summer 1987): 226–42.

67. *Sparta Ishmaelite*, June 17, 1887, 2, col. 3; *Sandersville Mercury*, June 21, 1887, 1, col. 3; *Milledgeville Union Recorder*, June 21, 1887, 1, cols. 5, 6; *Augusta Chronicle*, June 14, 1887, 2, col. 1; *Atlanta Constitution*, June 14, 1887, 1, col. 5; *Cleveland Gazette*, June 25, 1887, 2, col. 7.

68. *Sparta Ishmaelite*, June 17, 1887, 2, col. 3.

69. *Savannah Tribune*, August 6, 1887, 2, col. 1.

70. David Dickson Estate Records, Probate Court of Hancock County.

Chapter 4   The Death of a Lady

1. Willard B. Gatewood, Jr., *Aristocrats of Color: The Black Elite, 1880–1920* (Bloomington: Indiana University Press, 1990).

2. Hortense Powdermaker, "The Channeling of Negro Aggression by the

Cultural Process," in *The Making of Black America: Essays in Negro Life and History*, ed. August Meier and Elliot Rudwick (New York: Atheneum, 1969), 98; David C. Rankin, "French Romanticism, Free Colored Poetry, and the Politics of Reconstruction," paper presented at the Southern Historical Association Annual Meeting, November 12, 1987; Williamson, *Crucible of Race*, 67; Brown, "Weaving Threads of Community."

3. Records of David Dickson's Estate, Probate Court Records, Drawer "David Dickson," Hancock County Courthouse.

4. *Atlanta Constitution*, July 19, 1887, 6, col. 1; *Sparta Ishmaelite*, March 18, 1885, 3, col. 2; Deposition of Dr. W. H. Foster, who lived one block over from Amanda America Dickson at 320 Greene Street, *Nathan Toomer v. The Pullman Palace Car Co.*

5. *Augusta City Directory*, 1888 (Atlanta: R. L. Polk, 1888). According to the *Augusta City Directory* for 1886, the bridges in Augusta charged tolls: buggies and one horse, each way $.20; carts each way $.25; with wood, $11.25, cattle $.10, "loose"; horse and rider $.10; sheep, goats, and hogs, each way, $.05.

6. Dickson Family Oral History, Appendix 2.1; *Atlanta Constitution*, July 19, 1887, 6, col. 1; J. Morgan Kousser, "Separate but Not Equal: The Supreme Court's First Decision on Racial Discrimination in Schools," Social Science Working Paper, Number 204, California Institute of Technology, March 1978, 7; *Cleveland Gazette*, October 23, 1886, 1, col. 3.

7. Richard Henry Lee German, "The Queen City of the Savannah: Augusta, Georgia, During the Urban Progressive Era, 1890–1917" (Ph.D. dissertation, University of Florida, 1971).

8. L. D. Whitson, *Sketches of Augusta, Georgia, Sandersville, Sparta, Madison, Waynesboro, and Aiken, South Carolina* (Atlanta: N.p., 1885), 8–52; German, "Queen City," 23; *Augusta City Directories* for 1886 and 1890.

9. German, "Queen City," 36, 85.

10. Ibid., 89, 91.

11. The First Presbyterian Church of Augusta had twenty-five black members in 1883 and twelve in both 1891 and 1904 (Horace Calvin Wingo, "Race Relations in Georgia, 1872–1908" [Ph.D. dissertation, University of Georgia, 1969]).

12. Georgia Women's Temperance Union Records, Box 20, folder 45, 1891, Georgia Department of Archives and History.

13. John C. Ladeveze and Robert A. Harper were descended from Raymond Ladeveze, a white refugee from the Haitian revolution. Harper had been a free person of color in antebellum Augusta. He was educated as a musician

and composer in Boston and New York by his white father. Harper returned to Augusta, where he accumulated a fortune that placed him in the top 1 percent of wealthy free people of color in the state (Kousser, "Separate but Not Equal"). Judson W. Lyons later became register of the United States Treasury (1898–1906); (Kenneth Coleman and Charles Stephen Gurr, eds., *Dictionary of Georgia Biography*, 2 vols. [Athens: University of Georgia Press, 1983]); *Augusta City Directory*, 1886.

14. Anne R. Lockhart Hornsby, "Shifts in the Distribution of Wealth Among Blacks in Georgia, 1890–1915" (Ph.D. dissertation, Georgia State University, 1980), 114, 118, 119, 120, gives the wealth of Amanda America and her sons: Amanda America Dickson, $25,600; Julian H. Dickson, $15,344; and Charles Green Dickson, $12,686.

15. According to Hornsby, "Shifts," 200, 37 percent of wealthy black Georgians in 1890 had inherited their wealth, whereas in 1915 only 1 percent of the same group had inherited their wealth. See also E. Franklin Frazier, *Black Bourgeoisie: The Rise of a New Middle Class in the United States* (New York: Macmillan, 1957); Willard B. Gatewood, Jr., "Aristocrats of Color, North and South: The Black Elite, 1890–1920," *Journal of Southern History* 54 (February 1988): 3–20; Murray, *Proud Shoes*. The U.S. Census of 1890 lists the total black population in Georgia as 858,815 broken down as 773,682 blacks, 72,072 mulattoes, 8,795 quadroons, and 470 octoroons. Julian and Charles Dickson would have been classified as octoroons. In 1900, 67.3 percent of the black population of Georgia was still illiterate (Hornsby, "Shifts," 105, 118–20).

16. *Augusta City Directories* 1886, 1887, 1888.

17. Ibid.

18. Ibid.

19. *Nathan Toomer* v. *Pullman Palace Car Company*, Deposition of John M. Crowley, January 4, 1894, Maryland Department of Archives and History, Annapolis; William S. McFeely, *Frederick Douglass* (New York: Norton, 1991).

20. *Nathan Toomer* v. *Julian Dickson, Charles G. Dickson, and Julia Dickson*, Hancock County Superior Court, filed July 18, 1899.

21. *Atlanta Constitution*, June 19, 1887, 6, col. 2.

22. Deed Book W, 510–11, Hancock County Courthouse; *Sparta Ishmaelite*, July 29, 1887, 3, col. 2; U.S. Census of 1900; Paine College Alumni Association listings in the *Annual Catalogue* of 1912, 56–57. George and Isabella Walton are buried in the Toomer family plot in the Cedar Grove Cemetery in Augusta. George died October 15, 1908, and Isabella died on February 15, 1909.

23. Richmond County Deed Book 30, 756, March 26, 1889, EEEE, 77,

March 14, 1891; Hancock County Tax Digest for 1892, Hancock County Court-house.

24. U.S. Census of 1900.

25. Russell Duncan, *Freedom's Shore: Tunis Campbell and the Georgia Freedmen* (Athens: University of Georgia Press, 1986), xii; Drago, *Black Politicians and Reconstruction in Georgia,* 47; Wingo, "Race Relations," 2, 9; John Michael Matthews, "Studies in Race Relations in Georgia, 1890–1930" (Ph.D. dissertation, Duke University, 1970).

26. *Atlanta Constitution,* July 19, 1887, 5, cols. 1–2; Clarence A. Bacote, "Negro Proscriptions, Protests, and Proposed Solutions in Georgia, 1880–1908," *Journal of Southern History* 25 (1959): 471–98.

27. George Fredrickson, *The Black Image in the White Mind: The Debate on Afro-American Character and Destiny, 1817–1914* (New York: Torch Books, 1972), 273; Jacquelyn Dowd Hall, *Revolt Against Chivalry: Jessie Daniel Ames and the Women's Campaign Against Lynching* (New York: Columbia University Press, 1979), 135.

28. Rev. C. E. Dowman et al., eds., *The Possibilities of the Negro in Symposium: A Solution to the Negro Problem Psychologically Considered. The Negro Is Not a Beast* (Atlanta: Franklin Printing and Publishing Co., 1904), 102–3.

29. Wingo, "Race Relations"; *Houston Home Journal,* July 21, 1892, 2, col. 3.

30. Deed Book L, 124–25, Houston County Courthouse, for a mother Kit, a mulatto; Nathan 20, mulatto; Walter 18, mulatto; Patsy 16, mulatto; Fanny 14, mulatto; Tucker 8, mulatto; Tom 6, mulatto; and Claudette 4, mulatto. The family was valued at $7,000 (Deed Book S, 532, ibid.).

31. Houston County Tax Digest 1869, 421; U.S. Census of 1870, 14th District, 85; U.S. Census of 1880, 14th District, 3, Supervisor's Dist. 5, Enumeration Dist. 31, line 43; Houston County Agricultural Census of 1879.

32. *Nathan Toomer* v. *The Pullman Palace Car Company,* deposition of L. D. Stant; Darwin T. Turner quoting Jean Toomer in the introduction to *Cane* (1923; reprint New York: Liveright, 1975), xi; Willard B. Gatewood, Jr., and Kent A. Leslie, "A Sort of a Mystery: Jean Toomer's Father," *Georgia Historical Quarterly* 77 (1993): 789–809.

33. *Nathan Toomer* v. *The Pullman Palace Car Company,* deposition of Dr. Thomas D. Coleman.

34. Michael F. Rouse, *A Study of the Development of Negro Education Under Catholic Auspices in Maryland and the District of Columbia* (Baltimore: Johns Hopkins University Press, 1935), 42. An examination of the archives of the

Oblate Sisters of Providence revealed that Amanda America Dickson did not attend that institution.

35. "Love and Law Untangled in a Case That Came from Georgia," and "Not Devoid of Romance," abstracted by Gordon B. Smith, Case Files Frank/ Walton, Box 50, File 658, 3-27-6-10, Baltimore Criminal Court, Maryland State Archives.

36. *Nathan Toomer* v. *The Pullman Palace Car Company*, deposition of William H. Green, general manager of the Richmond and Danville Railroad.

37. Ibid., deposition of L. D. Stant, director of the cleaning crew for the Pullman Palace Car Company in Columbia, South Carolina.

38. Ibid.

39. "Anodyne, Greek: pain. Relieving pain. A medicine which relieves pain; anodynes include opium, morphine, codeine, aspirin and others" (William Alexander Newman Dorland, ed., *Illustrated Medical Dictionary*, 25th ed. (Philadelphia: W. B. Saunders, 1974), 100–101.

40. *Nathan Toomer* v. *The Pullman Palace Car Company*, depositions of Dr. Eugene Foster and Dr. W. H. Foster.

41. Barbara Sicherman, "The Uses of Diagnosis: Doctors, Patients, and Neurasthenia," *Journal of the History of Medicine* 32 (January 1977): 33–35, quoting George M. Beard, *A Practical Treatise on Nervous Exhaustion (Neurasthenia): Its Symptoms, Nature, Sequences, and Treatment*, 2d ed. (New York, 1881), 11–85; George M. Beard, *American Nervousness: Its Causes and Consequences* (New York: G. P. Putnam's Sons, 1881), 7–8. According to Sicherman, other famous neurasthenics were William James, Jane Addams, and Virginia Woolf, as well as Dr. Beard himself. Descriptions of neurasthenia in the nineteenth century are similar to descriptions of Epstein-Barr syndrome today.

42. Death Certificate of Amanda D. Toomer: forty-three years old; color —colored; nativity—Georgia; occupation—housewife; married, in Richmond County Courthouse, Augusta, Ga.

43. The hearse and carriages cost $25.00; *Nathan Toomer* v. *The Pullman Palace Car Company*. Evidence used in the lawsuit included a bill from Haggie Brothers Funeral Home for the cost of the casket, $500; *Union Recorder*, June 20, 1893, 1, col. 1.

44. *Atlanta Constitution*, June 12, 1893, 2, col. 2; Tribute paid by "A Friend," *Augusta Chronicle*, June 13, 1893, 2, col. 6. I am grateful to Gordon B. Smith for this reference. The entrance to the Cedar Grove Cemetery is on Watkins Street in Augusta. According to the *Savannah Morning News*, "Amanda Toomer (or

Dickson), the wealthy colored woman who was buried in the colored cemetery of Augusta last week was buried with some valuable jewelry on her person. A policeman is guarding the grave to prevent robbery" (June 19, 1893, 6, col. 1).

45. *Houston Home Journal,* June 15, 1893, 2, col. 2; *Atlanta Constitution,* June 2, 1893, 2, col. 2, June 12, 1893, 2, col. 1; *Savannah Morning News,* June 13, 1893, 6, col. 1; *Savannah Tribune,* June 17, 1893, 2, col. 1; *Atlanta Constitution,* June 12, 1893, 2, col. 1; *Augusta Chronicle,* June 12, 1893, 5, col. 1.

46. *Sparta Ishmaelite,* January 18, 1895, 3, col. 3. In all of the newspaper articles there is great confusion about the size of David Dickson's bequest. Estimates range from $250,000 to $1 million. Charles Dubose had recorded the inventory of the estate in the Sparta courthouse as a public record; consequently, the estimate in the *Sparta Ishmaelite* of $400,000 is probably the most accurate. The 1888 *Augusta City Directory* lists Theodore Markwalter as the proprietor of a "steam and marble and granite works" and sculptor, 529 and 531 Broad, residence 533 Broad Street.

47. *Atlanta Constitution,* June 12, 1893, 2, col. 2; *Augusta Chronicle,* June 13, 1893, 2, col. 6.

48. *Augusta Chronicle,* June 13, 1893, 2, col. 6.

49. Barbara Welter, *Dimity Convictions: The American Woman in the Nineteenth Century* (Athens: Ohio University Press, 1976); Kent Anderson Leslie, "A Myth of the Southern Lady: Proslavery Rhetoric and the Proper Place of Woman," *Sociological Spectrums* 6 (1986): 31–49; Ann Firor Scott, *The Southern Lady: From Pedestal to Politics, 1830–1930* (Chicago: University of Chicago Press, 1970).

50. Beverly Lynn Guy-Sheftall, " 'Daughters of Sorrow': Attitudes Toward Black Women, 1880–1920" (Ph.D. dissertation, Emory University, 1984), 155–56.

51. *Nathan Toomer* v. *The Pullman Palace Car Company,* deposition of Nathan Toomer; deposition of Dr. William H. Foster; Drew Gilpin Faust, "Culture, Conflict and Community: The Meaning of Power on an Antebellum Plantation," *Journal of Social History* 14 (Fall 1980): 83–98.

52. Estate Records, Amanda America Dickson, Richmond County Courthouse, Augusta, Ga.; David Dickson's will, Probate Court, Hancock County Courthouse. The property embraced by item seven of the will included all of David Dickson's $309,000 estate except $20,000 which he bequeathed to friends and relatives and 5,500 acres of land (of 17,000 acres), which Dickson gave to his brother Henry Dickson (2,000) and T. J. Warthen.

53. Agreement between Nathan Toomer and Julian and Charles Dickson, Record Book 55, 408–13, Richmond County Courthouse, Augusta, Ga.

54. *Nathan Toomer* v. *The Pullman Palace Car Company*, brief of Nathan Toomer.

55. Gatewood, *Aristocrats of Color*, 3–20.

56. *Nathan Toomer* v. *The Pullman Palace Car Company*, brief of Nathan Toomer; brief for the defendant, April 8, 1894.

57. Ibid., deposition of Dr. William Foster, January 3, 1894.

58. Ibid., testimony of Dr. Thomas C. Coleman, January 3, 1894; testimony of Dr. Kendall; deposition of Dr. Foster; verdict.

59. Letter from Nina Pinchback to Nathan Toomer, July 8, 1897, and "Mother's Dates," *Writings*, autobiographical, "Incredible Journey," notes from Chapter 1, part 2, Jean Toomer Papers, Beinecke Rare Book and Manuscript Library, Yale University; *Nina Eliza Pinchback Toomer, Complainant* v. *Nathan Toomer, Defendant*, in the Supreme Court of the District of Columbia, Equity No. 19,043.

60. *Nathan Toomer* v. *Julian Dickson, Charles Dickson, Julia Dickson*, Superior Court of Hancock County, deposition of Mariah Nunn, September 22, 1899; deposition of Thomas McNair, September 22, 1899.

61. Ibid., deposition of Sally Chapman, July 29, 1901.

62. Ironically, Judge Frank Lightfoot Little, who had witnessed David Dickson's will, was one of the lawyers for Nathan Toomer.

63. African-American Dickson Family Oral History, Appendix 2.1.

64. Deed Book FF, 600–601, Clerk of the Superior Court, Hancock County Courthouse.

Bibliography

Primary

General

Alvord, J. W. *Letters from the South Relating to the Condition of Freedmen, Addressed to Major General O. D. Howard, Commissioner, Bureau R. F. and A. L.* Washington, D.C.: Howard University Press, 1870.

Atlanta University Catalogues, 1876–1900. Atlanta University, Woodruff Library, Special Collections.

Augusta City Directories, 1885–1900. Richmond County–Augusta Public Library, Augusta, Ga.

A Century of Population Growth: From the First Census of the United States to the 12th, 1790–1900. Washington, D.C.: U.S. Bureau of the Census, 1909.

Confederate War Records, Including Pardons of David Dickson and Henry Toomer. Library of Congress, Washington, D.C.

Dickson, David. *A Practical Treatise on Agriculture to Which Is Added the Author's Published Letters.* Macon, Ga.: Burke, 1870.

Georgia Women's Christian Temperance Union Records. Box 20, 1890–93. Georgia Department of Archives and History, Atlanta.

Hancock County Court of Ordinary. *Register of the Free Persons of Color, 1855–1862.*

Henderson, Lillian, comp. *Roster of the Confederate Soldiers of Georgia, 1861–1865.* Hapeville, Ga.: Longino and Porter, 1959.

Hurd, John Codman. *Law of Freedom and Bondage in the United States.* 2 vols. Boston, 1858.

Johnston, Richard Malcolm. "Early Educational Life in Middle Georgia." *Report of the Secretary of the Interior,* House Document No. 5. vol. 5, pt. 2, Fifty-fourth Cong., 1st sess; House Document No. 5, pt. 1, Fifty-fourth Cong., 2d sess.

Lamar, Lucius Q. C., ed. *A Compilation of the Laws of the State of Georgia, 1810–1819.* Augusta: W. S. Hannon, 1821.

Prince, Oliver H., ed. *A Digest of the Laws of the State of Georgia.* Athens: Privately published, 1837.

Supreme Court of Georgia. *Reports,* Georgia Department of Archives and History, Atlanta.

U.S. Census of 1820, 1830, 1840, 1850, 1860, 1870, 1880, 1890, 1900, 1910.

Waddell, James. *Biographical Sketch of Linton Stephens.* Atlanta: Dodson and Scott, 1877.

White, George. *Statistics of the State of Georgia: Including an Account of Its Natural, Civil, and Ecclesiastical History; Together with a Particular Description of Each County, Notices of the Manners and Customs of Its Aboriginal Tribes, and a Correct Map of the State.* Savannah: W. Thorne Williams, 1849.

Whitson, L. D. *Sketches of Augusta, Georgia, Sandersville, Sparta, Madison, Waynesboro, and Aiken, South Carolina.* Atlanta: N.p., 1885.

Diaries

Andrews, Eliza Frances. *The War-Time Journal of a Georgia Girl, 1864–1865.* New York: D. Appleton, 1908.

Andrews, Garnett. *Recollections of an Old Georgia Lawyer.* Atlanta: Franklin Printing House, 1870.

Burge, Dolly Sumner Hunt. *The Diary of Dolly Sumner Hunt Burge.* 1902. Reprint, edited by James I. Robertson, Jr. Athens: University of Georgia Press, 1960.

Butler, John C. *Historical Review of Macon and Central Georgia Containing Many Interesting and Valuable Reminiscences Connected with the Whole State, Including Numerous Incidents Never Before Published and of Great Historical Value.* Macon, 1879.

Chesnut, Mary Boykin. *A Diary from Dixie.* Boston: Houghton Mifflin, 1961.

Cooper, Anna Julia. *A Voice from the South: By a Black Woman of the South.* 1892. Reprint, New York: Negro University Press, 1968.

De Tocqueville, Alexis. *Democracy in America.* 1835. Reprint, New York: New American Library, 1956.

Dubose, Kate Richards. Diary. Private Collection.

Fort, Kate Haynes. *Memories of the Fort and Fannin Families.* Chattanooga, Tenn.: Press of Macgowan and Cooke, 1903.

Harris, Nathaniel E. *Autobiography: The Story of an Old Man's Life with Reminiscences of Seventy-five Years.* Macon: J. W. Burke, 1925.

Jacobs, Harriet A. *Incidents in the Life of a Slave Girl, Written by Herself.* 1861. Reprint, Cambridge, Mass.: Harvard University Press, 1987.

Kemble, Frances Anne. *Journal of a Residence on a Georgian Plantation in 1838–1839.* 1863. Reprint, Athens: University of Georgia Press, 1984.

Miller, Benton, of Hancock County, Georgia. Diary. Georgia Department of Archives and History, Atlanta.

Moragne, Mary E. *The Neglected Thread: A Journal from the Calhoun Community, 1836–1842.* Edited by Delle M. Craven. Columbia: University of South Carolina Press, 1951.

Richards, Samuel P. Diary, 1883–1900. Atlanta Historical Society, Atlanta, Georgia. (Richards was Kate Richards Dubose's brother.)

Thomas, Ella Gertrude Clanton. *The Secret Eye: The Journal of Ella Gertrude Clanton Thomas, 1848–1889.* Edited by Virginia Ingraham Burr. Chapel Hill: University of North Carolina Press, 1990.

U.S. Bureau of the Census. *Negro Population in the United States, 1790–1900.* Washington, D.C.: U.S. Bureau of the Census, 1909.

Contemporary Newspapers

Atlanta Journal and Constitution.
Augusta Chronicle. University of Georgia.
Central Georgian (Sandersville). University of Georgia.
Cleveland Gazette
Federal Union (Milledgeville). University of Georgia.
Hancock Weekly Journal. Georgia College at Milledgeville.
Houston Home Journal. University of Georgia.
Macon Telegraph. University of Georgia.
New York Times.
Perry Home Journal. University of Georgia.
Sandersville Herald. University of Georgia.
Sandersville Mercury. University of Georgia.

Sandersville Progress. University of Georgia.

Savannah Morning News. University of Georgia.

Savannah Tribune. Savannah State, Savannah.

Southern Countryman, Southern Cultivator. Agrirama, Tifton, Ga.

Sparta Ishmaelite and Times Planter. University of Georgia.

Union Recorder (Milledgeville). University of Georgia.

Secondary

Books

Alexander, Adele. *Ambiguous Lives: Free Women of Color in Rural Georgia, 1789–1879.* Fayetteville: University of Arkansas Press, 1991.

Allmendinger, David F., Jr., ed. *Incidents of My Life: Edmund Ruffin's Autobiographical Essays.* Charlottesville: University Press of Virginia, 1990.

Ansley, Mrs. J. T. *History of the Georgia Women's Christian Temperance Union.* Columbus, Ga.: Filbert Printing Co., 1914.

Avery, L. W. *The History of the State of Georgia from 1850–1881.* New York: Brown and Derby, 1981.

Ayers, Edward L. *Vengeance and Justice: Crime and Punishment in the Nineteenth Century South.* New York: Oxford University Press, 1984.

Bacote, Clarence. *The Story of Atlanta University, 1865–1965.* Atlanta: Atlanta University, 1969.

Bancroft, Frederic. *Slave Trading in the Old South.* Baltimore: J. F. Furst, 1931.

Banks, Enoch. *The Economics of Land Tenure in Georgia.* New York: Columbia University Press, 1905.

Beard, George M. *American Nervousness: Its Causes and Consequences.* New York: G. P. Putnam & Sons, 1881.

———. *A Practical Treatise on Nervous Exhaustion (Neurasthenia): Its Symptoms, Nature, Sequences, and Treatment.* 2d ed. New York, 1881.

Beebe, Lucius. *Mr. Pullman's Elegant Palace Cars.* New York: Doubleday, 1961.

Bell, Hiram P. *Men and Things* (1905). Atlanta: Press of Foote and Davies, 1906.

Bell, Malcolm, Jr., *Major Butler's Legacy: Five Generations of a Slaveholding Family.* Athens: University of Georgia Press, 1987.

Bell, Velma. "Side Tour to Sparta." Federal Writers Project (1937) 1, University of Georgia Library Files.

Berkeley, Kathleen C. " 'Colored Ladies' Also Contributed: Black Women's

Activities from Benevolence to Social Welfare, 1866–1896." In *The Web of Southern Social Relations: Women, Family, and Education*, edited by Walter J. Fraser, Jr., K. Frank Saunders, Jr., and Jon L. Wakelyn, pp. 181–203. Athens: University of Georgia Press, 1985.

Berlin, Ira. *Slaves Without Masters: The Free Negro in the Antebellum South.* New York: Oxford University Press, 1974.

Bernhard, Virginia A., Betty Brandon, Elizabeth Fox-Genovese, and Theda Perdue, eds. *Southern Women: Histories and Identities.* Columbia: University of Missouri Press, 1992.

Berzon, Judith R. *Neither White nor Black: The Mulatto Character in American Fiction.* New York: New York University Press, 1978.

Birmingham, Stephen. *Certain People: America's Black Elite.* Boston: Little, Brown, 1977.

Blackford, L. Minor. *Mine Eyes Have Seen the Glory: The Story of a Virginia Lady, Mary Berkeley Minor Blackford, 1802–1896, Who Taught Her Sons to Hate Slavery and to Love the Union.* Cambridge, Mass.: Harvard University Press, 1954.

Blackwell, James E. "Social and Legal Dimensions of Interracial Liaisons." In *The Black Male in America*, edited by Doris Y. Wilkinson and Ronald L. Taylor, pp. 219–43. Chicago: Nelson-Hall, 1977.

Blassingame, John W. *Black Orleans, 1860–1880.* Chicago: University of Chicago Press, 1973.

———. *The Slave Community: Plantation Life in the Antebellum South.* New York: Oxford University Press, 1972.

Blessor, Carol, ed. *In Joy and in Sorrow: Women, Family, and Marriage in the Victorian South, 1830–1900.* New York: Oxford University Press, 1991.

Bonner, James C. *A History of Georgia Agriculture, 1732–1860.* Athens: University of Georgia Press, 1964.

Brodie, Fawn M. *Thomas Jefferson: An Intimate History.* New York: Norton, 1974.

Brooks, Robert P. *The Agrarian Revolution in Georgia, 1865–1911.* Madison: University of Wisconsin Press, 1914.

Bruce, Dickson D. *Black American Writing from the Nadir: The Evolution of a Literary Tradition, 1877–1915.* Baton Rouge: Louisiana State University Press, 1989.

Burton, Orville Vernon. *In My Father's House Are Many Mansions: Family and Community in Edgefield, South Carolina.* Chapel Hill: University of North Carolina Press, 1985.

Bynum, Victoria. *Unruly Women: The Politics of Social and Sexual Control in the Old South*. Chapel Hill: University of North Carolina Press, 1992.

Calhoun, Arthur W. *A Social History of the American Family*. 3 vols. Vol. 1: *The Colonial Period*; vol. 2: *From Independence Through the Civil War*; vol. 3: *From 1865–1919*. New York: Barnes and Noble, 1945.

Candler, Allen D., comp. *The Colonial Records of the State of Georgia*. Atlanta: Franklin Printing and Publishing Company, 1904.

Candler, Allen D., and Clement A. Evans, eds. *Georgia: Comprising Sketches of Counties, Towns, Events and Institutions and Persons Arranged in Cyclopedic Form*. 3 vols. Athens: State Historical Society, 1906.

Cash, W. J. *The Mind of the South*. New York: Vintage Books, 1941.

Cashin, Edward J. *The Story of Augusta*. Augusta, Ga.: Richmond County Board of Education, 1980.

Catterall, Helen Tunnicliff. *Judicial Cases Concerning American Slavery and the Negro*. 5 vols. Washington, D.C.: Carnegie Institution, 1932.

Censer, Jane Turner. *North Carolina Planters and Their Children, 1800–1860*. Baton Rouge: Louisiana State University Press, 1984.

Chappell, Absalom H. *Miscellanies of Georgia: Historical, Biographical, Descriptive, etc*. Atlanta: James F. Meegan, 1874.

Clark, Thomas, ed. *Travel in the Old South: A Bibliography*. 3 vols. Norman: University of Oklahoma Press, 1956.

Clarke, Erskine. *Wrestlin' Jacob: A Portrait of Religion in the Old South*. Atlanta: John Knox Press, 1979.

Clinton, Catherine. *The Other Civil War: American Women in the Nineteenth Century*. New York: Hill and Wang, 1984.

———. *Plantation Mistress: Woman's World in the Old South*. New York: Pantheon, 1982.

Clinton, Catherine, and Nina Silber, eds. *Divided Houses: Gender and the Civil War*. New York: Oxford University Press, 1992.

Cloves, W. Laird. *Black America: A Study of the Ex-Slave and His Late Master*. London: Cassell, 1891.

Coleman, Kenneth, gen. ed. *A History of Georgia*. Athens: University of Georgia Press, 1977.

Coleman, Kenneth, and Charles Stephen Gurr, eds. *Dictionary of Georgia Biography*. 2 vols. Athens: University of Georgia Press, 1983.

Corley, Florence Fleming. *Confederate City: Augusta, Georgia, 1860–1865*. Columbia: University of South Carolina Press, 1960.

Coulter, E. Merton. *James Monroe Smith: Georgia Planter Before Death and After*. Athens: University of Georgia Press, 1961.

——. *Travels in the Confederate States: A Bibliography*. Norman: University of Oklahoma Press, 1948.

Curry, Leonard P. *The Free Black in Urban America, 1800–1850*. Chicago: University of Chicago Press, 1981.

Daly, Mary. *Gyn/Ecology: The Meta Ethics of Radical Feminism*. Boston: Beacon Press, 1979.

Davis, Marianna W., ed. *Contributions of Black Women to America*. 2 vols. Columbia, S.C.: Kenday Press, 1982.

Day, Caroline Bond. *A Study of Some Negro-White Families in the United States*. Westport, Conn.: Negro University Press, 1932.

DeBats, Donald. *Elites and Masses: Political Structure, Communication, and Behavior in Antebellum Georgia*. New York: Garland, 1990.

DeBurg, William L. *The Slave Drivers: Black Agricultural Labor Supervisors in the Antebellum South*. New York: Oxford University Press, 1979.

Degler, Carl. *Neither Black nor White: Slavery and Race Relations in Brazil and the United States*. New York: Macmillan, 1971.

Dew, Thomas R. *The Debate in the Virginia Legislature of 1831 and 1832*. Richmond: T. W. White, Opposite the Tavern, n.d.

Dominguez, Virginia R. *White by Definition: Social Classification in Creole Louisiana*. New Brunswick, N.J.: Rutgers University Press, 1986.

Doris, Jonathan Truman. *Pardon and Amnesty Under Lincoln and Johnson: The Restoration of the Confederates to Their Rights and Privileges, 1861–1898*. Chapel Hill: University of North Carolina Press, 1953.

Dorland, William Alexander Newman, ed. *Illustrated Medical Dictionary*. 25th ed. Philadelphia: W. B. Saunders, 1974.

Douglas, Mary. *Purity and Danger: An Analysis of the Concepts of Pollution and Taboo*. Boston: Routledge & Kegan Paul, 1966.

Dowman, Rev. C. E., et al., eds. *The Possibilities of the Negro in Symposium: A Solution to the Negro Problem Psychologically Considered. The Negro is Not a Beast*. Atlanta: Franklin Printing and Publishing Co., 1904.

Drago, Edmund L. *Black Politicians and Reconstruction in Georgia: A Splendid Failure*. Baton Rouge: Louisiana State University Press, 1982.

——. *Initiative, Paternalism, and Race Relations: Charleston's Avery Normal Institute*. Athens: University of Georgia Press, 1990.

Drotning, Philip T. *A Guide to Negro History in America*. New York: Doubleday, 1968.

Dubin, Arthur D. *Some Classic Trains.* Milwaukee: Kalnsach, 1964.

Du Bois, Ellen Carol. *Feminism and Suffrage: The Emergence of an Independent Women's Movement in America, 1848–1869.* Ithaca: Cornell University Press, 1978.

Du Bois, W. E. B. *Darkwater: Voices from Within the Veil.* New York: Schocken Books, 1969.

———. "The Intermarriage of the Races." In *The Philadelphia Negro: A Social Study,* pp. 359–67. New York: Schocken Press, 1899.

———. *The Negro Landholder in Georgia.* U.S. Department of Labor, Bulletin No. 35. Washington, D.C., 1901.

———. *The Souls of Black Folk: Essays and Sketches.* Chicago: A. C. McClury, 1903.

Duncan, Russell. *Freedom's Shore: Tunis Campbell and the Georgia Freedmen.* Athens: University of Georgia Press, 1986.

Durr, Virginia Foster. *Outside the Magic Circle: The Autobiography of Virginia Foster Durr.* New York: Touchstone Books, 1985.

Edwards, Mary Roxie. *In Daddy Jesse's Kingdom.* Macon, Ga.: J. W. Burke, 1922.

Enock, Marvin Banks. *The Economics of Land Tenure in Georgia.* New York: Avis Press, 1905.

Faust, Drew Gilpin. *James Henry Hammond and the Old South: A Design for Mastery.* Baton Rouge: Louisiana State University Press, 1982.

———. *A Sacred Circle: The Dilemma of the Intellectual in the Old South, 1840–1860.* Baltimore: Johns Hopkins University Press, 1977.

———, ed. *The Ideology of Slavery: Proslavery Thought in the Antebellum South, 1830–1860.* Baton Rouge: Louisiana State University Press, 1981.

Felton, Rebecca Latimer. *Country Life in Georgia in the Days of My Youth: Also Addresses Before Georgia Legislature, Woman's Clubs, Women's Organizations and Other Noted Occasions.* Atlanta: Index Printing Company, 1919.

Fields, Barbara J. "Ideology and Race in America." In *Region, Race and Reconstructions: Essays in Honor of C. Vann Woodward,* edited by J. Moran and James M. McPherson, pp. 143–77. New York: Oxford University Press, 1982.

———. *Slavery and Freedom on the Middle Ground: Maryland During the Nineteenth Century.* New Haven: Yale University Press, 1985.

Fields, Mamie Garvin, with Karen Fields. *Lemon Swamp and Other Places: A Carolina Memoir.* New York: Free Press, 1983.

Finley, M. I. *Ancient Slavery and Modern Ideology.* New York: Pelican Books, 1983.

Fitzhugh, George. *Cannibals All! Or Slaves Without Masters*. 1857. Reprint, Cambridge, Mass.: Belknap Press of Harvard University Press, 1960.

————. *Sociology for the South: Or the Failure of Free Society*. 1854. Reprint, New York: Burt Franklin, 1965.

Flanders, Ralph B. *Plantation Slavery in Georgia*. Chapel Hill: University of North Carolina Press, 1933.

Flynn, Charles C., Jr. *White Land, Black Labor: Caste and Class in Late Nineteenth Century Georgia*. Baton Rouge: Louisiana State University Press, 1983.

Foucault, Michel. *The History of Sexuality*. Vol. 1: *An Introduction*. New York: Vantage, 1980.

Fox-Genovese, Elizabeth. *Within the Plantation Household: Black and White Women of the Old South*. Chapel Hill: University of North Carolina Press, 1988.

Franklin, John Hope. *The Free Negro in North Carolina, 1790–1860*. New York: Norton, 1943.

Franklin, Vincent P., and James D. Anderson, eds. *New Perspectives on Black Educational History*. Boston: G. K. Hall, 1978.

Frazier, E. Franklin. *Black Bourgeoisie: The Rise of a New Middle Class in the United States*. New York: Macmillan, 1962.

————. *The Negro Family in the United States*. 1939. Reprint, Revised and Abridged Edition, Chicago: University of Chicago Press, 1966.

Fredrickson, George. *The Arrogance of Race: Historical Perspectives on Slavery, Racism, and Social Inequality*. Middletown, Conn.: Wesleyan University Press, 1988.

————. *The Black Image in the White Mind: The Debate on Afro-American Character and Destiny, 1817–1914*. New York: Torch Books, 1972.

Friedman, Jean E. *The Enclosed Garden: Women and Community in the Evangelical South, 1830–1900*. Chapel Hill: University of North Carolina Press, 1985.

Friedman, Lawrence. *The White Savage: Racial Fantasies in the Post-Bellum South*. Englewood Cliffs, N.J.: Prentice-Hall, 1970.

Fuller, Chet. *Black Georgians in History*. Savannah Branch of the NAACP: Bicentennial Publications, 1976.

Gaines, Ernest J. *Of Love and Dust*. New York: Dial Press, 1967.

Gatewood, Willard B., Jr. *Aristocrats of Color: The Black Elite, 1880–1920*. Bloomington: Indiana University Press, 1990.

——, ed. *Free Man of Color: The Autobiography of Willis Augustus Hodges.* 1896. Reprint, Knoxville: University of Tennessee Press, 1982.

Genovese, Eugene. *Roll, Jordan Roll: The World the Slaves Made.* New York: Vintage, 1976.

——. *The World the Slaveholders Made.* New York: Vintage Books, 1971.

Giddings, Paula. *When and Where I Enter: The Impact of Black Women on Race and Sex in America.* New York: Bantam, 1984.

Gordon, Asa H. *The Georgia Negro.* Ann Arbor: Edward Brothers, 1937.

Gray, Lewis Cecil. *History of Agriculture in the Southern United States to 1860.* 2 vols. Washington, D.C.: Carnegie Institution, 1933.

Griggs, Sutton. *The Race Question in New Light.* Nashville: Orion, 1890.

Grimké, Angelina Emily. *Appeal to the Christian Women of the New South.* 1836. Reprint, New York: Arno Press, 1969.

Grimké, Sarah M. *Letters on the Equality of the Sexes and the Conditions of Women. Addressed to Mary S. Parker.* Boston: I. Knapp, 1838.

Gutman, Herbert G. *The Black Family in Slavery and Freedom, 1750–1925.* New York: Vintage, 1976.

Gwin, Minrose C. *Black and White Women of the Old South: The Peculiar Sisterhood in American Literature.* Knoxville: University of Tennessee Press, 1985.

Hahn, Steven. *The Roots of Southern Populism: Yeoman Farmers and the Transformation of the Georgia Upcountry, 1850–1890.* New York: Oxford University Press, 1983.

Hahn, Steven, and Jonathan Prude, eds. *The Countryside in the Age of Capitalist Transformation: Essays in the Social History of Rural America.* Chapel Hill: University of North Carolina Press, 1985.

Hall, Jacquelyn Dowd. *Revolt Against Chivalry: Jessie Daniel Ames and the Women's Campaign Against Lynching.* New York: Columbia University Press, 1979.

Handlin, Oscar, and Mary F. Handlin. "The Origins of Negro Slavery." In *The Origins of American Slavery and Racism,* edited by Donald L. Noel, pp. 21–44. Columbus: Charles E. Merrill, 1972.

Harley, Sharon, and Rosalyn Terborg-Penn, eds. *The Afro-American Woman: Struggles and Images.* Port Washington, N.Y.: Kennikat Press, 1978.

Harper, Chancellor, Governor Hammond, Dr. Simms, and Professor Dew. *The Proslavery Argument as Maintained by the Most Distinguished Writers of the Southern States: Containing Several Essays on the Subject.* Philadelphia: Lippincott, Grambo, 1853.

Harris, J. William. *Plain Folk and Gentry in a Slave Society: White Liberty and Black Slavery in Augusta's Hinterlands.* Middletown, Conn.: Wesleyan University Press, 1985.

Hawks, Joanne, and Sheila L. Skemp, eds. *Sex, Race, and the Role of Women in the South.* Jackson: University Press of Mississippi, 1983.

Hersh, Blanche Glassman. *The Slavery of Sex: Feminist-Abolitionists in America.* Urbana: University of Illinois Press, 1978.

Herskovits, Melville J. *The American Negro: A Study in Racial Crossing.* New York: Knopf, 1928.

Hickson, Bobbe Smith. *A Land So Dedicated: Houston County, Georgia.* Perry, Ga.: Houston County Library Service, 1977.

Historical Activities Committee of the National Society of Colonial Dames of America, in the State of Georgia. *Early Georgia Portraits, 1715–1870.* Athens: University of Georgia Press, 1975.

Holsey, Bishop Lucius Henry. *Autobiography, Sermons, Addresses and Essays.* Atlanta: Franklin Printing and Publishing Co., 1899.

Holt, Thomas. *Black Over White: Negro Political Leadership in South Carolina During Reconstruction.* Urbana: University of Illinois Press, 1977.

Hooks, Bell. *Ain't I a Woman? Black Women and Feminism.* Boston: South End Press, 1981.

Horton, James Oliver. *Free People of Color: Inside the African American Community.* Washington, D.C.: Smithsonian Institution Press, 1993.

Hundley, Daniel R. *Social Relations in Our Southern States.* 1860. Reprint, Baton Rouge: Louisiana State University Press, 1979.

Ione, Carole. *Pride of Family: Four Generations of American Women of Color.* New York: Summit Books, 1991.

Jackson, Luther Porter. *Free Negro Labor and Property Holding in Virginia, 1830–1860.* New York: D. Appleton-Century, 1942.

Janiewski, Dolores. "Sisters Under Their Skins: Southern Working Women, 1880–1950." In *Sex, Race, and the Role of Women in the South,* edited by Joanne V. Hawks and Sheila L. Skemp, pp. 13–35. Jackson: University Press of Mississippi, 1983.

Johnson, Guion Griffis. "The Changing Status of the Southern Woman." In *The South in Continuity and Change,* edited by John C. McKinney and Edgar T. Thompson, pp. 418–36. Durham, N.C.: Duke University Press, 1965.

Johnson, Michael P. *Toward a Patriarchal Republic: The Secession of Georgia.* Baton Rouge: Louisiana State University Press, 1977.

Johnson, Michael P., and James L. Roark. *Black Masters: A Free Family of Color in the Old South.* New York: Norton, 1984.

———. *No Chariot Let Down: Charleston's Free People of Color on the Eve of the Civil War.* Chapel Hill: University of North Carolina Press, 1984.

Johnston, James Hugo. *Race Relations in Virginia and Miscegenation in the South, 1776–1860.* Amherst: University of Massachusetts Press, 1970.

Jones, Anne Goodwyn. *Tomorrow Is Another Day: The Woman Writer in the South, 1859–1936.* Baton Rouge: Louisiana State University Press, 1981.

Jones, Jacqueline. *Labor of Love, Labor of Sorrow: Black Women, Work, and the Family from Slavery to the Present.* New York: Basic Books, 1985.

Jordan, Winthrop D. *White Over Black: American Attitudes Toward the Negro, 1550–1812.* Chapel Hill: University of North Carolina Press, 1977.

Jordan, Winthrop, and Shelia L. Skemp, eds. *Race and Family in the Colonial South.* Jackson: University Press of Mississippi, 1987.

Kerman, Cynthia Earl, and Richard Eldridge. *The Lives of Jean Toomer: A Hunger for Wholeness.* Baton Rouge: Louisiana State University Press, 1987.

King, Spencer B., Jr. *Georgia Voices: A Documentary History to 1872.* Athens: University of Georgia Press, 1966.

———, ed. *Georgia Voices: Readings in Georgia History to 1860.* Macon, Ga.: Mercer University Press, 1962.

Kinney, James. *Amalgamation! Race, Sex, and Rhetoric in the Nineteenth-Century American Novel.* Westport, Conn.: Greenwood Press, 1985.

Kletzing, H. F., and W. H. Crogman. *Progress of a Race, or The Remarkable Advancement of the Afro-American.* Atlanta: J. L. Nichols, 1897.

Klineberg, Otto, ed. *Characteristics of the Negro.* New York: Harper, 1944.

———, ed. *Characteristics of the American Negro.* New York: Harper and Brothers, 1944.

Knight, Lucian Lamar. *Reminiscences of Famous Georgians (1907).* Atlanta: Franklin-Turner Co., 1907–8.

Koger, Larry. *Black Slaveholders: Free Black Masters in South Carolina, 1790–1860.* London: MacFarland, 1985.

Kousser, J. Morgan, and James M. McPherson, eds. *Region, Race and Reconstruction.* New York: Oxford University Press, 1982.

Lebsock, Suzanne. *The Free Women of Petersburg; Status and Culture in a Southern Town, 1784–1860.* New York: Norton, 1984.

———. *A Share of Honour: Virginia Women, 1600–1945.* Best Products Foundation, 1984.

Lerner, Gerda. *Black Women in White America: A Documentary History*. New York: Pantheon, 1973.

———. *The Grimké Sisters from South Carolina: Pioneers for Woman's Rights and Abolition*. New York: Schocken Books, 1971.

———. *The Majority Finds Its Past: Placing Women in History*. New York: Oxford University Press, 1981.

Lewis, Jan. *The Pursuit of Happiness: Family and Values in Jefferson's Virginia*. New York: Cambridge University Press, 1983.

Linley, John. *Architecture of Middle Georgia: The Oconee Area*. Athens: University of Georgia Press, 1972.

Loewenberg, Bert James, and Ruth Bogin, eds. *Black Women in Nineteenth Century American Life: Their Words, Their Thoughts and Their Feelings*. University Park: Pennsylvania State University Press, 1976.

Madden, Thomas O., and Anne Miller. *We Were Always Free: The Maddens of Culpeper County, Virginia, a 200-Year Family History*. New York: Norton, 1992.

Majors, Monroe Alphus. *Noted Negro Women: Their Triumphs and Activities*. 1893. Reprint, Freeport, N.Y.: Books for Libraries Press, 1971.

Mathew, William M. *Edmund Ruffin and the Crisis of Slavery in the Old South: The Failure of Agricultural Reform*. Athens: University of Georgia Press, 1988.

McFeely, William S. *Frederick Douglass*. New York: Norton, 1991.

McLaurin, Melton A. *Celia, A Slave: A True Story of Violence and Retribution in Antebellum Missouri*. Athens: University of Georgia Press, 1991.

Meier, August. *Negro Thought in America, 1880–1915: Racial Ideologies in the Age of Booker T. Washington*. Ann Arbor: University of Michigan Press, 1963.

Memoirs of Georgia. Atlanta: Atlanta Southern Historical Society, 1895.

Mencke, John G. *Mulattoes and Race Mixture: American Attitudes and Images, 1865–1918*. Ann Arbor: University of Michigan Press, 1979.

Mills, Gary M. *The Forgotten People: Cane River's Creoles of Color*. Baton Rouge: Louisiana State University Press, 1977.

Mohr, Clarence L. *On the Threshold of Freedom: Masters and Slaves in Civil War Georgia*. Athens: University of Georgia Press, 1986.

Morgan, Dorothy. *When Servants Ride Horses: One Version of the David Dickson Story*. Privately published, 1992.

Morgan, Edmund S. *American Slavery, American Freedom: The Ordeal of Colonial Virginia*. New York: Norton, 1975.

————. *Virginians at Home: Family Life in the 18th Century.* Charlottesville: University Press of Virginia, 1952.

Morgan, Kathryn L. *Children of Strangers: The Stories of a Black Family.* Philadelphia: Temple University Press, 1980.

Mossell, N. F. *The Work of the Afro-American Woman.* Philadelphia: George S. Ferguson, 1894.

Murray, Pauli. *Proud Shoes: The Story of an American Family.* 1956. Reprint, New York: Harper & Row, 1978.

————. *Song in a Weary Throat: An American Pilgrimage.* New York: Harper & Row, 1987.

Myers, Robert Manson, ed. *The Children of Pride: The True Story of Georgia and the Civil War.* New Haven: Yale University Press, 1972.

Myrdal, Gunnar. *An American Dilemma.* New York: Harper & Row, 1944.

Nash, Gary B., and Richard Weiss, eds. *The Great Fear: Race in the Mind of America.* New York: Holt, Rinehart and Winston, 1970.

Neverdon-Morton, Cynthia. *African-American Women of the South and the Advancement of the Race, 1895–1925.* Knoxville: University of Tennessee Press, 1989.

Newman, Frances. *The Hard-Boiled Virgin.* 1926. Reprint, Athens: University of Georgia Press, 1980.

Noel, Donald L., ed. *The Origins of American Slavery and Racism.* Columbus, Ohio: Charles E. Merrill, 1972.

Northern, William Jonathan, ed. *Men of Mark in Georgia.* 6 vols. Atlanta: A. B. Caldwell, 1911.

Oakes, Jim. *The Ruling Race: A History of American Slaveholders.* New York: Knopf, 1982.

Orr, Dorothy. *A History of Education in Georgia.* Chapel Hill: University of North Carolina Press, 1950.

Owens, Harley P., ed. *Perspectives and Irony in American Slavery.* Jackson: University Press of Mississippi, 1976.

Owsley, Frank L. *Plain Folk in the Old South.* Baton Rouge: Louisiana State University Press, 1949.

Phillips, Ulrich B. *American Negro Slavery.* 1929. Reprint, Baton Rouge: Louisiana State University Press, 1966.

————. *A History of Transportation in the Eastern Cotton Belt to 1860.* New York: Columbia University Press, 1908.

————. *Life and Labor in the Old South.* Boston: Little, Brown, 1930.

Ponton, Mungo Melancthen. *Life and Times of Henry M. Turner*. Atlanta: A. B. Caldwell, 1917.

Potter, David M. *People of Plenty: Economic Abundance and the American Character*. Chicago: University of Chicago Press, 1954.

Powdermaker, Hortense. "The Channeling of Negro Aggression by the Cultural Process." In *The Making of Black America: Essays in Negro Life and History*, edited by August Meier and Elliot Rudwick, 2:94–105. New York: Atheneum, 1969.

Rabinowitz, Howard N. *Race Relations in the Urban South, 1865–1890*. New York: Oxford University Press, 1978.

Rable, George C. *Civil Wars: Women and the Crisis of Southern Nationalism*. Urbana: University of Illinois Press, 1989.

Range, Willard. *A Century of Georgia Agriculture, 1850–1950*. Athens: University of Georgia Press, 1954.

Rankin, David C. "French Romanticism, Free Colored Poetry, and the Politics of Reconstruction." Paper presented at the Southern Historical Association Annual Meeting, November 12, 1987.

Rawick, George P., ed. *The American Slave: A Composite Autobiography*. 19 vols. Contributions in Afro-American and African Studies, No. 11. Westport, Conn.: Greenwood Press, 1972.

———. *The American Slave: A Composite Biography*. Supplement, 12 vols. Westport, Conn.: Greenwood Press, 1977.

Redkey, Edwin A. *Respect Black: The Writings and Speeches of Henry McNeal Turner*. New York: Aran Press and New York Times, 1971.

Reuter, Edward Byron. *The American Race Problem: A Study of the Negro*. New York: Thomas Y. Crowell, 1927.

———. *The Mulatto in the United States*. Boston: R. E. Badger, 1918.

Reynolds, Harriet Dickson. *Several Dickson Lines: Many of Them Branches in Georgia*. Vol. 2, Supplement 2, compiled by the Author, 1972.

Richings, G. F. *Evidence of Progress Among Colored People*. Philadelphia: George S. Ferguson, 1896.

Roark, James L. *Masters Without Slaves: Southern Planters in the Civil War and Reconstruction*. New York: Norton, 1977.

Rouse, Jacqueline Anne. *Lugenia Burns Hope: Black Southern Reformer*. Athens: University of Georgia Press, 1989.

Rouse, Michael F. *A Study of the Development of Negro Education Under Catholic Auspices in Maryland and the District of Columbia*. Baltimore: Johns Hopkins University Press, 1935.

Rowbotham, Sheila. *Hidden from History: Rediscovering Women in History from the 17th Century to the Present*. New York: Vintage Books, 1974.

——. *Woman's Consciousness, Man's World*. New York: Penguin Books, 1981.

Rozier, John. *Black Boss: Political Revolution in a Georgia County*. Athens: University of Georgia Press, 1982.

——, ed. *The Granite Farm Letters: The Civil War Correspondence of Edgeworth and Sallie Bird*. Athens: University of Georgia Press, 1988.

Rubin, Gayle. "The Traffic in Women: Notes on the 'Political Economy' of Sex." In *Toward an Anthropology of Women*, edited by Rayna R. Reiter, pp. 157–210. New York: Monthly Review Press, 1975.

Rubin, Michele McNichols. "An Incomplete History of the Personal and Sexual Relations Between Blacks and Whites in America." Paper for "The Black Metropolis," a course taught by Dana White, April 30, 1981, Emory University.

Russell, Lester F. *Profile of a Black Heritage*. N.p.: Published by Lester F. Russell, 1977.

St. Clair-Abrams, Alexander. *Manual and Biographical Register of the State of Georgia for 1871–1872*. Atlanta, 1872.

Scarborough, Ruth. *The Opposition to Slavery in Georgia Prior to 1860*. Nashville: George Peabody College for Teachers, 1933.

Schweninger, Loren. *Black Property Owners in the South, 1790–1915*. Chicago: University of Chicago Press, 1990.

Scott, Anne Firor. *Making the Invisible Woman Visible*. Chicago: University of Chicago Press, 1984.

——. *The Southern Lady: From Pedestal to Politics, 1830–1930*. Chicago: University of Chicago Press, 1970.

——. "Women, Religion and Social Change in the South, 1830–1930." In *Religion and the Solid South*, edited by Samuel S. Hill, Jr. Nashville: Abingdon Press, 1972.

Scruggs, L. A. *Women of Distinction: Remarkable in Works and Invincible in Character*. Raleigh, N.C.: L. A. Scruggs, 1893.

Sherwood, Grace H. *The Oblates's Hundred and One Years*. New York: Macmillan, 1931.

Shivers, Forrest. *The Land Between: A History of Hancock County, Georgia, to 1940*. Spartanburg, S.C.: Reprint Company, 1990.

Smith, Daniel Blake. *Inside the Great House: Planter Family Life in Eighteenth-Century Chesapeake Society*. Ithaca: Cornell University Press, 1980.

Smith, Elizabeth Wiley. *The History of Hancock County, Georgia.* 2 vols. Washington, Ga.: Wilkes, 1974.

Smith, George. *Life and Times of George Foster Pierce.* Sparta, Ga: Hancock, 1888.

Smith, Lillian. *Killers of the Dream.* 1948. Reprint, New York: Norton, 1961.

———. *Strange Fruit.* New York: Regnal & Hitchcock, 1944.

Smith, Nellie May. *The Three Gifts of Life: A Girl's Responsibility for Race Progress.* New York: Dodd, Mead, 1919.

Smith, William A. *Lectures on the Philosophy and Practice of Slavery, with the Duties of Masters to Slaves.* Nashville: Stevenson & Evans, 1858.

Sobel, Michael. *The World They Made Together: Black and White Values in Eighteenth-Century Virginia.* Princeton: Princeton University Press, 1987.

Spruill, Julia Cherry. *Women's Life and Work in the Southern Colonies.* New York: Norton, 1972.

Stampp, Kenneth M. "Miscegenation." In *The Peculiar Institution: Slavery in the Antebellum South,* pp. 350–61. New York: Knopf, 1956.

Stanton, William R. *The Leopard's Spots: Scientific Attitudes Toward Race in America, 1815–1859.* Chicago: University of Chicago Press, 1960.

Stember, Charles Herbert. *Sexual Racism: The Emotional Barrier to an Integrated Society.* New York: Elsevier, 1976.

Sterling, Dorothy, ed. *We Are Your Sisters: Black Women in the Nineteenth Century.* New York: Norton, 1984.

Stetson, Erlene. "Studying Slavery: Some Literary and Pedagogical Considerations of the Black Female Slave." In *All the Women Are White, All the Blacks Are Men, but Some of Us Are Brave,* edited by Gloria T. Hull and Patricia Bell Scott, pp. 61–84. Old Westbury, N.Y.: Feminist Press, 1982.

Stonequist, Everett V. "Mulattoes in the United States" and "The American Negro." In *The Marginal Man: Study in Personality and Culture Conflict,* pp. 24–27, 106–19. New York: Charles Scribner and Son, 1937.

Stowe, Steven M. *All the Relations of Life: A Study in Sexuality, Family and Social Values in the Southern Planter Class.* Baltimore: Johns Hopkins Press, 1978.

———. *Intimacy and Power in the Old South: Ritual in the Lives of the Planters.* Baltimore: Johns Hopkins University Press, 1987.

Strickland, John Scott. "Traditional Culture and Moral Economy: Social and Economic Change in the South Carolina Low Country, 1865–1910." In *The Countryside in the Age of Capitalist Transformation,* edited by Steven Hahn and Jonathan Prude, pp. 141–78. Chapel Hill: University of North Carolina Press, 1985.

Terborg-Penn, Rosalyn. "Discrimination Against Afro-American Woman in the Woman's Movement, 1830–1920." In *The Afro-American Woman: Struggles and Images*, edited by Sharon Harley and Rosalyn Terborg-Penn, pp. 28–42. Port Washington, N.Y.: National Publications, 1978.

Terrell, Lloyd P., and M. S. Terrell. *Blacks in Augusta: A Chronology, 1741–1977*. Augusta: By the Author, 1977.

Thompson, C. Mildred. *Reconstruction in Georgia: Economic, Social, Political, 1865–1872*. New York: Columbia University Press, 1915.

Thorpe, Earl E. *Eros and Freedom in Southern Life and Thought*. Westport, Conn.: Greenwood Press, 1979.

Tindall, George B. "Mythology: A New Frontier in Southern History." In *The Idea of the South: Pursuit of the Central Theme*, pp. 1–16. Chicago: University of Chicago Press, 1964.

Toomer, Jean. *Cane*. 1923. Reprint, New York: Liveright, 1975.

Torrence, Ridgely. *The Story of John Hope*. New York: Macmillan, 1948.

Turner, Darwin. *The Wayward and the Seeking: A Collection of Writings by Jean Toomer*. Washington, D.C.: Howard University Press, 1980.

Veblen, Thorstein Bunde. *The Theory of the Leisure Class*. 1899. Reprint, New York: Penguin, 1969.

Wade, Richard C. *Slavery in the Cities: The South of 1820–1860*. 1964. Reprint, New York: Oxford University Press, 1980.

Washington, Booker T. *A New Negro for a New Century: An Accurate and Up-to-Date Record of the Upward Struggles of the Negro Race*. Chicago: American Publishing House, n.d.

Washington, Mrs. Booker T. "Club Work Among Negro Women." In *The New Progress of a Race: Remarkable Advancement of the American Negro*, edited by J. L. Nichols and W. B. Grogan, pp. 176–209. Napierville, Ill.: J. L. Nichols, 1920.

Welter, Barbara. *Dimity Convictions: The American Woman in the Nineteenth Century*. Athens: Ohio University Press, 1976.

White, Deborah Gray. *"Ar'n't I a Woman?" Female Slaves in the Plantation South*. New York: Norton, 1985.

White, John H., Jr. *The American Railroad Passenger Car*. 2 vols. Baltimore: Johns Hopkins University Press, 1984.

Wikramanayake, Marina. *A World in Shadow: The Free Black in Antebellum South Carolina*. Columbia: University of South Carolina Press, 1973.

Wiley, Bell Irvin. *Confederate Women.* Westport, Conn.: Greenwood Press, 1975.

Williams, Fannie Barrier. "The Club Movement Among Colored Women of America." In *The Colored American from Slavery to Honorable Citizenship,* edited by J. W. Gibson and W. H. Grogman, pp. 197–231. Atlanta: Hertel, Jenkins, 1905.

Williams, George. *The History of the Negro Race in America, 1619–1880.* New York: Putnam's Sons, 1883.

Williamson, Joel. *The Crucible of Race: Black-White Relations in the American South Since Emancipation.* New York: Oxford University Press, 1984.

———. *New People: Miscegenation and Mulattoes in the United States.* New York: Free Press, 1980.

Wirth, Louis, and Herbert, Goldhamer. "The Hybrid and the Problem of Miscegenation." In *Characteristics of the American Negro,* edited by Otto Klineberg, pp. 249–369. New York: Harper and Brothers, 1944.

Woods, Sister Frances Jerome. *Marginality and Identity: A Colored Creole Family Through Ten Generations.* Baton Rouge: Louisiana State University Press, 1972.

Woodson, Carter G. *The Education of the Negro Prior to 1861.* Washington, D.C., 1919.

———. *The Mind of the Negro as Reflected in Letters Prior to 1861.* Washington, D.C., 1919.

Woodward, C. Vann. *American Counterpoint: Slavery and Racism in the North-South Dialogue.* 1964. Reprint, New York: Oxford University Press, 1971.

———. *The Burden of Southern History.* Baton Rouge: Louisiana State University Press, 1960.

———. *The Strange Career of Jim Crow.* New York: Oxford University Press, 1955.

———, ed. *Mary Chesnut's Civil War.* New Haven: Yale University Press, 1981.

Woodward, C. Vann, and Elizabeth Muhlenfield, eds. *The Private Life of Mary Chesnut: The Unpublished Civil War Diaries.* New York: Oxford University Press, 1984.

Wyatt-Brown, Bertram. *Southern Honor: Ethics and Behavior in the Old South.* New York: Oxford University Press, 1982.

Articles

Abbott, Shirley. "Southern Women and the Indispensable Myth." *American Heritage* 42 (8) (1982): 82–91.

Anthony, Susan B. "The Status of Woman: Past, Present and Future." *Arena* 17 (May 1897): 901–8.

Bacote, Clarence A. "Negro Proscriptions, Protests, and Proposed Solutions in Georgia, 1880–1908." *Journal of Southern History* 25 (1959): 471–98.

———. "Some Aspects of Negro Life in Georgia, 1880–1908." *Journal of Negro History* 43 (1958): 186–213.

Barlett, Irving H., and C. Glenn Camber. "The History and Psychodynamics of Southern Womanhood." *Women's Studies* 2 (1974): 9–24.

"Black and Mulatto Populations of the South." *De Bow's Review* 8 (June 1850): 587–88.

Bloch, Ruth. "American Feminine Ideals in Transition: The Rise of the Moral Mother, 1785–1815." *Feminist Studies* 4 (June 1978): 101–26.

Boatright, Eleanor. "The Political and Civil Status of Women in Georgia, 1783–1860." *Georgia Historical Quarterly* 25 (December 1941): 301–24.

Bonner, James C. "Genesis of Agricultural Reform in the Cotton Belt." *Journal of Southern History* 9 (November 1943): 473–500.

———. A Georgia County's Historical Assets." *Emory University Quarterly* 9 (March 1953): 24–30.

———. "The Plantation Overseer and Southern Nationalism as Revealed in the Career of Garland D. Harmon." *Agricultural History* 19 (January 1945): 1–11.

———. "Profile of a Late Ante-Bellum Community." *American Historical Review* 49 (July 1944): 633–80.

Brooks, Robert Preston. "A Local Study of the Race Problem: Race Relations in the Eastern Piedmont Region of Georgia." *Political Science Quarterly* 26 (1911): 193–221.

Brown, Elsa Barkley. "Weaving Threads of Community: The Richmond Example." Paper presented at the Southern Historical Association Convention, Norfolk, Virginia, November 12, 1988.

Bruce, Josephine B. "What Has Education Done for Colored Women?" *Voice of the Negro* 1 (July 1904): 294–98.

Bryant, Jonathan M. "Race, Class and Law in Bourbon Georgia: The Case of David Dickson's Will." *Georgia Historical Quarterly* 71 (Summer 1987): 226–42.

Bullock, Penelope. "The Mulatto in American Fiction." *Phylon* 6 (1945): 78–82.

Burroughs, Nannie H. "Not Color but Character." *Voice of the Negro* 1 (July 1904): 294–98.

Burton, Orville Vernon. "Anatomy of an Antebellum Rural Free Black Community: Social Structure and Social Interaction in Edgefield District, South Carolina, 1850–1860." *Southern Studies* 21 (Fall 1982): 294–325.

Carlson, E. T. "The Nerve Weakness of the 19th Century." *International Journal of Psychiatry* 9 (1970–71): 50–54.

Carson, Roberta. "The Loyal League in Georgia." *Georgia Historical Quarterly* 20 (June 1936): 125–153.

Cartwright, Samuel A. "Report on the Diseases and Physical Peculiarities of the Negro Race." *Southern Quarterly Review* 22 (July 1852): 49–63.

Cazenave, Noel A. " 'A Woman's Place': The Attitudes of Middle Class Black Men." *Phylon* 44 (March 1983): 12–32.

Censer, Jane Turner. "Smiling Through Their Tears: Antebellum Southern Women and Divorce." *American Journal of Legal History* 25 (1981): 24–47.

Clark, E. Culpepper. "Sara Morgan and Francis Davison: Raising the Woman's Question in Reconstruction in South Carolina." *South Carolina Historical Magazine* 81 (January 1980): 8–23.

Clark, William Bedford. "The Serpent of Lust in the Southern Garden." *Southern Review* 10 (1974): 805–22.

Clinton, Catherine. "Bloody Terrain: Freedwomen, Sexuality, and Violence During Reconstruction." *Georgia Historical Quarterly* 76 (Summer 1992): 313–32.

———. "Their Due: Education of Planters' Daughters in the Early Republic." *Journal of the Early Republic* 2 (1982): 39–60.

Coulter, E. Merton. "Henry M. Turner, Georgia Negro Preacher-Politician During the Reconstruction Era." *Georgia Historical Quarterly* 48 (1964): 371–410.

———. "Negro Legislators in Georgia During the Reconstruction Period." *Georgia Historical Quarterly* 52 (1968): 16–52.

———. "Southern Agriculture and Southern Nationalism Before the Civil War." *Journal of Agricultural History* 4 (July 1930): 77–91.

Craven, Avery Odell. "The Agricultural Reformers of Ante-Bellum South." *American Historical Review* 33 (January 1928): 302–14.

Davis, Angela Y. "Reflections on the Black Woman's Role in the Community of Slaves." *Black Scholar* 3 (December 1971): 3–15.

DeBats, Donald. "Elites and Masses: Political Structure, Communication, and Behavior in Antebellum Georgia." *Georgia Historical Quarterly* 76 (Spring 1992): 152–53.

Degler, Carl N. "What Ought to Be and What Was: Women's Sexuality in the

Nineteenth Century." *American Historical Review* 79 (December 1974): 67–
90.

de Graffenreid, Mary Clare. "The Georgia Cracker in the Cotton Mill." *Century Magazine* 61 (February 1891): 483–98.

Dellinger, J. Elmer. "Hospital Work for Negro Women." *Spelman Messenger* 18 (March 1902): 1–7.

Destler, Chester M. "David Dickson's 'System of Farming' and the Agricultural Revolution in the Deep South, 1850–1885." *Journal of Agricultural History* 31 (1957): 30–39.

Dew, Thomas E. "On the Characteristic Differences Between the Sexes and on the Position and Influence of Women in Society." *Southern Literary Messenger* 11 (July, August 1835): 621–32, 672–91.

Drago, Edmund L. "How Sherman's March Through Georgia Affected the Slaves." *Georgia Historical Quarterly* 57 (Fall 1973): 361–75.

———. "Militancy and Black Women in Reconstruction Georgia." *Journal of American Culture* 1 (Winter 1978): 838–44.

Du Bois, W. E. B. "The Negro Landholder in Georgia." *Bulletin of the Department of Labor*, July 1901, 647–777.

———. "The Relation of the Negro to the Whites in the South." *Annals of the American Academy of Political and Social Sciences* 18 (July 1901): 121–40.

———. "The Work of Negro Women in Society." *Spelman Messenger* 18 (February 1902): 1–3.

Duvall, Severn. "Uncle Tom's Cabin: The Sinister Side of the Patriarchy." *New England Quarterly* 36 (March 1963): 3–22.

Eskew, Glenn T. "Black Elitism and the Failure of Paternalism in Postbellum Georgia: The Case of Bishop Lucius Henry Holsey." *Journal of Southern History* 58 (November 1991): 637–66.

Faust, Drew Gilpin. "Culture, Conflict and Community: The Meaning of Power on an Antebellum Plantation." *Journal of Social History* 14 (Fall 1980): 83–98.

Flanders, Ralph B. "The Free Negro in Antebellum Georgia." *North Carolina Historical Review* 9 (1932): 250–72.

———. "'Planters' Problems in Antebellum Georgia." *Georgia Historical Quarterly* 14 (March 1930): 17–40.

———. "Two Plantations and a County in Ante-Bellum Georgia." *Georgia Historical Quarterly* 12 (March 1928): 1–37.

Foby. "The Management of Servants." *Southern Cultivator* 11 (August 1853): 227.

Frazier, E. Franklin. "Children in Black and Mulatto Families." *American Journal of Sociology* 39 (July 1933): 12–29.

Gatewood, Willard B., Jr. "Aristocrats of Color: The Black Elite, 1890–1920." *Journal of Southern History* 54 (February 1988): 3–20.

Gatewood, Willard B., Jr., and Kent A. Leslie. "A Sort of a Mystery: Jean Toomer's Father." *Georgia Historical Quarterly* 77 (1993): 789–809.

Govan, Thomas P. "Banking and the Credit System in Georgia, 1810–1860." *Journal of Southern History* 4 (1938): 164–84.

Grantham, Dewey S. "History, Mythology, and the Southern Lady." *Southern Literary Journal* 3 (Spring 1971): 98–108.

Gray, Virginia Gearhart. "Activities of Southern Women, 1840–1860." *South Atlantic Quarterly* 27 (July 1978): 265–79.

Greenacre, Phyllis, M.D. "Child Wife as Ideal: Sociological Considerations." *American Journal of Ortho-Psychiatry* 17 (1947): 167–71.

Greenblatt, Milton. "Thomas Jefferson's Women." *Psychohistory Review* 19 (Winter 1991): 233–54.

Guy-Sheftall, Beverly. "Male Attitudes Toward Black Women, 1880–1917." An Interdisciplinary Essay on File in the Institute for the Liberal Arts, Emory University, June 1980.

H.C. "On the Management of Negroes." *Southern Agriculturist* 7 (July 1834): 368.

Hagler, D. Harland. "The Ideal Woman in the Antebellum South: Lady or Farm Wife." *Journal of Southern History* 46 (August 1980): 405–18.

Haller, John S., Jr. "Neurasthenia: The Medical Profession and the 'New Woman' of Late Nineteenth Century." *New York Journal of Medicine* 71 (1971): 473–82.

Harper, C. W. "Black Aristocrats: Domestic Servants on the Antebellum Plantation." *Phylon* 46 (June 1985): 123–35.

Harper, Frances W. "The National Women's Christian Temperance Union." *AME Church Review* 5 (1889): 242–45.

Harris, Olivia. "Households and Their Boundaries." *History Workshop* 13 (Spring 1982): 143–52.

Higginbotham, Evelyn Brooks. "African-American Woman's History and the Meta Language of Rape." *Signs* 12 (2): 251–74.

Hill, Mozell C., and Thelma D. Ackiss. "Social Classes: A Frame of Reference for the Study of Negro Society." *Social Forces* 22 (October 1943): 92–98.

Hine, Darlene Clark. "Female Slave Resistance: The Economics of Sex." *Western Journal of Black Studies* 3 (Summer 1979): 123–27.

Hoffert, Sylvia D. "Mary Boykin Chesnut: Private Feminist in the Civil War South." *Southern Studies* 16 (1977): 81–99.

———. "This 'One Great Evil': The Sexual Practice That Northern Abolitionists Exploited, Southern White Men Concealed, and Proper Ladies Never Discussed." *American History Illustrated* 12 (May 1977): 37–41.

Hogeland, Ronald W. "'The Female Appendate': Feminine Lifestyles in America, 1820–1868." *Civil War History* 17 (1971): 101–14.

Holsey, Lucius Henry. "Amalgamation and Miscegenation." *CME Church Bulletin* (1899).

Horton, James Oliver. "Freedom's Yoke: Gender Conventions Among Antebellum Free Blacks." *Feminist Studies* 12 (Spring 1986): 51–76.

Hunt, Patricia K. "Clothing as an Expression of History: The Dress of African-American Women in Georgia, 1880–1910." *Georgia Historical Quarterly* 76 (Summer 1992): 459–71.

Hunter, Frances L. "Slave Society on the Southern Plantation." *Journal of Negro History* 7 (January 1922): 1–10.

Hutchinson, George B. "Jean Toomer and the 'New Negroes' of Washington [in 1920s]." *American Literature* 63 (December 1991): 683–92.

J.T. "Negro Mania." *Southern Quarterly Review* 21 (January 1852): 153–75.

Jay, Nancy. "Gender and Dichotomy." *Feminist Studies* 7 (Spring 1981): 38–56.

Jefferson, Olive Ruth. "The Southern Negro Women." *Chatauquan* 8 (1893): 91.

Jeffrey, Julie Roy. "Women in the Southern Farmer's Alliance: A Reconsideration of the Role and Status of Women in the Late Nineteenth Century South." *Feminist Studies* 3 (Fall 1975): 72–91.

Johnson, James. "Woman's Exalted Station." *A.M.E. Church Review* 8 (1892): 402–6.

Johnson, Kenneth R. "Kate Gordon and the Woman-Suffrage Movement in the South." *Journal of Southern History* 38 (August 1972): 365–92.

Johnson, Michael P., and James L. Roark. "'A Middle Ground': Free Mulattoes and the Friendly Moralist Society of Antebellum Charleston." *Southern Studies: An Interdisciplinary Journal* 21 (Fall 1982): 246–65.

Johnson, Whittington B. "Free Blacks in Antebellum Augusta, Georgia: A Demographic and Economic Study." *Journal of Richmond County History* 14 (Winter 1982): 10–21.

Johnston, Richard Malcolm. "Early Education in Middle Georgia." *Georgia Journal*, January 7, 1823, 839–60, 1699–1733.

Jones, Alton Dumar. "The Child Labor Reform Movement in Georgia." *Georgia Historical Quarterly* 49 (1965): 396–417.

Jones, Jacqueline. " 'My Mother Was Much of a Woman': Black Women, Work and the Family Under Slavery." *Feminist Studies* 8 (Summer 1982): 235–69.

Kaplan, Sidney. "The Miscegenation Issue in the Election of 1864." *Journal of Negro History* 34 (July 1949): 274–343.

———. "The Octoroon: Early History of the Drama of Miscegenation." *Journal of Negro History* 20 (1951): 547–57.

King, Richard H. "Marxism and the Slave South." *American Quarterly* 39 (1977): 117–31.

Kondert, Nancy T. "The Romance and Reality of Defeat: Southern Women in 1865." *Journal of Mississippi History* 35 (May 1973): 141–52.

Kousser, J. Morgan. "Separate but Not Equal: The Supreme Court's First Decision on Racial Discrimination in Schools." *Journal of Southern History* 46 (February 1980): 18–44.

Kraditor, Aileen S. "Tactical Problems of the Woman Suffrage Movement in the South." *Louisiana Studies* 5 (Winter 1966): 289–307.

Lebsock, Suzanne. "Free Black Women and the Question of Matriarchy: Petersburg, Virginia, 1784–1820." *Feminist Studies* 8 (Summer 1982): 235–69.

Lerner, Gerda. "Early Community Work of Black Women." *Journal of Negro History* 59 (April 1974): 158–67.

Leslie, Kent Anderson. "A Myth of the Southern Lady: Antebellum Pro-Slavery Rhetoric and the Proper Place of Woman." *Sociological Spectrums* 6 (1986): 31–49.

———. "Southern Women in Bi-Racial Families in the Antebellum Period: A Case Study, Amanda America Dickson." *Mind and Nature* 3 (January 1981): 55–58.

MacDougal, G. Elise Johnson. "The Double Task: The Struggle of Negro Women for Sex and Race Emancipation." *Survey* 53 (March 1, 1925): 689–91.

Macmillian, M. B. "Beard's Concept of Neurasthenia and Freud's Concept of the Actual Neurosis." *Journal of the History of Behavioral Science* 12 (1976): 376–90.

McAdoo, Laura Sterrette. "Woman's Economic Status in the South." *Arena* 21 (1899): 741–56.

McCord, Louisa. "Carey on the Slave Trade." *Southern Quarterly Review* 25 (1854): 115–84.

———. "Diversity of the Races: Its Bearing upon Negro Slavery." *Southern Quarterly Review* 19 (April 1851): 329–419.

———. "Enfranchisement of Women." *Southern Quarterly Review* 21 (April 1852): 322–41.

———. "Justice and Fraternity." *Southern Quarterly Review* 15 (July 1849): 356–74.

———. "Negro and White Slavery." *Southern Quarterly Review* 20 (July 1851): 118–32.

———. "The Right to Labor." *Southern Quarterly Review* 16 (October 1849): 138–60.

McDowell, Rogers W. "Free Negro Legislation in Georgia Before 1865." *Georgia Historical Quarterly* 16 (1932): 27–37.

Matthews, John M. "Negro Republicans in the Reconstruction of Georgia." *Georgia Historical Quarterly* 60 (Summer 1976): 145–64.

Mehlinger, Louis R. "The Attitude of the Free Negro Toward African Colonization." *Journal of Negro History* 1 (June 1916): 276–301.

Meier, August, and David Lewis. "History of the Negro Upper Class in Atlanta, Georgia, 1890–1958." *Journal of Negro Education* 28 (Spring 1959): 128–39.

Mendenhall, Marjorie Stratford. "Southern Women of a Lost Generation." *South Atlantic Quarterly* 23 (1934): 234–53.

Mills, Gary. "Coincoin: An Eighteenth Century 'Liberated Woman.' " *Journal of Southern History* 42 (May 1976): 205–22.

———. "Miscegenation and the Free Negro in Antebellum 'Anglo' Alabama: A Re-examination of Southern Race Relations." *Journal of American History* 68 (June 1981): 16–34.

Moffat, Adalene. "Views of a Southern Woman." *Crisis* 2 (August 1911): 160–62.

Mohr, Clarence L. "Before Sherman: Georgia Blacks and the Union War Effort." *Journal of Southern History* 45 (August 1979): 331–52.

Mora, G. "Antecedent to Neurosis." *International Journal of Psychiatry* 9 (1970–71): 57–60.

Moses, Wilson Jeremiah. "Domestic Feminism, Conservatism, Sex Roles, and Black Women's Clubs, 1893–1896." *Journal of Social and Behavioral Sciences* 24 (Fall 1978): 166–77.

N.B.P. "The Treatment of Slaves in the South." *Southern Quarterly Review* 21 (January 1852): 209–20.

Nobles, Wade W. "African Root and American Fruit: The Black Family." *Journal of Social and Behavioral Sciences* 19–20 (Spring 1974): 52–64.

Painter, Nell. "Miscegenation and the Maintenance of Power." Paper presented at Georgia 200 Years, Athens, Ga., October 1985.

Palmer, Edward N. "Negro Secret Societies." *Social Forces* 23 (December 1944): 207–12.

Parkhurst, Jessie W. "The Role of the Black Mammy in the Plantation Household." *Journal of Negro History* 23 (July 1938): 349–69.

Porter, Dorothy B. "Early Manuscript Letters Written by Negroes." *Journal of Negro History* 24 (1939): 199–210.

Potter, David. "The Enigma of the South." *Yale Review* 51 (Autumn 1961): 142–51.

Range, Willard. "The Prince of Southern Farmers." *Georgia Review* 2 (Spring 1948): 92–97.

Redkey, Edwin S. "Bishop's Turner's African Dream." *Journal of American History* 54 (1967): 271–90.

Rockwell, A. D. "Some Causes and Characteristics of Neurasthenia." *New York Medical Journal* 58 (1893): 589–91.

Rogers, W. McDowell. "Free Negro Legislation in Georgia Before 1865." *Georgia Historical Quarterly* 16 (March 1932): 30–32.

Sanday, Peggy. "Toward a Theory of the Status of Women." *American Anthropologist* 75 (1973): 1682–1700.

Schafer, Judith K. " 'Open and Notorious Concubinage': The Emancipation of Slave Mistresses by Will and the Supreme Court in Antebellum Louisiana." *Louisiana History* 28 (Spring 1987): 165–82.

Schweninger, Loren. "Property Owning Free African-American Women in the South, 1800–1870." *Journal of Women's History* 1 (Winter 1990): 13–44.

———. "Prosperous Blacks in the South, 1790–1880." *American Historical Review* 95 (February 1990): 31–56.

Scott, Anne Firor. "Making the Invisible Woman Visible." *Journal of Southern History* 38 (November 1972): 629–38.

———. "The 'New Woman' in the New South." *South Atlantic Quarterly* 61 (Autumn 1962): 473–83.

———. "Women's Perspective on the Patriarchy in the 1850s." *Journal of American History* 61 (June 1974): 52–64.

Seidel, Kathryn L. "The Southern Belle as an Antebellum Ideal." *Southern Quarterly* 15 (1977): 387–401.

Shaw, Stephanie J. "Black Women and the Creation of the National Association of Colored Women." *Journal of Women's History* 2 (Fall 1991): 10–25.

Sicherman, Barbara. "The Uses of a Diagnosis: Doctors, Patients, and Neurasthenia." *Journal of the History of Medicine* 32 (1977): 33–55.

Sides, Sudie Duncan. "Southern Women and Slavery." *History Today* 20 (January 1970): 54–60.

Smith-Rosenberg, Carroll. "The Hysterical Woman: Sex Roles and Role Conflict in 19th Century America." *Social Research* 30 (1972): 652–78.

Steckel, Richard H. "Miscegenation and the American Slave Schedules." *Journal of Interdisciplinary History* 11 (Autumn 1980): 251–63.

Taylor, A. Elizabeth. "Revival and Development of the Woman Suffrage Movement in Georgia." *Georgia Historical Quarterly* 42 (December 1974): 339–54.

Tillman, Katherine Davis. "Afro-American Women and Their Work." *A.M.E. Church Review* 12 (1895): 477–99.

Toll, William. "Free Men, Freedmen, and Race: Black Social Theory in the Gilded Age." *Journal of Southern History* 44 (November 1978): 571–96.

Toplin, Robert Brent. "Between Black and White: Attitudes Toward Southern Mulattoes, 1830–1861." *Journal of Southern History* 45 (May 1979): 185–200.

Turner, Darwin. "Chapters from *Earth Being*, an Unpublished Autobiography." *Black Scholar* 2 (January 1971): 2–13.

Wade-Gayles, Gloria. "Black Women Journalists in the South, 1880–1905: An Approach to the Study of Black Women's History." *Callaloo* 4 (February–October 1981): 138–52.

Walker, Alice. "The Search of Our Mother's Gardens, the Creativity of Black Women in the South." *MS* 2 (May 1974): 64–70.

Walters, Ronald G. "The Erotic South: Civilization and Sexuality in American Abolitionism." *American Quarterly* 25 (May 1973): 177–201.

Washington, Mrs. Booker T. "Social Improvement of the Plantation Woman." *Voice of the Negro* 1 (July 1904): 288–90.

Watson, Annah Robinson. "The Attitude of Southern Women in the Suffrage Question." *Arena* 11 (February 1895): 363–68.

Weatherly, W. G. "Race and Marriage." *American Journal of Sociology* 15 (January 1919): 433–53.

Weiman, David F. "Farmers and the Market in Antebellum America: A View from the Upcountry." *Journal of Economic History* 47 (1987): 627–47.

Wells, Charles E. "The Hysterical Personality and the Feminine Character: A Study of Scarlett O'Hara." *Comprehensive Psychiatry* 17 (March–April 1976): 353–59.

Welter, Barbara. "The Cult of True Womanhood, 1820–1860." *American Quarterly* 18 (Summer 1966): 151–74.

Whittington, B. Johnson. "Free African-American Women in Savannah, 1800–

1860: Affluence and Autonomy Amid Adversity." *Georgia Historical Quarterly* 76 (Summer 1992): 260–83.

Wight, Willard E. "Negroes in the Georgia Legislature: The Case of F. H. Fyall of Macon County, Georgia." *Georgia Historical Quarterly* 44 (1960): 85–97.

Williams, Sylvanie Francaz. "The Social Status of the Negro Woman." *Voice of the Negro* 1 (July 1904): 298–300.

Wood, Ann Douglas. " 'The Fashionable Diseases': Women's Complaints and Their Treatment in Nineteenth Century America." *Journal of Interdisciplinary History* 4 (Summer 1973): 25–52.

Woodson, Carter G. "The Beginnings of Miscegenation of Whites and Blacks." *Journal of Negro History* 3 (October 1918): 335–53.

Work, Monroe N., ed. "Some Negro Members of Reconstruction Conventions and Legislatures and of Congress." *Journal of Negro History* 5 (January 1920): 63–125.

Wright, Edward R. "Comments: Interracial Marriage: A Survey of Statutes and Their Interpretations." *Mercer Law Review* 1 (1949): 83–90.

Yant, Martin. "Father Healy: A Negro, a Building, a Dream." *Georgetown Today*, September 1971, 4–9.

Yates-Silome, Josephine. "The National Association of Colored Women." *Voice of the Negro* 1 (July 1904): 283–87.

Yoder, Parton. "Private Hospitality in the South." *Mississippi Valley Historical Review* 47 (1960): 419–33.

Zanger, Jules. "The 'Tragic Octoroon' in Pre–Civil War Fiction." *American Quarterly* 18 (Spring 1966): 62–70.

Theses and Dissertations

Alexander, Adele. "Ambiguous Lives: Free Women of Color in Middle Georgia, 1787–1879." M.A. thesis, Howard University, 1987.

Bacote, Clarence. "The Negro in Georgia Politics, 1880–1908." Ph.D. dissertation, University of Chicago, 1955.

Bonner, James C. "Agricultural Reform in the Georgia Piedmont, 1820–1860." Ph.D. dissertation, University of North Carolina, 1944.

Brooks, Evelyn. "The Woman's Movement in the Black Baptist Church, 1880–1920." Ph.D. dissertation, University of Rochester, 1970.

Brown, Kathleen Mary. "Gender and the Genesis of a Race and Class System in Virginia, 1630–1750." Ph.D. dissertation, University of Wisconsin, Madison, 1990.

Brown, Nathaniel Baker, Jr. "The Role of Cooperatives in Alleviating Long-term Rural Poverty: A Case Study in Hancock County, Georgia." Ph.D. dissertation, University of Michigan, 1978.

Burgess, Hugh Otis. "A Study of Prosperity in Georgia, 1840–1850." Master's thesis, University of Georgia, 1926.

Burton, Adams Olin. "The Negro and the Agrarian Movement in Georgia, 1874–1908." Ph.D. dissertation, Florida State University, 1973.

Byrne, William. "The Burden and Heat of the Day: Slavery and Servitude in Savannah, 1733–1865." Ph.D. dissertation, Florida State University, 1979.

Christler, Ethel Maude. "Participation of Negroes in the Government of Georgia, 1867–1870." Ph.D. dissertation, Atlanta University, 1932.

Cimbala, Paul Alan. "The Terms of Freedom: The Freedman's Bureau and Reconstruction in Georgia, 1865–1870." Ph.D. dissertation, Emory University, 1983.

Clark, William Bedford. "The Serpent of Lust in the Southern Garden: The Theme of Miscegenation in Cagle, Twain, Faulkner and Warren." Ph.D. dissertation, Louisiana State University and Agricultural and Mechanical College, 1973.

Clary, George Esmond. "The Founding of Paine College: A Unique Venture in Interracial Cooperation in the New South, 1882–1903." Ph.D. dissertation, University of Georgia, 1965.

Coleman, Willie Mae. "Keeping the Faith and Disturbing the Peace: Black Women from Anti-Slavery to Women's Suffrage." Ph.D. dissertation, University of California, Irvine, 1982.

Corley, Florence Fleming. "Higher Education for Southern Women: Four Church Related Colleges in Georgia, 1900–1920." Ph.D. dissertation, Georgia State University, 1985.

De Treville, John Richard. "The Little New South: Origins of Industry in Georgia's Fall-Line Cities, 1840–1865." Ph.D. dissertation, University of North Carolina, 1986.

Dorris, Ronald. "The Bacchae of Jean Toomer." Ph.D. dissertation, Emory University, 1979.

Flynn, Charles Lenean. "White Land, Black Labor: Property, Ideology, and the Political Economy of Late Nineteenth Century Georgia." Ph.D. dissertation, Duke University, 1980.

Gay, Dorothy Ann. "The Tangled Skein of Romanticism and Violence in the Old South: The Southern Response to Abolitionism and Feminism." Ph.D. dissertation, University of North Carolina, 1975.

German, Richard Henry Lee. "The Queen City of the Savannah: Augusta, Georgia, During the Urban Progressive Era, 1890–1917." Ph.D. dissertation, University of Florida, 1971.

Gifford, James Maurice. "The African Colonization Movement in Georgia, 1817–1860." Ph.D. dissertation, University of Georgia, 1977.

Gillespie, Earl Wallace. "Temperance and Prohibition in Antebellum Georgia." Master's thesis, University of Georgia, 1961.

Graham, William L. "Patterns of Intergroup Relations in the Cooperative Establishment, Control, and Administration of Paine College (Georgia) by Southern Negro and White People: A Study of Intergroup Process." Ph.D. dissertation, New York University, 1955.

Griffin, John Chandler, Jr. "Jean Toomer: American Writer (A Biography)." Ph.D. dissertation, University of South Carolina, 1976.

Guy-Sheftall, Beverly Lynn. " 'Daughters of Sorrow': Attitudes Toward Black Women, 1880–1920." Ph.D. dissertation, Emory University, 1984.

Harris, John William, Jr. "A Slaveholding Republic: Augusta's Hinterland Before the Civil War." Ph.D. dissertation, Johns Hopkins University, 1982.

Hodes, Martha Elizabeth. "Sex Across the Color Line: White Women and Black Men in the Nineteenth-Century American South." Ph.D. dissertation, Princeton University, 1991.

Hornsby, Anne R. Lockhart. "Shifts in the Distribution of Wealth Among Blacks in Georgia, 1890–1915." Ph.D. dissertation, Georgia State University, 1980.

Hume, Richard L. "The 'Black and Tan' Constitutional Conventions of 1867–1869 in Ten Former Confederate States: A Story of Their Membership." Ph.D. dissertation, University of Washington, 1969.

Jenkins, William Thomas. "Antebellum Macon and Bibb County, Georgia." Ph.D. dissertation, University of Georgia, 1966.

Jones, Anne. "Idol, Equal and Slave: White Female Identity and White Male Guilt, a Study of Female Role Definition in the Antebellum South." Ph.D. dissertation, American University, 1980.

Jones, Jacqueline. "The 'Great Opportunity': Northern Teachers and the Georgia Freedman, 1866–74." Ph.D. dissertation, University of Wisconsin, Madison, 1976.

Jones, Rubye M. "The Negro in Colonial Georgia, 1735–1805." Master's thesis, Atlanta University, 1938.

King, Francine. "A Documentary Source Book: A Review of the African-American Woman in the Savannah River Valley Before the Civil War–History, Analysis, with 177 Accompanying Documents." Ph.D. dissertation, Clark University, 1993.

Koch, Mary Levin. "A History of the Arts in Augusta, Macon, and Columbus, Georgia, 1800–1860." Master's thesis, University of Georgia, 1983.

Lewis, Vashti Cruther. "The Mulatto Woman as a Major Female Character in Novels by Black Women, 1892–1937." Ph.D. dissertation, University of Iowa, 1981.

Matthews, John M. "The Negro in Georgia Politics, 1865–1880." Master's thesis, Duke University, 1938.

———. "Studies in Race Relations in Georgia, 1890–1930." Ph.D. dissertation, Duke University, 1970.

McGuire, May Jennie. "Getting Their Hands on the Land: Black Farmers in St. Helena Parish, 1861–1900." Master's thesis, University of South Carolina, 1982.

Mohr, Clarence Lee. "Georgia Blacks During Secession and Civil War, 1859–1865." Ph.D. dissertation, University of Georgia, 1975.

O'Brien, Kenneth. "The Savage and the Child in Historical Perspective: Images of Blacks in Southern White Thought, 1830–1915." Ph.D. dissertation, Northwestern University, 1974.

Owens, James Leggette. "The Negro in Georgia During Reconstruction, 1864–1872: A Social History." Ph.D. dissertation, University of Georgia, 1975.

Porter, Michael Leroy. "Black Atlanta: An Interdisciplinary Study of Blacks on the East Side of Atlanta, 1890–1930." Ph.D. dissertation, Emory University, 1974.

Ramsey-Berkley, Carlyle. "The Public Black College in Georgia, 1903–1965." Ph.D. dissertation, Florida State University, 1973.

Reddick, James Lawson. "The Negro in the Populist Movement in Georgia." M.A. thesis, Atlanta University, 1937.

Reidy, Joseph Patrick. "Masters and Slaves, Planters and Freedmen: The Transition from Slavery to Freedmen in Central Georgia, 1820–1880." Ph.D. dissertation, Northern Illinois University, 1982.

Roth, Darlene Rebecca. "Matronage Patterns in Women's Organizations, Atlanta, Georgia, 1890–1940." Ph.D. dissertation, George Washington University, 1978.

Rouse, Jacqueline Anne. "Lugenia D. Burns Hope: A Black Woman Reformer in the South, 1871–1947." Ph.D. dissertation, Emory University, 1983.

Sides, Sudie Duncan. "Women and Slaves: An Interpretation Based on the Writings of Southern Women." Ph.D. dissertation, University of North Carolina, 1969.

Smith, Albert Colby. "Down Freedom's Road: The Contours of Race, Class and Property Crime in Black-Belt Georgia, 1866–1910." Ph.D. dissertation, University of Georgia, 1982.

Sweat, Edward Forrest. "The Free Negro in Antebellum Georgia." Ph.D. dissertation, University of Michigan, 1957.

Thornberry, Jerry John. "The Development of Black Atlanta, 1865–1885." Ph.D. dissertation, University of Maryland, 1977.

Wardlaw, Ralph W. "Negro Suffrage in Georgia, 1867–1930." M.A. thesis, University of Georgia, 1932.

Weiner, Marli Frances. "Plantation Mistress/Female Slave: Gender, Race, and South Carolina Women, 1830–1880." Ph.D. dissertation, University of Rochester, 1985.

Wingo, Horace Calvin. "Race Relations in Georgia, 1872–1908." Ph.D. dissertation, University of Georgia, 1969.

Wolfe, Allis. "Women Who Dared: Northern Teachers of the Southern Freeman, 1862–1872." Ph.D. dissertation, City University of New York, 1982.

Wright, C. T. "The Development of Education for Blacks in Georgia, 1865–1900." Ph.D. dissertation, Boston University Graduate School, 1977.

Index